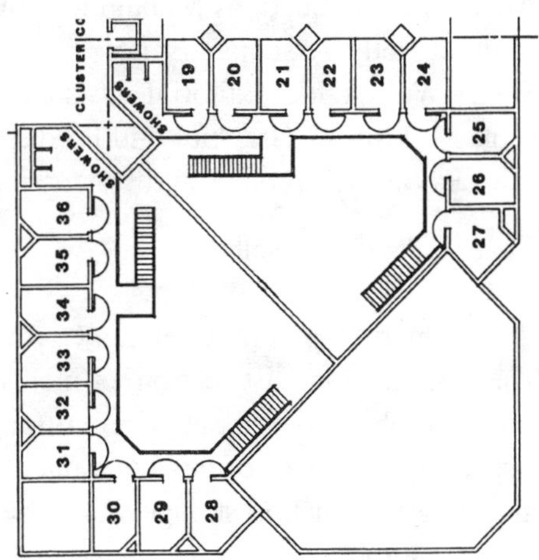


# Unit Management in Prisons and Jails



Robert B. Levinson, Ph.D.

American Correctional Association
Lanham, Maryland

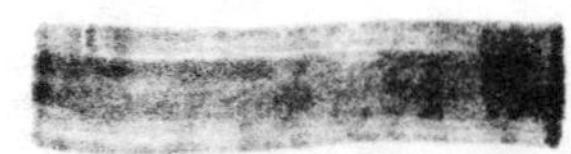

Cover by Michael Selby



Printed in the United States of America by Kirby Lithographic, Co., Inc., Arlington, VA.

ISBN 1-56991-079-0

This publication may be ordered from:

American Correctional Association
4380 Forbes Boulevard
Lanham, Maryland 20706-4322
1-800-222-5646

For information on publications and videos available from ACA, contact our worldwide web home page at: http://www.corrections.com/aca.

Library of Congress Cataloging-in-Publication Data

Levinson, Robert B.
Unit management in prisons and jails / Robert B. Levinson.
p. cm.
Includes bibliographical references (p. ) .
ISBN 1-56991-079-0 (pbk.)
1. Prison administration—United States. 2. Jails—United States--Administration. I. Title.
HV9469.L39 1998
365'.068—dc21 98-20708
CIP

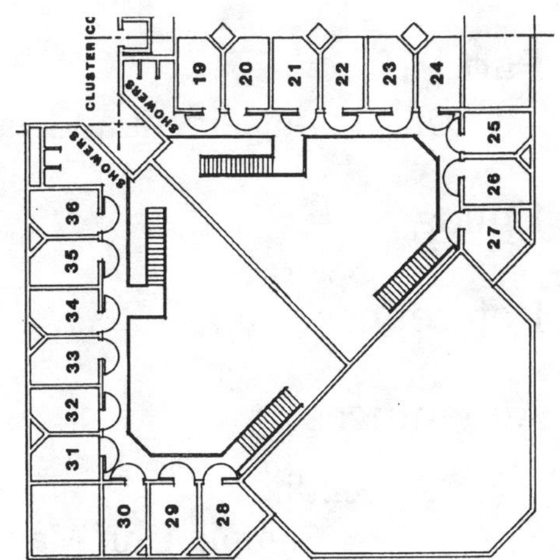


# Table of Contents

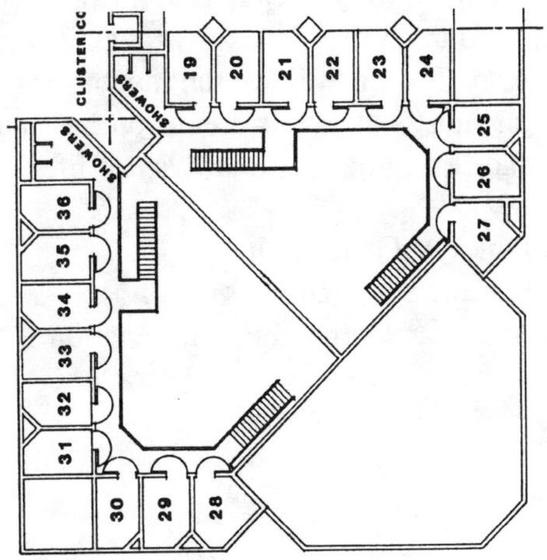


# Foreword

In the 1970s, when the Federal Bureau of Prisons began implementing unit management, it was a revolutionary experiment in correctional theory. Now, more than twenty years later, unit management is a proven method in correctional facility operation. What began as the Demonstration Counseling Project, funded by Attorney General Robert F. Kennedy in the 1960s, developed into a system that has been used by the correctional departments of many states and other countries, including Australia, the United Kingdom, Canada, and Israel.

Unit management can increase contact between staff and inmates, foster increased interpersonal relationships, and lead to more knowledgeable decisions as a result of staff dealing with a smaller, more permanent group of inmates. The specific requirements of unit management differ from one jurisdiction to another, but the goal is universal—effective correctional administration.

In *Unit Management in Prisons and Jails*, Robert Levinson describes unit management's humble beginnings at the National Training School in Washington, D.C., and recounts its rise to becoming a system that revolutionized prison management. Dr. Levinson introduces readers to the concept of unit management and carefully walks them through each step involved with implementing this method. The appendices include a sample manual and unit plan to assist individuals with the details of unit management. Aside from prisons, jails also have adopted this idea (unit management is called "direct supervision" in a jail setting). This book includes a chapter on these types of jails by Kenneth Kerle.

As one of the people most responsible for the development and implementation of unit management, Dr. Levinson speaks with authority. He was with the Bureau of Prisons when it was just an idea on paper, and he saw it grow from one institution to another. Now, as Dennis Johnson, assistant correctional services administrator with the Bureau of Prisons says, "Unit management is now a philosophy and not a program. It is the way we run institutions. It is a way of life for the Bureau of Prisons and for most states." Dr. Levinson has made *Unit Management in Prisons and Jails* an excellent guide for this "way of life."

James A. Gondles, Jr.
Executive Director
American Correctional Association

*"Man, it took me 25 years just to learn what to leave out."*

—Dizzy Gillespie

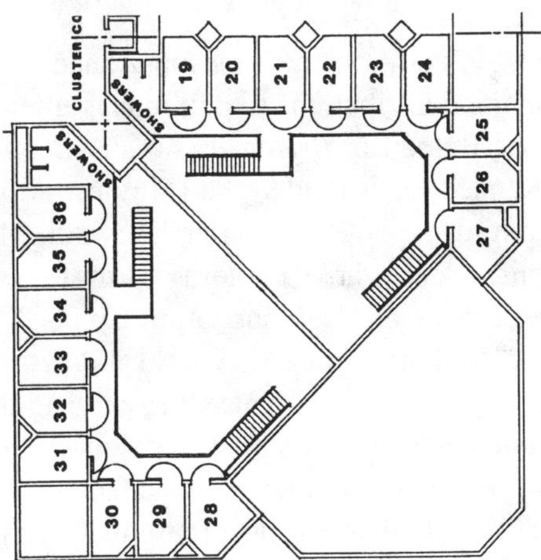


# Introduction and Acknowledgments

Not too many years ago, I met a corrections official from New South Wales, Australia, who was traveling in the United States on a Churchill Fellowship. During the course of our conversation, he mentioned that his correctional system was about to begin unit management. Since this is a subject in which I have long had an interest, I asked what they were planning to do. "Oh," he replied, "we're going to follow the Danish model."

This colloquy is illustrative of the worldwide dispersal that the unit management concept has achieved. The National Criminal Justice Reference Service, for example, in addition to Australia, lists citations on unit management from the United Kingdom, Canada, and Israel. In 1991, Roy E. Gerard, Assistant Director (retired), Federal Bureau of Prisons, asked:

> Who is responsible for developing the unit management concept? Across the country, I am frequently introduced as "the father of unit management." If providing support during the early years of its development qualifies a person as a parent, then I accept responsibility. However, if I am the father, then Bob Levinson was the attending physician and Norman Carlson (Director of the Federal Bureau of Prisons) paid the hospital bills . . . In truth, there were many fathers of unit

> management. The concept evolved over a number of years. It brought together many well-recognized and long-endorsed elements of effective correctional administration. This made unit management's road to acceptance a little smoother.

In addition to those mentioned, a large number of other individuals have made major contributions to unit management: H. G. "Gus" Moeller, assistant director, Federal Bureau of Prisons, who shepherded the grant from Attorney General Robert F. Kennedy that funded the Demonstration Counseling Project, immediate precursor to unit management; Charles E. Smith, M.D., medical director, Federal Bureau of Prisons, under whose authority Howard L. "Kitch" Kitchener and I functioned as codirectors of the Demonstration Counseling Project; Allan Childers, superintendent at the National Training School in Washington, D.C., where the Demonstration Counseling Project was housed; Elvin Elliott, Frank Wilson, and William Young who were unit management's first correctional counselors in the Demonstration Counseling Project's "Experimental" Cottage—Jefferson Hall—and Stephen Keating, the classification and parole officer (case manager) for the delinquents in this experimental group.

Truly, success has many fathers. Names of other significant contributors are listed in the references and the index. Bringing it all together in this one volume is a quick trip to nostalgia.

I have long thought that we all have an obligation to leave this a better world than we found it. Serendipity always plays a critical role. But it was—and is—great to have been at the center of all who made unit management happen!

*Robert B. Levinson*

Dedicated to family and friends who constitute a *very* special unit:

- Anna, Betty, Brooke, Eric, Jana, Jason, Joel, Ken, Mackenzie, and of course, Aria and Bravo;

- Al, Bill, Charlie, Chuck, Craig, Doug, Elvin, Frank, Gil and Ruth Ann, Herb, JD, Jim, Jerry, Joe, Kitch, Larry, Lowell, Marty, Norm and Pat, Ray, Roy and Penny, and the staff (back then) of the Federal Bureau of Prisons.

Thanks!

RBL

*Unitization is the talk of the yard. Old cons tend to view it with suspicious eye; they've been through administrative manipulations before and are still incarcerated. And, first terms are speculating the unit system is a major move toward correctional reform, and are more optimistic. Possibly a combination of the two views is the most fruitful for everyone to adopt, for unitization represents changes in both directions.*

—*The T.I. News* (inmate newspaper),
Federal Correctional Institution,
Terminal Island, California
May 2, 1975

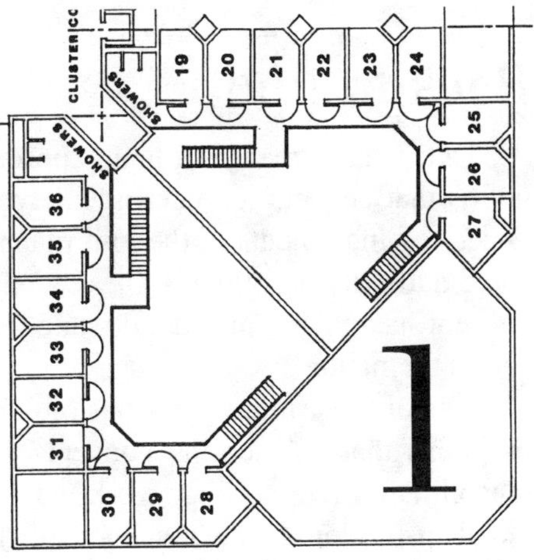


# What is Unit Management?

## Introduction

They don't build institutions the way they used to! Gone are the "panopticons" and the "telephone poles" of yesteryear. They have been replaced by campus-style facilities. Why and how this has occurred forms the background for this volume.

With unit management in place, however, far more than the physical architecture changes. Yet, buildings are "form givers," according to Gary Mote, AIA, then Assistant Director, Federal Bureau of Prisons, at a National Workshop on Unit Management (1988). Prisoners respond to expectations—both those expressed by the staff and the expectations inherent in buildings. Architecture can increase one's sense of being both safe and secure. This occurs through designs which allow direct supervision—without physical barriers. Such a design fosters maximum staff-inmate contact, and permits mutually beneficial relationships to develop. In contrast:

> Mini-control centers, in corridors and secure booths in living units from which officers observe inmates and push buttons, convey the impression that this is a very dangerous place—and no one is safe (Mote, 1988).

In 1975, the Federal Bureau of Prisons opened a Federal Correctional Institution in Butner, North Carolina that was the first secure facility for adult prisoners designed around a unit management concept. Its schematic is the progenitor of modern prison designs used throughout the world. By 1996, two-thirds of the states responding to a questionnaire (27 of 41) from the Wisconsin Department of Corrections said that they used unit management.

# Background

Unit management is a team approach to inmate management. It incorporates the notion that cooperation is most likely in small groups that have lengthy interactions. Other key ingredients in the unit management mixture are decentralization and delegated authority. Employing these ideas has led to the success that this management concept has gained in federal, state, and local correctional systems, including jails, across the nation.

One of the primary missions of corrections is to develop and operate correctional programs that balance the concepts of punishment, deterrence, incapacitation, and rehabilitation (counseling, work, education, and training) for individuals in correctional institutions. Unit management helps provide this balance. This management approach relies on continuous communication among staff and between staff and inmates. Clearly written policies, participatory management, and an emphasis on teamwork contribute to improved conditions.

Staff and inmates gain many benefits from adopting the procedures integral to unit management. Two of the advantages apply to staff:

- Unit management fosters the development of correctional and managerial skills.
- The use of a multidisciplinary team improves communication and cooperation with other institutional departments.

Three additional unit management benefits concern inmates:

- It increases the frequency/intensity of relationships[1] between inmates and staff, which results in better communication and program planning.
- Decentralized management results in decisions about inmates being made more quickly by people who really know them.
- It results in increased program flexibility, since each unit can develop the type of program appropriate for its own population.

Foremost among these benefits are the advantages of a more personalized and responsive approach to the management of inmates. Because decision-making personnel are in close proximity to those about whom the decisions are to be made—the inmates under their control—the amount of violence in institutions that have adopted unit management has decreased significantly (*see* Part 6—Does Unit Management Work?).

# Definition

Unit management has been called many things—some of which should not be said in polite society. Officially,

> Unit management is an approach to inmate and institutional administration designed to improve control and relationships by dividing a large institution population into smaller, more manageable groups, in order to improve the delivery of correctional services.
>
> Roy E. Gerard,
> Assistant Director (retired), Federal Bureau of Prisons

Other definitions include that of an Ohio warden: Unit management is a method for controlling inmate behavior; and, the sign in the office of the superintendent of the Palmer Correctional Center in the Alaska Department of Corrections states:

**[ Unit management is NOT a program; it is a more effective way to manage programs. ]**

Developing an institution's architectural plans[2] around a unit management concept has changed not only how the Bureau of Prisons (and everyone else) builds prisons, it also has altered jail construction. The Federal Prison System's Metropolitan Correctional Centers—the first jails designed around the unit management concept—demonstrated that jails could be more than just places to warehouse people while they undergo the trial process. During the development of the architectural program for the first of these metropolitan correctional centers (in New York City, 1975) John Minor (a member of the Bureau's planning task force) proposed the term "functional unit management."[3] In 1973, Levinson and Gerard, suggested that prisons are like cities, and in this context, units are "neighborhoods" (Johnson, 1996).

# History of Unit Management

Unit management did not spring full-blown from the brow of some bureaucrat during a morning shower. Many independent developments in corrections, especially within the Federal Bureau of Prisons, eventually led to functional unit management.

Prior to the 1950s, newly admitted inmates appeared before a group of institution department heads (for example, the chief of classification, the director of education, the prison industries superintendent, the medical director, the chief of psychology services, the chief of security, and so forth) who constituted the classification committee. At this meeting, the prisoners were informed about the programs and work in which they would be involved during their period of incarceration. Inmates had little input.

Moreover, these decisions were made by staff who had minimal direct daily contact with the prisoners whose programs they were determining.

Nevertheless, the "committee" was an improvement over the prior practice of a single staff member classifying an institution's entire inmate population. Policy dictated that the classification committee's recommendations were forwarded to the deputy warden (or the warden) for a final decision. Caseworkers, then, would call inmates to their office and inform them about the final outcome.

During the mid- to late-1950s, the Federal Reformatory at El Reno, Oklahoma, and later the Federal Youth Center in Ashland, Kentucky—both under Warden John Galvin—developed classification teams. Each team (at a minimum) consisted of a department head and a case manager. These classification teams made recommendations concerning the case manager's caseload of inmates, who resided in living quarters that were scattered throughout the institution.

In October 1961, the Demonstration Counseling Project, a research study, codirected by this author and Howard L. Kitchener, began at the National Training School for Boys in Washington, D.C.; Allan Childers was the superintendent. Among other innovations, this project gathered together in one housing unit, the delinquents on the caseload of one case manager (known as the classification and parole officer, at that time). Prior to the initiation of the Demonstration Counseling Project, the delinquents that became the project's experimental group had been housed in living quarters spread throughout the training school.

Staffing in the experimental cottage was enriched by the addition of three "correctional counselors." These were experienced correctional officers who were given additional training in counseling techniques. The functions performed by these individuals closely paralleled those of the liaison officers, a concept developed by John Galvin at the Federal Youth Center, Englewood, Colorado. The interdisciplinary staff in the experimental cottage were authorized to make specified classification/reclassification decisions and to conduct counseling, recreation, and other in-unit programs.

The Demonstration Counseling Project, then, was the initial approximation of what eventually became unit management. The latter, essentially, is a modification for an adult inmate population of the "cottage" system found in many state training schools for juvenile delinquents.

Research results from the Demonstration Counseling Project (1963) showed meaningful improvement in the areas of institutional adjustment, educational achievement, and positive psychological changes when the experimental group was compared with a randomly selected control group (who had continued with the Training School's traditional approach). Postrelease follow-up showed that the experimental group remained in the community free of new law violations for a significantly longer period of time than the control group. For releasees who later "failed" in the community, recommitment offenses for the experimental group were substantially less serious than those committed by the control group.

Subsequent to the completion of the Demonstration Counseling Project, its living unit management concept was expanded from one cottage to include the entire National Training School population. When staff compared data with that obtained during the prior period of operation under the traditional (centralized) management style, the results showed positive findings similar to those found under the original Demonstration Counseling Project.

In 1963, Warden Joseph Bogan established a "unit system" at the Englewood, Colorado Federal Youth Center. In addition to the traditional correctional officers, each inmate living area had a "unit officer." These unit officers were teamed with a caseworker and maintained an office in the housing unit to which their caseload had been assigned. At Englewood, the unit classification team consisted of one department head, the caseworker, and the unit officer.

When the U.S. Congress passed the Narcotic Addict Rehabilitation Act in 1966, the Bureau of Prisons became firmly involved in drug rehabilitation. Initially, Narcotic Addict Rehabilitation Act treatment units were established at three facilities: the Federal Correctional Institution at Danbury, Connecticut; the Federal Reformatory for Women at Alderson, West Virginia; and the Federal Correctional Institution at Terminal Island, California. These drug treatment units operated on a semiautonomous basis within institutions that had a traditional, centralized approach to inmate management.

The operational success of the Narcotic Addict Rehabilitation Act program (Narcotic Addict Rehabilitation Act, 1975) encouraged the spread of unit management throughout the Bureau of Prisons. Staffing for these Narcotic Addict Rehabilitation Act units became the "ideal" pattern for future specialized functional units under unit management, such as treatment-intensive programs for sex offenders, inmates with mental health needs, and so forth. The staffing pattern for these types of units included one unit manager (administrator), a psychologist, a caseworker, and for each fifty inmates, two correctional counselors. Units with one hundred inmates were staffed with an additional caseworker and two additional correctional counselors.

Subsequently, other Narcotic Addict Rehabilitation Act program components have become prototypes for all functional units. Drug abuse treatment programs now have been established in every facility of the Bureau of Prisons.

Current Bureau of Prisons'programs that are implemented as part of unit management include three levels of substance abuse programs. The first level is education—inmates receive forty hours of information on what drugs are and what they do. The second level, nonresidential treatment, is for prisoners who have experimented with drugs or are occasional users. They are exposed to a group of programs and some counseling.

The third level is residential drug abuse treatment, which is similar to a a therapeutic community and lasts for 500 hours—nine months. Inmates at this level are housed together. Under the Crime Control Act of 1994, they receive one year off their sentence for completing the program and are eligible for transitional services—six months in a halfway house. Because of the sentence-lowering component, many inmates claim they have a substance abuse problem, but the determination is based on the presentence investigation report, which documents the need to be in such a program. For program entrance, the unit staff does the initial review and will make referral to the drug treatment specialist who makes a subsequent review to *see* if an inmate is eligible for an interview. After the initial recommendation, the case manager is responsible to *see* if the inmate is eligible for a year off. However, no inmate who is adjudged violent is eligible for a sentence reduction, Delores Stephens, Assistant

Administrator for Policy Development and Training, Bureau of Prisons, Washington, D.C. told ACA staff.

However, we are getting ahead of the history. In January 1969, the Robert F. Kennedy Youth Center opened in Morgantown, West Virginia. Roy E. Gerard, who had been an Associate Warden at Englewood and followed Childers as superintendent at the National Training School for Boys, was the Kennedy Youth Center's first warden. This federal facility was architecturally designed in accord with unit management concepts.

In addition to being the first institutionwide implementation of unit management, the Kennedy Youth Center also employed a specific internal inmate classification system, AIMS—Adult Inmate Management System, based on Quay's (1984) typology. This was a later version of Quay's 1971 formulation for juveniles. Quay's AIMS approach identifies and houses together inmates who are similar to each other, and allows character-driven management and treatment strategies to be offered to inmates in different housing units (*see* Part 5—Internal Classification).

A study of the Kennedy Youth Center considered the total institutional climate, including both staff and inmate attitudes, and their opinions about the facility's management and correctional programs. Data were compared to similar information from a comparable federal youth center and two nonfederal institutions—one using a traditional management and treatment approach and the other using an approach similar to the Kennedy Youth Center.

Results showed overwhelmingly more positive attitudes on the part of both staff and inmates, and better inmate-staff relationships at Kennedy. In general, the findings indicated a better institutional climate at the Kennedy Youth Center and the State Residential Treatment Center for Delinquents, which used a management and treatment approach similar to Kennedy's.

These positive experiences (bolstered by the favorable evaluation results) led to expanding unit management during the 1970s to all youth and young adult facilities within the federal prison system. In 1972, functional unit management was established by Warden Elwood "Woody" Toft, first at the Federal Correctional Institution in Seagoville, Texas, and, then at the Federal Correctional Institution in El Reno, Oklahoma. Between 1968 and 1976, the number of functional units within the Bureau of Prisons grew from 4 to 141.

However, the transition into unit management was not always an easy one. Resistance to a change of this pervasive nature abounded. Nevertheless, by mid-1976, unit management was operating in all the Bureau of Prisons' institutions, except the six penitentiaries, where problems of antiquated facilities, huge populations, and limited staffing blocked its implementation.

> The breakthrough for moving unit management into the penitentiaries came as a result of a series of incidents at, and surrounding, the U.S. Penitentiary in Lewisburg, Pennsylvania. Inmate violence . . . had become a source of concern to the public, the Congress, the Judiciary, and the Bureau of Prisons. As a result, a Board of Inquiry was ordered [convened] by the Bureau in June of 1976. A major recommendation of

> this Board was that the penitentiary should "establish a complete unit management system" (Smith and Fenton, 1978).

Following Lewisburg, the federal penitentiaries at Terre Haute (in 1977), Atlanta (in 1978), and Leavenworth and McNeil Island (in 1979) all implemented unit management. According to a 1983 audit of the Bureau of Prisons' Unit Management System, conducted by the Audit Staff of the Justice Management Division of the U.S. Department of Justice, ". . . all but four of the Bureau's forty-three institutions have unit management. There is a total of 181 units. Of this total, 34 [19 percent] are drug or alcohol program units."

And in 1998, unit management is considered the norm for all Bureau of Prisons' facilities. The modified mission statement for the Bureau of Prisons' as of September 1998 is to "determine inmate programs and encourage prosocial institution and community behaviors that benefit inmates, staff, victims, and society. This is accomplished through functional unit management and effective interaction," Delores Stephens, Assistant Adminsitrator for Policy Development and Training at the Bureau of Prisons in Washington, D.C. explained to American Correctional Association staff.

To implement its mission, vital functions of the Bureau of Prisons are reviewed during a program review, sometimes called in other places an 'audit.' These include the following issues, Dolores Stephens of the Bureau of Prisons told ACA staff in September, 1988:

1. To insure inmates are appropriately classified to promote institution and public safety
2. To insure staff evaluate the needs of inmates and recommend appropriate programs through front-end intervention and effective communication, program evaluation, and follow-up
3. To insure staff are accessible to the inmates
4. To insure staff are appropriately trained
5. To insure case management coordinators and units managers provide oversight and quality control of case management and unit operations

Many state and local jurisdictions across the nation also began to express interest in, and to adopt, unit management as their approach to inmate management. Acceptance and growth have continued during the 1980s and 1990s. For example, at the international level:

- In 1984 in the United Kingdom, the Prison Service's Control Review Committee, citing a "new generation" of prison designs in the United States—"made up of self-contained units . . . with decentralized unit management"—recommended that a new system of special units, "designed to cater to prisoners presenting control problems which could not be dealt with in normal prison conditions," be established (Prison Service, 1984); such special units currently operate at Hull and Woodhill.

- The Correctional Service of Canada indicated its intent to implement unit management in all of its institutions (Correctional Service of Canada, 1990), and developed several documents that describe how this has been done (Correctional Service of Canada, 1985, 1986, 1990, and 1992).[4]
- The New Zealand Department of Justice stated, in its management plan for 1993-1994, that it was implementing unit management.
- The Correctional Services in South Africa, in a March 1995 report, has endorsed the concept of unit management.
- The two 600-bed institutions—Fulham Correctional Centre, Victoria, Australia and Junee Correctional Center, New South Wales, Australia—which opened March 1997 and June 1996, respectively, "will be managed in accordance with progressive unit management principles . . . ."
- At its first new correctional facility, Tzalmon Prison in Kallanit, Israel, the new concepts of modular housing and unit management were introduced to the Israeli government.

In summary, the antecendents of unit management were in institutions for juveniles. They spread to other types of facilities (minimum-security and medium-security prisions, then the penitentiaries), initially in federal adult institutions and jails, and then in a number of state jurisdictions and international systems.

A familiar expression in corrections is: what goes around, comes around. It is somewhat ironic that today's adult facilities, faced with the prospect of increasing numbers of "jadults"—juveniles, teenagers, and young adults (McMillen and Hill, 1977)—are looking to unit management for answers. These young offenders, charged with serious offenses, have been waived from the juvenile justice system and incarcerated in adult institutions. Their need for protection presents adult institution administrators with severe problems (Levinson and Greene, in press).

Johnson (1996) offers a different perspective concerning the role of unit management in prisons. He discusses ways in which prisoners "attempt to carve out a private prison world composed of niches or sanctuaries." Inmates seek a "haven from stress" and ways to avoid victimization (*see also*, Toch, 1997, pp. 201-206).

> Prisons that use a unit management system are considerably better organized than other prisons. . . . As a general matter, prisons run on a functional unit model are safer, more humane, and more readily adapted to correctional programming than are traditional, undifferentiated prisons.
>
> Functional unit management offers a flexible approach to the classification and management of different groups. With a functional unit management structure in place, special-risk or special-needs inmates can be readily offered a coherent routine that at once addresses their situation and also integrates them, in varying degrees, into the life of the larger prison (Johnson, 1996, p. 262).

## TABLE 1.1: TEN COMMANDMENTS OF UNIT MANAGEMENT

1. Unit management must be understood by and have the support of the top-level administration.

2. Unit management requires three sets of written guidelines:
   - a policy statement issued by the central office
   - an institution procedures manual
   - a unit plan for each unit

3. In the Table of Organization, Unit Managers are at department-head level, giving them responsibility for both staff and inmates assigned to their unit; and the table shows them and the head of security reporting to the same supervisor.

4. Each unit's population size is based on its mission:
   - General Unit—150-250 inmates; in other words, two caseloads
   - Special Unit—75-125 inmates

5. Inmates and unit staff are permanently assigned to the unit; correctional officers are stationed for a minimum of nine months.

6. Staffing consists of:

| | General Unit | Special Unit |
|---|---|---|
| Unit manager | 1 | 1 |
| Case manager | 2 | 1 |
| Correctional counselor | 2 | 1 |
| Unit secretary | 1 | 1 |
| Mental health staff | ½ | 1 |
| Part-time staff | * | * |

   *(education, recreation, volunteers)
   Correctional officers—24-hour coverage

7. In addition to correctional officer coverage, unit staff provide twelve-hour supervision Monday through Friday and eight hours on each weekend day.

8. Staff offices are located on the unit (or as near to it as possible).

9. Unit personnel receive initial, and ongoing, formal training regarding their roles and responsibilities.

10. Unit management audits (conducted by knowledgeable central or regional office staff) occur on a regularly scheduled basis (minimum, once a year).

A corrections professional from North Carolina recently remarked: "If it wasn't for unit management, we wouldn't know how else to run a large institution."

# Essential Components of Unit Management

In a *Federal Probation* article (1973), Levinson and Gerard characterized a functional unit as a small self-contained inmate living and staff office area, operating semiautonomously within the confines of a larger institution. As unit management grew in popularity and was implemented in a variety of settings, "innovative" modifications also have proliferated; some of these have so stretched the concept that they raise a number of questions:

(1) While flexibility is a hallmark of unit management, how far can a unit's operation deviate from the 1973 definition and still be considered unit management?

(2) What are unit management's minimum must-have features?

# Unit Management's "Ten Commandments"

To the degree that the ten attributes listed in Table 1.1 (on page 9) are absent, unit management will fail. These requisites concern two major goals unit management is designed to help attain:

(1) to establish a safe, humane environment (for both staff and inmates) which minimizes the detrimental effects of confinement, and

(2) to deliver a wide variety of counseling, social, education, and vocational training programs designed to aid offenders to make a successful return to the community.

The following subsections elaborate on unit management's Ten Commandments (Gerard, 1991):

## (1) Support

Because unit management results in a major reorganization of the traditional ways in which correctional institutions function, it must have the clear and continuing support from the highest levels of top management. The importance of this attribute is suggested by the nature of some of the changes which unit management introduces. For example:

- It requires a willingness to change department policy so that it reflects a chain-of-command that includes unit managers at a department-head level—in other words, at the same level as each institution's highest uniformed (security staff) officer. At the state level, this is often a major; in federal institutions, it is a captain.
- It "breaks down" the traditional separation between "treatment" and "security" staff.

- It introduces new career opportunities.
- It necessitates changes in position descriptions and post orders.
- It requires a willingness to convert some current positions to other functions to comply with unit management's staffing pattern.

Leadership must be expressed from the central (and regional) office(s), institution, and unit levels. A commitment to unit management at each echelon is imperative to the successful implementation of this concept.

## (2) Guidelines

The pervasive changes that unit management fosters require that clear, written guidance is available, which outlines these new functions. Three documents are needed:

- A policy statement concerning unit management, issued by the central office and signed by the director/commissioner of the corrections department
- An institution procedures manual, signed by the warden, which specifies how the central office policy that pertains to unit management will be implemented at his or her institution (*see* Appendix 1)
- A unit plan written by each unit manager (and approved by his or her supervisor), which describes that unit's operation within the parameters established by both central office policy and the institution's procedures manual (*see* Appendix 2)

## (3) Department Heads

Functional units have been compared to mini-institutions, headed by "mini-wardens." The scope of unit managers' responsibility requires that they have the authority to function at a commensurate level. Unit managers must be department heads to deal effectively with staff in all other departments throughout the institution.

Equally important, unit managers and the chief of security should report to the same supervisor; *see* Unit Table of Organization, page 32. This ensures rapid and fair resolution of the conflicts that will arise regarding areas of overlapping responsibility. Unit management cannot function in a vacuum. Mutual cooperation and assistance are imperative.

## (4) Size

The size of the inmate population should be commensurate with the mission of each unit. A general population unit consists of two caseloads of inmates, each of 75 to 125 individuals; in other words, a total of 150 to 250 prisoners. Special program-intensive units (to which inmates are assigned because they have a need for a specific type of in-unit treatment regimen) are smaller—from 75 to 125 prisoners. Examples of special units include those with treatment programs for inmates with mental health problems, sex offenders, substance abusers, and so forth.

When determining how many units an institution has, it is important to avoid confusing the number of living areas and the number of units. The number of units in a facility equals the number of unit managers. And, it is that number which is used to assess the adequacy level of each unit's size. For example, an institution with six living areas (buildings or cell blocks), each with 175 inmates, has three unit managers (each supervising two living areas). This is not within the recommended staffing guideline. Unit size is determined by dividing the total number of unit managers (3) by the total number of inmates (6 x 175), regardless of the number of living areas. In this example, the result is 350 prisoners per unit, which is too many.

## (5) Stability

In many ways, traditional correctional procedures recapitulate the chaotic preinstitutional existence of most offenders. For example, continually moving inmates from one housing area to another breaks up potentially positive staff-inmate relationships. This type of situation results when, say, inmates are designated to units by their job assignments (for example, all kitchen workers live together). When a job change occurs, it results in a prisoner moving to a different unit. Or when, as a consequence of frequently (daily, weekly, monthly) rotating correctional officers, inmates experience ever-changing rule interpretations. Both of these situations are unnecessary and destructive.

Unit management replaces this type of disorder with a more dependable structure. Under unit management, unit staff is assigned on a permanent basis. Although unit correctional officers may rotate among all three shifts (midnight, day, and evening), this rotation occurs within one unit, where the correctional officers are stationed for a minimum of nine months.

Additionally, inmates stay in one unit for the entire time they spend at that institution. If prisoners are placed in punitive segregation, when released from there, they return to their original unit.[5] This avoids inmates being able to manipulate the system. The philosophy is, if offenders cannot "make it" in a particular unit, then they cannot "make it" in that institution. There is no "passing around" of problem cases. On the other hand, if inmates do well, they are not moved to a different living area—an "honor dorm." Offenders newly admitted to the unit should have the opportunity to observe positive role models.

**[ Cooperation is most likely in small groups with lengthy interactions. ]**

## (6) Staffing

An adequate number of unit personnel is required. The minimum staffing for a general population functional unit (in addition to twenty-four-hour correctional officer coverage) consists of six full-time personnel: one unit manager, two case managers,[6] two correctional counselors,[6] and one secretary or clerk-typist. Each general unit also has assigned to it the following part-time, ancillary personnel: an education adviser, a recreation specialist, and a unit psychologist.

Special units are smaller and usually consist of one caseload. They serve a specially selected population and have a staff consisting of: one unit manager, one secretary, one case manager, one correctional counselor, and a full-time unit psychologist. This enables special unit personnel to develop intensive in-unit treatment programs specifically designed to meet the needs of their particular population. A unit of all early risers (for example, kitchen workers) does not qualify as a special unit, whereas one with an intensive in-house program for mentally retarded inmates does (*see also* Unit Types, pages 42-45).

Per-unit staffing among the ten states participating in the 1988 National Institute of Corrections Workshop—exclusive of twenty-four-hour correctional officer coverage—ranged from three to seven (the average was five, the mode six). A significant consequence of understaffing is that coverage by unit staff for twelve hours during the week and eight hours on weekends becomes impossible. This, in turn, results in an increased likelihood of "turf battles"(*see* page 41).

Having competent staff is crucial. In addition to personnel with trained competency in the requisite skills required for each individual position, staff must have a personal resolve and commitment to the principles of unit management.

## (7) Coverage

Unit personnel supplement round-the-clock correctional officer staffing by providing twelve hours of coverage Monday through Friday and eight hours on weekends and holidays. In other words, a properly staffed unit (with six staff members) covers 66 of the week's total of 168 hours. Every counselor, case manager, and unit manager works evening hours at least once a week. To stay abreast of unit and facility activities, unit managers work a weekend and/or holiday at least once every quarter; such workdays will not be assigned unequally to counselors.

## (8) Office space

Office space for all full-time unit staff is located on, or adjacent to, the housing unit. This fosters the development of a "unit team concept." It also helps create positive inmate-staff relationships since the prisoners have easy access to personnel charged with decision-making responsibility about their case.

## (9) Training

Because of the nontraditional aspects of unit management, staff must receive initial and ongoing training regarding their roles and responsibilities. We strongly recommended that this training should include, at least for unit managers (and, preferably, for all unit staff), an on-site visit to a currently operating, well-established functional unit.

Competent staff must be performing at a level of high quality for unit management to be effective. One aspect of meeting this condition is that unit managers must be directly involved in the annual performance ratings of their staff.

Currently, according to Terry Tibbals of Ohio's South Regional Office, all staff hired by the Ohio Department of Rehabilitation and Correction receive four weeks of pre-service training and one week of on-the-job training at the facility in which they will work. In addition, the Corrections Training Academy offers additional courses to unit management staff throughout each year. Each facility is also responsible for providing forty hours of annual in-service training that includes eight hours of job specific training.

## (10) Audits

Periodic (twelve-to-eighteen-month) formal, on-site reviews of unit management should be conducted by the central office unit management coordinator (or this person's regional office counterpart, if there is one). The intent of these audits is to assess policy compliance and obtain statistical data. This information provides the basis for initiating modifications designed to maximize unit management's overall effectiveness and efficiency throughout the department of corrections.

Performing this review function requires trained staff who use a formal unit management audit form (*see* an example in Appendix 3). The same basic audit form will be used for all units; however, it may be augmented with additional items to fit the needs of different unit types within the system.

In addition to monitoring for compliance with policy, a systematic approach to data collection is necessary. It assists in determining whether the system's goals for unit management have been attained and provides a basis for remedial action.

For example, regional directors in Ohio "were asked to set the review of the application of the Unit Management Concept as a priority. . . . " On-site reviews of unit management were conducted at twenty of the jurisdiction's twenty-two institutions. Their findings are listed in terms of security, safety, staff-to-inmate ratio, and administrative efficiency. "With few exceptions [unit management] was found to be functioning as originally designed. . . . [T]he adoption of Unit Management in Ohio has been extremely beneficial."

In a 1998 letter from the South Regional Ofice of the Ohio Department of Rehabilitation and Correction to the American Correctional Association, Terry Tibbals writes that Ohio's mission statement for unit management is as follows:

> Unit management enhances accountability, security and communication by dividing large groups of offenders into smaller groups supervised by teams of trained staff located in close proximity to other living area; correctional services delivery is improved through early problem resolution and mediation by staff familiar with assigned caseloads.
>
> Unit management works very well with the ideals of Total Quality Management (TQM). With all levels of staff involved in the unit management concept, staff are afforded

the opportunity to review and make suggestions regarding the overall operation of unit management in each facility and department wide. This continually improves our operations and the delivery of services to the offenders housed in our facilities.

# Operational Minimums

A National Institute of Corrections-sponsored technical assistance project for the American Federation of State, County, and Municipal Employees' founding Congress of AFSCME Corrections United, was conducted October 13-14, 1993, in Columbus, Ohio. Sixty-six members attending a workshop indicated the situation concerning unit management at their own state facility by circling a "yes" or "no" for each of unit management's "Ten Commandments" (*see* page 9). As shown in Table 1.2, representatives from sixteen different state systems completed the questionnaire—some states were represented by more than one person.

Despite the requirements for operational success, as shown in Table 1.2, only one institution (in Ohio) was reported as functioning in accord with all of unit management's "Ten Commandments." Two other Ohio facilities reported being in compliance with eight (and another two with five) of the "Commandments." (In 1998, according to Terry Tibbals, from the Ohio Department of Rehabilitation and Correction, Ohio still adheres to each of the Ten Commandments of unit management in many of their thirty-one facilities. However, due to space constraints and crowding issues, they do not meet the requirements listed under the fourth commandment, regarding the population size, in several of their facilities.) At the other extreme, while none of the participants reported "zero" compliance, Nevada and Oregon reported complying with just one of the ten criteria. Six states—Illinois, Nevada, New York, Ohio, Pennsylvania, and Texas—had more than one participant at the conference and, therefore, appear more than once in the table.

**Table 1.2: Number of Unit Management "Commandments" Followed (By State)**

10 — OH

9 — AZ, MD, MN

8 — OH*, WI

7 — PA, TN

6 — IL, KY, PA, TX

5 — IL, OH*, PA, TX

4 — NY*, PA*, WI

3 — CT, PA*, NV*

2 — IL*, NV, PA, VA

1 — NV, OR

[* = two replies]

In May 1997, sixty-two participants were involved in a week-long unit management training program at Appalachian State University that was sponsored by the North Carolina Division of Prisons. As part of a training exercise, these individuals—central office personnel, superintendents, assistant superintendents, captains, lieutenants, unit managers, assistant unit managers, and sergeants—indicated which of unit management's "Ten Commandments" were followed at their facility, in North Carolina, by circling "yes" or "no" on a form. Fifty-four surveys were returned. The percent of "yes" replies on each survey item ranged from 100 percent [staff offices located on/near unit] to 39 percent [have recommended staffing pattern].

Twelve participants gave their institution 10 "yes" responses; these represented seven different facilities (out of the thirteen that had staff at the training session). Two of these facilities received all "yes" responses from three staff members (of the five that were in attendance from each of these institutions). The largest spread in number of "yes" responses received by the same institution ranged from a low of two to a high of eight "yes" replies.

The discrepancies found in the two training program data sets indicate either the lack of a department of corrections' policy on unit management or inconsistencies in following it. They highlight the question: When is a unit "doing" unit management? In a recent letter from the North Carolina Division of Prisons, Director Daniel Stienke stated that as a result of these training exercises, they recognized the importance of developing division standards for unit management and have formed a task force to adopt divisonwide policy.

## What Unit Management is Not

> "The organization design is based on the 'unit management concept' in which each of the buildings are run by a counselor and assisted jointly [sic] by a sergeant. . . . The following points are important.
>
> A. The Unit management team is governed by three people with the lieutenant having more [authority] though not substantially more than the counselor and sergeant.[7] The team has discretion to decide such issues as: clothing, property, phone calls, and recreation policy for the inmates in its building. There are five buildings, each has a unit management team.
>
> B. The Unit Management Review Committee (UMRC) consists of two captains from the perimeter team and the treatment program supervisor. Decisions between the buildings need to be coordinated. . . . The UMRC approves or disapproves of building [team] decisions, taking the security needs of the institution as a whole into account.

C. The Chief of Security, as the top uniformed official in the institution . . . means that the chief will influence UMRC decisions.

D. . . . The UMRC does not have the final say on building policies. Teams dissatisfied with UMRC decisions can appeal to the executive committee [which consists of the Assistant Warden for Operations, the Assistant Warden for Treatment, and the Chief of Security] . . . ."

Extract from a case study developed for the *Program on Correctional Leadership and Innovation* of the Wharton School; no date.

This description fails to comply with unit management requirements in the following five ways:

1. The unit is understaffed—only three personnel [paragraph A]
2. The unit team leader—a lieutenant—is not at a department-head level [paragraph A]
3. The unit team's decisions [sic] are approved or disapproved by the Unit Management Review Committee [paragraph B]; therefore, they are not decisions but recommendations
4. The chief of security controls unit team decision-making [paragraph C]
5. The five administrative layers that are listed are too many—unit, Unit Management Review Committee, chief of security, executive committee, and warden [paragraphs A, B, C, D]

## Therapeutic Community

Another differentiation needs to be made. How does unit management differ from a therapeutic community? According to Dr. Maxwell Jones, (1980, pp. 34-35), the father of the therapeutic community concept, there are twenty-one "principles essential in putting together a therapeutic community in a prison setting." Some—four and one-half—but far from all, of these also describe a functional unit.

Unlike a therapeutic community, in unit management, clients and staff do not volunteer to work as a problem-solving group. Confidentiality concerning all that goes on in the unit is not "totally respected" as it is in a therapeutic community. Prison authorities do delegate some responsibility and authority to the unit, but not to the extent found in a therapeutic community. And, unlike a therapeutic community, in a unit management situation, decision-making by consensus is not a goal from the start.

As in a therapeutic community, the unit manager does have access to prison authorities at all times. However, traditional prison rules are not modified to accommodate the unit as happens in a therapeutic community environment. Further, in a unitized institution there is not an inevitable crisis between unit management and the prison's administrators. Consequently, a facilitator acceptable to both the institution's hierarchy and the functional unit is not required, as it is in a therapeutic situation. In unit management, there is not an inverse relationship between the growth potential of the inmates and the degree of staff intervention.

Under unit management, inmates may have as much responsibility as they are competent to manage—but they are not given the amount of authority they get in a therapeutic community. Only to a limited degree (*see* Advisory Council, pages 72-73) do a unit's residents nominate their own leaders, and those individuals do not represent the culture carriers for their peers. Under unit management, discipline and other important decisions are not delegated to the inmates.

Unit management personnel are prepared, as a consequence of inmate turnover, to recycle basic principles; this process does not have the "peaks and valleys" regarding the level of the staff's supervisory role that are anticipated in a therapeutic community. Growth in the direction of social maturity is not an immediate goal for unit management staff, although, ultimately, it may be for the unit's inmates.

Follow-through with inmates leaving a functional unit is not the ultimate goal of unit management. And, only to a limited degree in a functional unit is the "treatment" process one of "two-way communication of content and feeling, listening and interaction, and problem-solving leading to learning." In unit management, treatment and training do not overlap, so one cannot talk of treating staff and training inmates as well as vice versa.

When asked how unit management is similar to the therapeutic community, Joseph Lehman, Secretary of the Washington State Department of Corrections said "the advantages of the therapeutic community is that it enhances the structure of communication. The therapeutic community achieves consensus about the norms, and the staff reinforces them; this is where we should be headed in unit management to insure continuity of communication" (conversation with ACA staff, September 1998).

As in a therapeutic community, under unit management larger numbers of inmates can be broken down into groups of optimal size—twenty prisoners or less. Generally, units are larger. Unit management does not apply these twenty-one principles during a daily community meeting of staff and inmates, followed by a process review involving all personnel although some of this occurs at each unit's weekly/biweekly inmate advisory council and unit town hall sessions.

A useful distinction between unit management and therapeutic communities emerged during a conference dialog (Toch, 1980; Chapter 13). The dialog involved the following individuals: Maxwell Jones, M.D., the originator of the therapeutic community concept and a leader in its implementation in mental hospitals and other rehabilitation settings; Fritz Redl, Ph.D., a pioneer in the use of residential treatment facilities for delinquent youths; George DeLeon, the Director of Research for the Phoenix House Foundation, Inc.; Hans Toch, Professor of Psychology, School of Criminal Justice, State University of New York at Albany; and this author.

Jones: "But the essence of what Fritz [Redl] said is that the inmates who are isolated [in a therapeutic community or a unit] get a group identity. Through that group identity they begin to feel that they are real people. And, I think that's one of the goals we're after."

Redl: "As long as we understand that what we are talking about here is, primarily, helping the system function and helping the individual keep out of trouble."

Levinson: "But it's also helping that therapeutic group. If the environment in which that therapeutic community is [located is] a more safe and humane one, then whatever is going on in that unit is likely to have greater benefit."

DeLeon: "I'm happy now. I think an important distinction is beginning to appear, and we're talking less about a rehabilitation model and more about an impact model. I would argue that drawing such distinctions dictates what kind of dependent variables you're going to look at. For example, the key variables that I see are management operations, 'Are you having a positive impact on the institution?' A very different approach than 'Have we applied a therapeutic rehabilitative model here . . . ?'"

Toch: "But you have no objections to gravy, right? I mean Bob Levinson can say, 'I'm happy on account of we haven't had a riot in two years, and the murder rate has dropped.' And now, nobody is upset and he can do what therapy he wants to do. If after five years he can show a reduction in his recidivism rate and people are functioning better, which may be his real goal, is that O.K.? If you have demonstrated improvement in the prison, it doesn't hurt if you also get change in people, does it?"

In 1998, Missouri had two therapeutic communities that used 'pure unit management.' These two communities at the Ozark Correctional Center and at the Maryville Treatment Center have received good external evaluations. A third therapeutic community in a maximum-security prison does not use unit management.

In the two Missouri therapeutic communities that do use unit management, they do not classify the inmates on any internal classification system (*see* Part 5 on Internal Classification) because the inmates are there for treatment and soon will be out in the community and must know how to get along there. In the therapeutic community, the inmates are in units called "families." They are expected to help one another and not exploit each other. All the correctional officers are trained to deliver services in the treatment milieu. The therapeutic communities are under the domain of the Division of Offender Rehabilitative Services, which includes education and mental health delivery and treatment, George Lombardi of the Missouri Department of Corrections explained (conversation with ACA staff, September 1998).

# Summary

So, then, how does one recognize a unit? It is unit management when the following conditions occur:

- A small number of inmates
- who, based on a specific methodology, are assigned to live together
- throughout their stay in the facility
- and it also has a multidisciplinary staff consisting of the following individuals:
  - — one unit manager
  - — two correctional counselors
  - — one clerk/secretary
  - — twenty-four-hour correctional officer coverage
  - — two casemanagers
- whose staff offices are located on the unit
- the unit manager has supervisory responsibility over them, which includes scheduling unit staff to work (on a rotation basis) in the evenings and on weekends, in addition to the on-duty unit correctional officers
- the unit staff have administrative authority for all within-unit aspects of inmate living and programming

# Endnotes

1 European nations place much more reliance on personal contact, personal relationships with inmates, and personal communication skills than seems to be the case in the United States, according to Professor Darrel Cheatwood, personal communication (1991).

2 The Federal Correctional Institution in Butner, North Carolina was the first secure, adult prison built in accord with unit management concepts.

3 The original name has, subsequently, been shortened to "Unit Management."

4 Correctional Service of Canada. 1990. *Unit Management Principles of Correctional Operations—A Discussion Paper*. Correctional Service of Canada. Ottawa, Canada..

5 Currently, inmates in Missouri who are assigned to administrative segregation are in a separate unit management group. "We experimented with it the other way [with inmates returning to their original unit] but found it was not practical with overcrowded facilities and the need to use every bed. If it is at all possible to place the inmate back in the unit, this is done, but if there is no bed there, then when the inmate completes administrative segregation time, the inmate is sent to another unit wherever the bed is.

"Another advantage to having a separate unit management for administrative segregation cases is that the staff there know the policies and procedures for the unit and because of this there is less legal exposure. Due to severe crowding, the idea of the unit 'owning' the inmate had to be discarded when the inmate was sent to administrative segregation," George Lombardi, director of adult institutions for the Missouri Department of Corrections, told ACA staff (September 1998).

6 Exact titles are not important; having adequate staff to perform these functions is what counts.

7 The warden (personal communication) described this as 34 percent, 33 percent, and 33 percent, respectively.

*If you put a pile of pebbles together carefully enough, you get a cathedral.*

—Anonymous

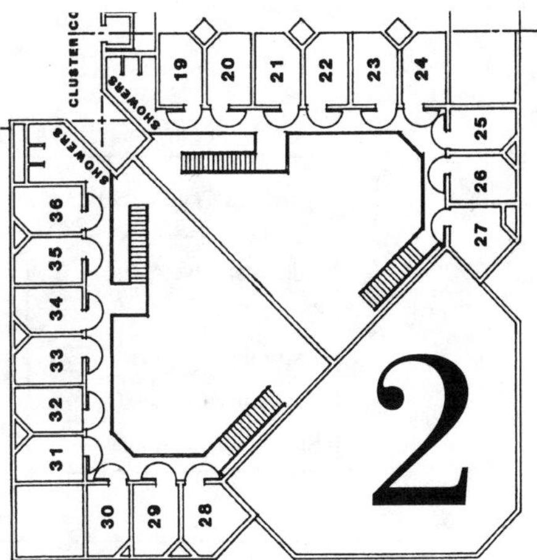


# Managing Unit Management

## Chain of Command

Unit management not only changes the relationships between staff and inmates, it also fundamentally alters the ways in which correctional personnel interrelate with one another. Often, when unit management begins in a department of corrections, it starts at a single institution (*see* Implementation section, pages 48-62). As its benefits begin to be recognized, the concept proliferates. Other institutions "get into" unit management, and it becomes increasingly apparent that this "new kid on the block" is here to stay. When this occurs, top-level administrators begin to realize that a new configuration of the agency's management functions will be needed at all levels.

## Central Office

Typically, in the central office table of organization, the unit management section finds a home in the correctional programs division—either as a subsection within, or as a separate entity on a par with, case management. The "marriage" of programs and security, which unit management fosters at the institution level, often prompts a similar restructuring in the central office. That is, both unit management and security become part of one chain of command; consequently, the chiefs of these two sections report to the same associate director (*see* Central Office Table of Organization, Figure 2.1, next page).

# FIGURE 2.1 CENTRAL OFFICE TABLE OF ORGANIZATION*

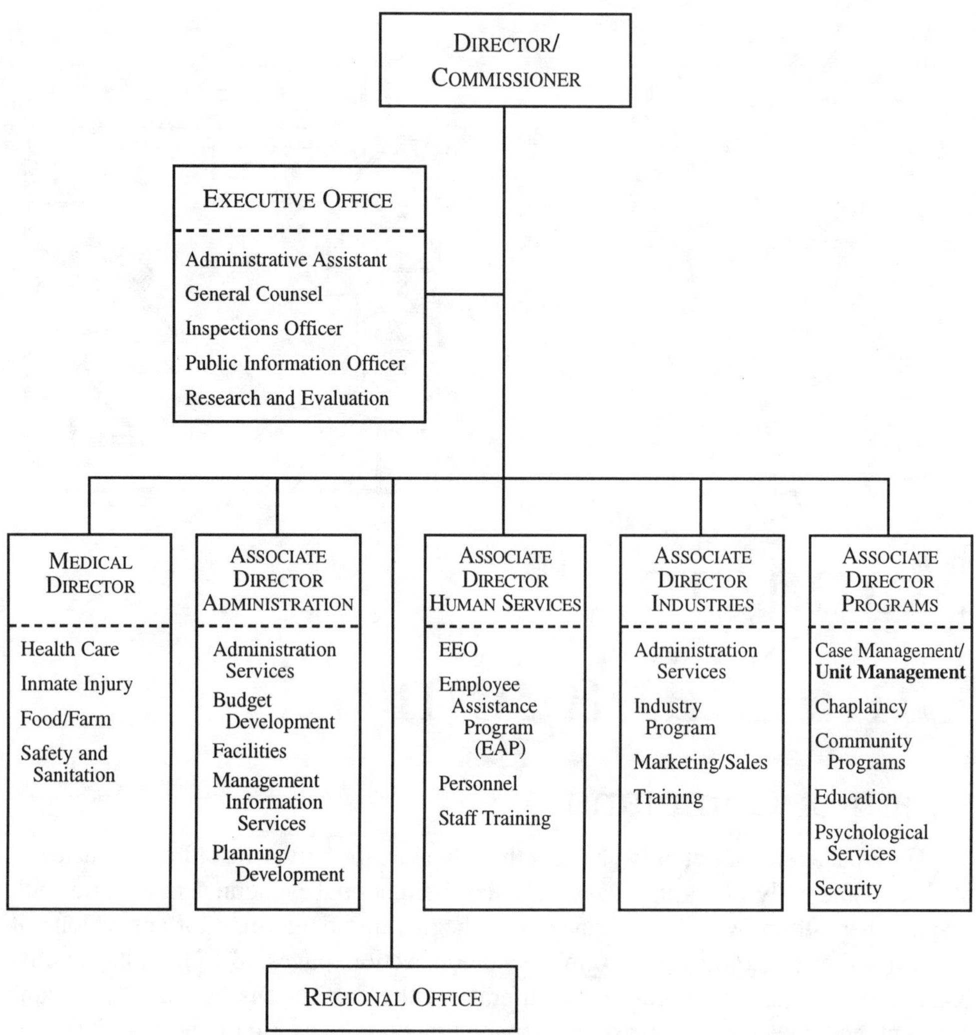


* Specific titles may differ, the important considerations are the functions that each staff member performs.

At the central office level, the unit management section is responsible for:

- Developing a systemwide unit management policy
- Monitoring the development and implementation of unit management
- Coordinating and providing unit management training for all department of corrections staff (at its training academy), and special, discipline-relevant training for unit managers and other unit staff.

- Conducting a yearly conference for regional unit management specialists
- Furnishing technical assistance to state or local agencies
- Coordinating unit management research and evaluation

## Regional Office

Figure 2.2 (*see* page 26) depicts unit management at the regional office level, where the unit management specialist is responsible for:

- Providing technical assistance to unit staff at institutions within his or her region
- Assisting with the planning/implementing of a unit manager training program for newly appointed unit managers
- Arranging/conducting a yearly training conference for the region's unit managers
- Conducting annual unit management program reviews (audits) at each of the region's facilities
- Monitoring and coordinating unit management activities throughout the region
- Ensuring that routine (such as monthly/quarterly/annual) institution data collection efforts are completed in a timely fashion
- Ensuring that all research/evaluation efforts are coordinated with the central office
- Providing input for the development of central office policy regarding unit management

## Institution Level

Figure 2.3 (*see* page 27) depicts the location of unit management on the table of organization of a typical institution. Unit managers are at the third level in the chain of command.

**[ Warden ⟶ Deputy Warden ⟶ Unit Manager ]**

Within each facility, unit management is the responsibility of the same supervisor who has jurisdiction over security services, such as the deputy warden for programs in the table of organization shown in Figure 2.3. This reduces tension that typically exists between the program and the correctional (security) services through regularly scheduled (weekly) staff meetings. It also helps ensure that any problems which do arise will be resolved at the appropriate administrative level, in other words, below the warden's office.

# FIGURE 2.2 REGIONAL OFFICE TABLE OF ORGANIZATION*

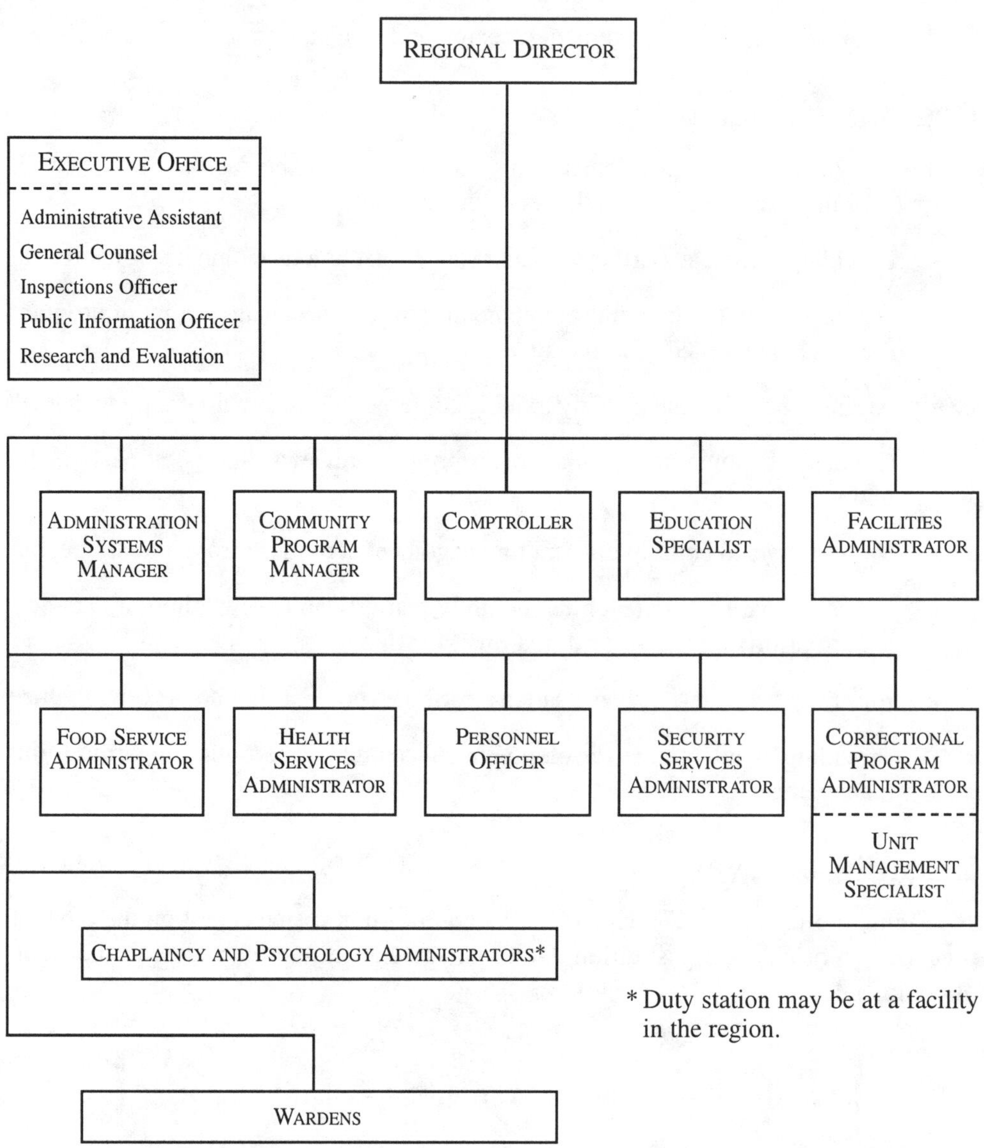


* If a jurisdiction does not have regional offices, then these responsibilities are assumed by the central office, and a larger unit management section will be necessary.

# Centralized Versus Decentralized Management

A major concept in the unit management approach is the notion of a decentralized approach to institutional management. Traditional (centralized) correctional settings follow a hierarchial-management structure. That is, there is a chain of command in which decision-making is a top-down function; while information may flow up and down, only upper-level staff decides.

Unit management "flattens" this decision hierarchy by subdividing facilities into smaller, semi-autonomous sections (units) whose staff has specified decision-making authority. The unit manager's level of authority is circumscribed. Not everything is decentralized in a unitized correctional facility; a number of critical operations remain centralized as shown in Table 2.1. This ensures a level of internal coherence. It allows for decentralized decision-making without permitting the facility to "go off in all directions."

## FIGURE 2.3 INSTITUTION LEVEL TABLE OF ORGANIZATION

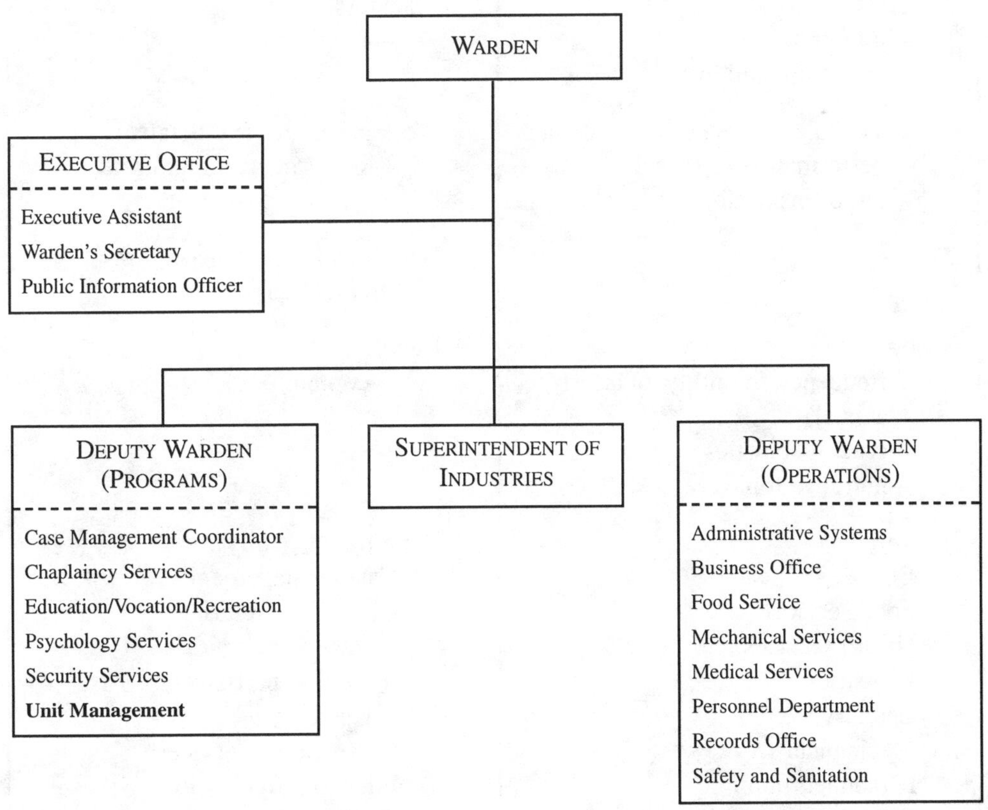

## TABLE 2.1: INSTITUTION OPERATIONS/DEPARTMENTS

| REMAIN CENTRALIZED | BECOME DECENTRALIZED |
|---|---|
| Operations: | Operations: |
| Inmate-to-unit assignment procedures | Inmates assigned to beds |
| Coordinating inmate program assignments | Classification decisions |
| Length of "program day" | Assigning inmates to programs |
| Institutionwide meetings:<br>—who attends<br>—where held<br>—how often (minimum)<br>—major agenda items | Unit meetings:<br>—when held<br>—how often (beyond minimum)<br>—how long<br>—additional agenda items |
| Disciplinary procedures (major reports) | Disciplinary procedures (minor reports) |
| Transfers:<br>—interunit<br>—out of institution | Transfers:<br>—intra-unit |
| Work schedules (correctional staff*):<br>—performance appraisals*<br>—out of institution | Work schedules (unit staff*):<br>—performance appraisals |
| | Health and safety inspections (living areas) |
| Reports:<br>—frequency (monthly, quarterly, annual)<br>—type of statistics<br>—narrative topics | Reports:<br>—content |
| Departments:<br>Business office<br>Food service<br>Health services<br>Industries<br>Laundry<br>Mechanical services<br>Personnel/training<br>Safety and sanitation | Departments (fully):<br>Case management<br>Clerical/secretarial<br><br>Departments (partially):<br>Chaplaincy<br>Correctional services<br>Education/recreation<br>Psychology |

* with input from unit staff

The left-hand column in Table 2.1 displays the institution components that remain centralized when a facility becomes unitized, while the right-hand column shows those aspects of the institution that become decentralized. This means that all of the activities and departments listed in the left-hand column operate in the same way for every unit. In other words, they continue to function in the traditional (nondecentralized) fashion. Unit management changes the way in which the activities/departments listed in the right-hand column function (*see* the next section). It allows each unit a degree of flexibility.

The top half of Table 2.1 (both columns) concerns institutional operations and procedures; the bottom half of the table lists institution departments. Among the latter, some departments are fully decentralized while others are only partially decentralized. These distinctions are clarified in the following section.

# Staff Roles

It is important that all players are aware of their role in unit management. This information should be available in written policy statements, which clearly define the scope of each staff member's authority and the level of responsibility; *see also* Unit Management—Table of Organization, page 32.

## Institution

### Warden

As indicated previously, decentralization and delegated authority are key elements. Nevertheless, within every facility, the warden retains final authority and responsibility. For unit management to be effective, a high degree of autonomy must be vested in each unit manager. Wardens must ensure that the proper degree of decision-making authority has been delegated. The prime objective of unit management is to have semi-autonomous functional units. The benefits of unit management are not achieved by architecture or merely by placing additional personnel within housing areas. However, some aspects of decentralization can be a mixed blessing (*see* unit management issues, pages 41-45).

### Deputy Warden

The warden will ensure that the same deputy warden has supervisory responsibility over both unit management and correctional (security) services. The deputy warden (usually for programs) will function as the institution's leader of unit management. The responsibilities of the deputy warden for operations continue pretty much the same as in a traditionally organized facility.

The deputy warden in charge of unit management will establish written guidelines and parameters. These are contained in an institution procedures manual (*see* Appendix 1) which will:

- Ensure some consistency across the facility's units

- Permit sufficient latitude for the unit managers to individualize each unit's operations
- Create a cost center (budget) for each unit manager—to cover expenses involved in the independent management of minor unit supplies, services, programs, and so forth

As the supervisor of unit management, the deputy warden needs to develop an extensive network for communicating with the unit managers. This should include regularly scheduled group meetings (preferably weekly) attended by all unit managers—or acting unit managers, when the unit manager is absent due to vacation, sick leave, or for other reasons.

## Case Management Coordinator

This staff member functions as a resource person for both the institution's administration (such as the deputy warden) and for unit management. This individual is responsible for the following:

- Ensuring quality case management work
- Regularly auditing case management areas
- Training unit case managers
- Orienting nonunit staff to case management functions[1]

While the case management coordinator has no direct supervisory authority over unit staff, this individual must work closely with each unit manager to achieve common objectives (*see also* the Performance Rating Section, page 167, in the Unit Management Procedures Manual, Appendix 1.)

## Chief of Security

The chief of security (the highest uniformed officer, usually a captain or a major) is the department head with the primary responsibility for maintaining the institution's security. This person serves as an adviser, consultant, and monitor to other department heads in matters pertaining to security (for example, counts and shakedowns).

Unit managers and the chief of security have areas of overlapping responsibility, such as searches for within-unit contraband. Consequently, it is imperative that they maintain a cooperative working relationship. Combining the technical expertise of the major with the unit manager's firsthand knowledge of the unit's inmate population will enhance the orderly running of the facility and the quality of its staff's decision-making.

Unit managers will have a persuasive voice in selecting the correctional officers assigned to the regular posts in their unit—including the morning, day, and evening shifts. Moreover, unit managers will be consulted before changes take place that affect the correctional officers working in their unit.[2]

Generally, unit correctional officers did not rotate out of a unit in less than nine months (preferably not under one year). (However, at the Bureau of Prisons, this has changed so that correctional officers are not compromised in their positions due to ethical lapses and/or inmate manipulation.) If the rotation schedule requires more frequent change—such as every three months—moves will occur within the unit, among the three shifts (*see also*, Performance Rating Section, page 167, in Unit Management Procedures Manual, Appendix 1). Additionally, correctional officers assigned to a unit will not be "pulled" by security unless a genuine emergency exists, such as when the warden or someone acting in this position formally declares such a situation.

### Shift Supervisor

Correctional supervisors and shift commanders (such as the captain or a lieutenant) have delegated authority for institution security matters during the absence of the chief of security. Among their other responsibilities, they serve as consultants to unit managers regarding unit security and have jurisdiction over the nonunit areas of a facility. When no unit team personnel are on duty (such as during the midnight shift), the shift supervisor's responsibilities expand to include unit security. At such time, the unit correctional officers are directly supervised by the shift commander. The traditional notion that "The shift commander tells it, and that's the way it goes," has to change if unit management is to be successful.

## Unit

The table of organization (Figure 2.4 on the next page) shows the relationships among unit staff and between unit personnel and other departments within a unitized correctional facility.

### Unit Manager

The unit manager is the administrator, supervisor, coordinator, trainer, and monitor for a multidisciplinary staff team assigned to work in his or her unit. Included among these administrative responsibilities is the expectation that unit managers will help deliver quality programs and services to all inmates assigned to their unit. Moreover, as a department head, the unit manager will perform additional administrative functions, such as serving as the institution duty officer.

In terms of the career backgrounds of unit managers, all ten systems participating at the National Workshop on Unit Management (1988) reported that in their jurisdictions, both "treatment" and "security" personnel were eligible for (and had been placed in) these positions. This supports the philosophy expressed from unit management's beginning; namely, that this management approach is strengthened when its unit managers come from any discipline found in a typical correctional institution.

Since "unit manager" was a newly created position title, how were the first unit managers trained? The originators of the concept, the directors of the Demonstration Counseling Project trained them; however, for the most part, these "new kids on the block" learned on the job. Subsequently, staff newly promoted to this position were

# FIGURE 2.4 UNIT MANAGEMENT TABLE OF ORGANIZATION

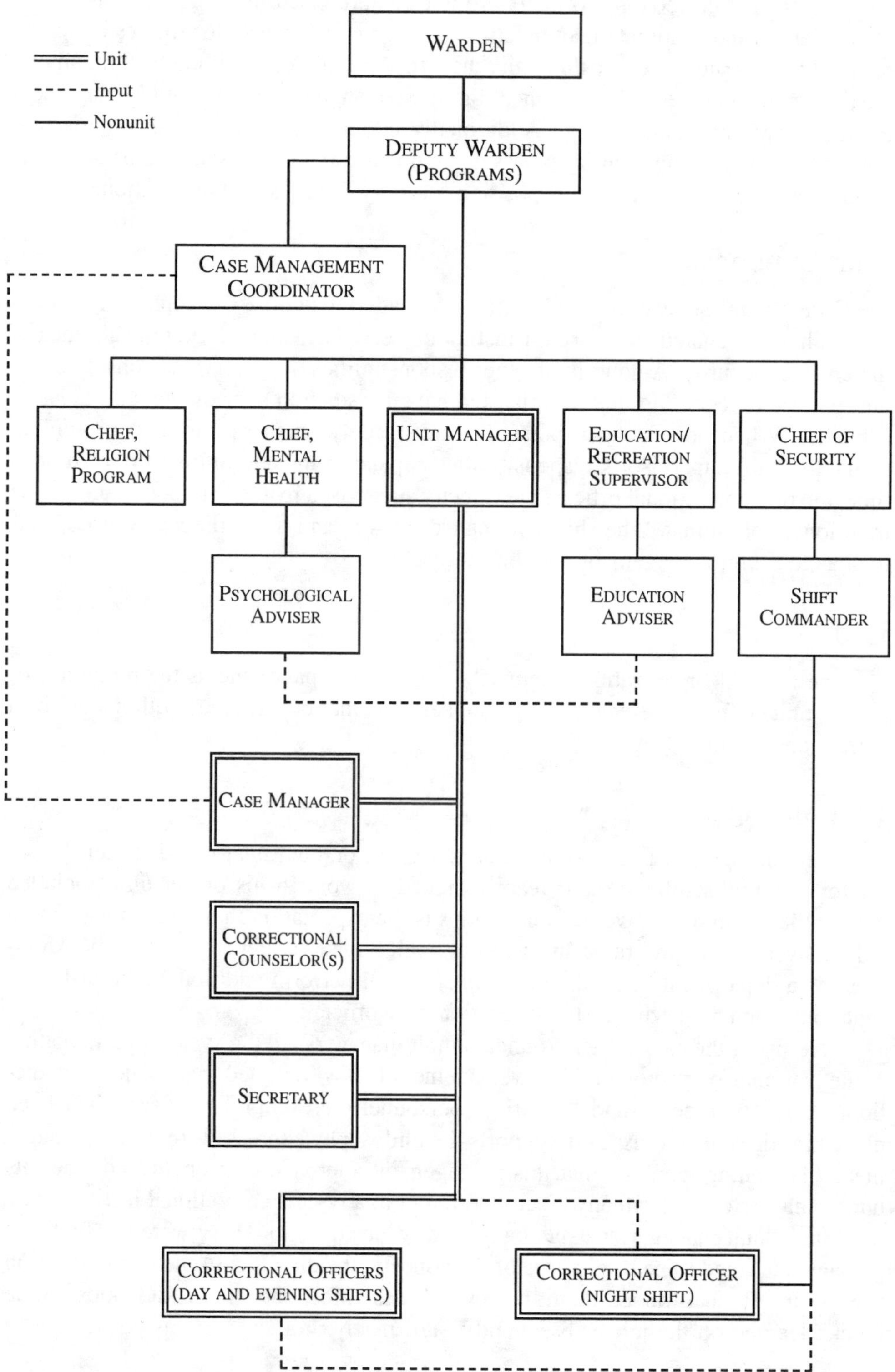

sent by the Bureau of Prisons to existing units where they "shadowed" role model unit managers during a week of apprentice-like training. Then, a training curriculum was developed and incorporated into the offerings provided at the Bureau's Training Academy. Now, several disciplines offer special training in unit management on an as-needed basis.

A unit manager has supervisory responsibility for the unit's case managers, correctional counselors, and secretary. The unit manager also serves as joint supervisor of the unit's correctional officers, and for the unit's part-time personnel (education adviser, recreation specialist, staff psychologist, and so forth (*see also*, Performance Rating Section, page 168, in the Unit Management Procedures Manual, Appendix 1). Every unit manager must ensure that the individual, policy-dictated responsibilities of all unit personnel are accomplished.

The large number of responsibilities of the unit manager can lead to the unit's needs or demands controlling the unit manager rather than vice versa; therefore, being able to delegate is an important managerial skill. Within-unit responsibilities of unit managers include obligations in the following nine general areas (for a discussion in greater detail, *see* the Institution's Unit Management Procedures Manual, Appendix 1; pages 153-157):

1) Administrative
2) Security
3) Safety, Sanitation, and Facilities Management
4) Unit Programs
5) Human Resource Development
6) Supervision
7) Quality Control
8) Financial
9) Strategic Planning

As conceptualized by the U.S. Naval Corrections Branch (Butler, n.d.):

> The dual role of the [Unit Manager—first, maintaining of security within the unit and second, providing counseling to those confined in their unit and facilitate behavior change]. . . requires. . . bridging of the traditional chasm which often separates security and treatment staffs in correctional facilities.

## Case Manager

Under the unit manager's direct supervision, case managers are responsible for all case management matters concerning inmates on their caseload and other duties as assigned by the unit manager. Usually, this does not include clerical functions.

Since the unit manager will not always possess case management expertise, he or she will need to work very closely with the facility's case management coordinator to ensure that all unit case managers are adequately supervised and trained. This will help guarantee that the case managers' work meets recognized standards of professional quality (*see also*, Performance Rating Section, page 168, in the Unit Management Procedures Manual, Appendix 1).

Case managers must be easily accessible to prisoners on their caseload and to other unit and institution personnel. Additional responsibilities include:

1. Interviewing inmates newly assigned to their caseload within twenty-four hours of assignment
2. Developing an inmate's visiting list in collaboration with a correctional counselor
3. Preparing an individualized treatment plan for consideration by the unit's classification team in collaboration with each inmate newly assigned to their caseload (Note: work and basic education will be required for all inmates)[3]
4. Completing necessary initial classification instrument(s) for presentation to the unit's classification team within thirty days of the inmate's admission
5. Reviewing monthly reports concerning in-program progress (for example, work or school) for all inmates on their caseload
6. Completing necessary reclassification instrument(s) for presentation to the unit's classification team (at least annually for every inmate on their caseload)
7. Conducting "debriefing" sessions with inmates after every meeting that individuals on their caseload have with a formal unit or institution committee
8. Initiating and conducting an individual interview with each inmate on their caseload at least once every three months (more frequently, such as every other month, in a special unit)
9. Conducting a formal individual and/or group counseling/therapy session with unit inmates on their caseload—regularly scheduled (at least weekly) and lasting thirty to ninety minutes—maybe with the unit psychologist as coleader
10. Attending and being a voting member at any formal unit committee meeting, which involves an inmate on their caseload
11. Attending and providing written information to any institution committee making decisions pertaining to an inmate on their caseload
12. Visiting, at least once, every inmate on their caseload whose stay in punitive segregation (or the infirmary) exceeds five days
13. Providing back-up to assist inmates on the caseload of the unit's other case manager, when that individual is absent

## Correctional Counselor

In many jurisdictions, the introduction of unit management brings a new type of staff member into the prison setting—the correctional counselor, also known as an inmate relations (or liaison) officer or correctional services coordinator. These are specially trained correctional officers (usually at the level of a sergeant) who function under the unit manager's direct supervision. Continuing training is provided by the unit's psychology adviser. These staff members have been relieved of their usual security responsibilities and, now, deal with the day-to-day problems of institutional living encountered by their caseload of inmates.[4]

There is a continuing discussion as to whether these individuals should remain in uniform. Some contend that it makes the term correctional officer more meaningful; others say that the officer's uniform is an additional barrier in establishing a relationship between inmates and counselors.

Each correctional counselor is teamed with a case manager (they both have the same caseload of inmates), so that they can "back up" each other. For example, their days off should not overlap. Correctional counselors also will perform other assignments as specified by the unit manager. Normally, these do not include duties of the correctional officer. In the absence of the unit manager, they may function as the acting unit manager, when they are so assigned.

Correctional counselors must be readily accessible to prisoners on their caseload to meet the following major responsibilities, which should occupy approximately one-half of the counselor's on-duty time:

1. Assisting in resolving inmates' day-to-day problems
2. Conducting formal/informal group/individual counseling and crisis-intervention sessions

Additional correctional counselor duties include:

3. Interviewing inmates newly admitted to the unit as part of a formal intake screening and orientation process
4. Developing general knowledge about all of the unit's inmates and detailed information about individuals on their own caseload
5. Assisting in the preparation of a visiting list for inmates on their caseload
6. Conducting a fifteen-minute individual interview, at least monthly, with every inmate on their caseload
7. Touring the unit daily
8. Serving as a member of the unit's classification team
9. Being on the unit's disciplinary committee

10. Visiting, at least monthly, work and training sites for inmates on their caseload and interacting with (and seeking information from) the work/training supervisors
11. Providing grievance forms, on request, to inmates on their caseload after making every effort to resolve complaints informally
12. Visiting, at least weekly, inmates on their caseload who have been placed in segregation and/or the institution's infirmary
13. Coordinating inmate telephone sign-up list (when this type of procedure is used), inmate trust fund activities, and inmate compliance with personal property policies
14. Sponsoring at least one in-unit inmate group such as Alcoholics Anonymous
15. Assisting the recreation specialist in conducting recreation and leisure-time activities for the unit's inmates
16. Assisting, at the direction of the unit manager, other unit staff in performing their duties, including correctional officers, case managers, the secretary, and part-time staff
17. Serving as policy and procedures expert to unit inmates, their families and friends, other federal, state, and local agencies, and to the general public

## Unit Secretary

Under the direct supervision of the unit manager, the unit secretary's primary duties (at which this individual spends the most time) are, by definition, secretarial and clerical in nature. These include:

1. Preparing unit reports (weekly, monthly, quarterly, annual) and general correspondence
2. Creating and/or maintaining unit and inmate files
3. Doing general filing
4. Preparing inmate records when prisoners transfer out of the institution
5. Preparing unit staff schedules
6. Monitoring sick, annual, and training leave for unit personnel
7. Performing the unit's data entry
8. Serving as a liaison with other departments in the facility

Unit managers should encourage career development and the generation of a professional image by enhancing the secretary's job responsibilities. This will involve training for, and participation in, other unit/institution activities, such as taking minutes at a unit's various meetings. A department of corrections' unit secretary's manual should be developed by the jurisdiction to provide guidance and to serve as a reference source for these employees.

To facilitate access and improve the interaction/relationship between unit staff and prisoners, inmate records should be kept in a safe, secure area on the unit. Prior to complete recordkeeping on computers and in systems which are not yet computerized, changing from centralized to decentralized management of inmate files raised a number of important but competing issues, for example, maintaining the security and confidentiality of records versus ease of access. Some systems maintained two records for each inmate. One (containing court material and confidential information) was kept in a centralized records office. The second, kept on the unit, held information used on a daily basis, such as program assignments, monthly reports, disciplinary reports or outcomes, and so forth. The problem became avoiding multiple records which all had to be updated continually and easily could have become misplaced. Since a large number of correctional systems have computerized their inmate records, they avoid many of these concerns provided that each unit management office: (1) has its own computer terminal and (2) inmates are totally excluded from all contact with any computer modems.

The general consensus at the National Workshop on Unit Management (1988) was that records should be kept on the units. Adequate measures can be taken to ensure their security. Legal documents might be centralized, but the unit's file should contain copies. And, everyone at this conference was looking forward to computerized recordkeeping, which is still not a reality in all systems.

## Unit Correctional Officer

The unit correctional officer has primary responsibility for matters relating to unit security and sanitation, inmate accountability, and custody. This includes performing counts, shakedowns, cell and room inspections, bar taps, escort duties, laundry and clothing checks, and so forth. The unit correctional officers supervise the unit's inmate orderlies (assigned by the unit classification team) and help prepare their monthly performance (inmate) pay report. While these correctional officers may be assigned other responsibilities by the unit manager, those duties cannot conflict with the position's primary (security) functions.

Unit correctional officers are supervised by the unit manager, except for officers assigned to the midnight shift, who are supervised by the shift supervisor. Security matters affecting a particular unit, when no unit staff is on duty, will be handled by the correctional officer and the shift commander. The correctional officer will make an appropriate notation in the unit's logbook concerning the event and the actions taken. This will ensure that the matter comes to the attention of unit staff when they come on duty—the unit manager (or acting unit manager) will initial this entry every day.

Ideally, officers assigned to a unit's regular duty shifts (midnight, day, evening) should remain in that unit for a minimum of nine months. In Missouri, they may rotate at three-month intervals among the three watches, with the exception of the correctional officer whose effectiveness may have been compromised by misconduct or ethical issue and who should be allowed to move out before this period of time elapses.

The unit manager will provide written input for each unit correctional officer's performance evaluation.

In Missouri, despite the benefit of having a stable staff, the staff may move out of a unit at their discretion. "They can bid out of the unit according to their seniority or skill level, according to the terms of the contract with AFSCME, the union. However, there is not much movement out of the housing units. Yet, there is some movement by promotion or transfer," George Lombardi, director of adult institutions explained (conversation withACA staff, September 1998).

Since they are valuable members of the unit team, other personnel will solicit both positive and negative input concerning unit inmates from the unit's complement of correctional officers. This information may be provided in written form (in a daily log) or through the officers' attendance at unit meetings, when possible. The unit's correctional officers will write a signed comment in the unit's logbook at the end of each shift. This will be initialed by the officer coming on duty, to ensure that important information is being shared. The unit manager (or the staff member "acting" during his or her absence) will initial these logbook comments when he or she comes on duty each day.

Ohio's Department of Rehabilitation and Correction found (Unit Management Inspection and Evaluation Report, 1991):

> Through unit management the number of "eyes" in the living areas increases. No longer are correctional officers isolated in the inmate housing areas. Unit staff assists with such traditional corrections officer's duties as head counts, cell shakedowns, and inmate pack-ups. . . . With more staff in the inmate housing areas, inmates are better managed, illegal activities can be curtailed, unit cleanliness maintained, and inmates made accountable for their job and program attendance, as well as their behavior.

## Part-time Unit Staff

Except for a psychologist in each special unit, other institutional personnel (such as the general unit's psychologist, education adviser, recreation specialist, and chaplain) provide every unit with part-time services. Part-time unit personnel may be assigned to up to two units. They are under the direct supervision of their own department head. Consequently, their annual performance evaluations are not completed by unit managers. However, unit managers must provide written input for those evaluations, concerning such administrative issues as:

- Availability
- Responsiveness to staff and inmate requests
- Timeliness of reports
- Attendance at specified unit meetings, such as classification and reclassification sessions

## Unit Psychologist

Under the direct supervision of the facility's chief psychologist, a general unit's psychologist furnishes the unit team with expertise concerning psychological diagnoses, counseling, psychotherapy, training, development, and research/evaluation methodology. As mentioned previously, the ideal would be to have a unit psychologist, but the economic realities mitigate against this.[5] However, if there is a psychologist in this role, this person, in collaboration with the unit manager, should develop a specific schedule so that unit staff and inmates know which days (minimum of two per week) that the psychologist will be available in their unit.

The psychologist attends the initial classification meetings. Preferably, this individual also will participate in all reclassifications and program reviews, but the latter is not mandatory. When not in attendance, the unit psychologist is expected to supply written reports.

Each unit psychologist helps train case managers and correctional counselors in counseling techniques. In addition, a unit psychologist conducts therapy with some of the unit's inmates.[6]

In a special unit, the unit psychologist is a full-time staff member. In addition to performing the duties just outlined (but at a more intensive level) and involving a larger number of inmates, this person plays a major role in developing, and subsequently, evaluating the special unit's treatment regimen.

The chain of command also will differ for a psychologist in a special unit. It will be similar to that of the unit's case manager(s). That is, the unit manager is the psychologist's primary supervisor (performance evaluator). The unit manager receives written input from the institution's chief psychologist on issues concerning the unit psychologist's professional capabilities.

## Education Adviser

The unit's part-time education adviser is a member of the education department. This individual functions under the supervisor of education, but the unit manager provides written input into the education adviser's annual performance evaluation.

The education adviser is the unit's consultant and liaison on education and vocational training programs, and recreation/leisure-time activities. The education adviser attends initial classification meetings, and preferably, also participates in all reclassifications and program reviews, but the latter is not mandatory. When unable to attend, the education adviser provides a written report showing the level of progress made and any continuing education or vocational training needs for each inmate being reviewed.

# Other Staff

Although it is preferable to identify the following personnel with specific units, since no staff member should be assigned to more than two units, some institutions may not have a sufficient number of personnel in their recreation and chaplaincy sections. (Under minimal staffing circumstances, the following areas would remain centralized in an otherwise unitized institution.)

## Recreation Specialist

Unless there is a separate department that handles recreation and leisure-time activities, these staff members are usually in the institution's department of education. Unit managers will have input into performance evaluations (that are written by the supervisor of education) for the recreation specialist assigned to their unit.

Under unit management and the decentralized management style it fosters, the role of the recreation specialist changes. Instead of an emphasis on traditional "varsity" sports, intramural activities become the primary focus. This approach, which includes both large-muscle games as well as leisure-time activities (table games, leathercraft, painting, and other projects), increases the number of inmate participants and helps set up "healthy" interunit competitions.

Recreation specialists focus on arranging round-robin tournaments in a wide variety of individual and team games. The first round is within the unit level to establish "unit champions." Then, these champions play the best from the other units. This culminates in an awards ceremony and banquet for the institutionwide champions.

Similar "competitions" should be organized, and monthly awards made, to the unit with the highest academic achievement, the highest average work-report ratings, the best unit sanitation, the unit with the fewest disciplinary reports, and so forth.

**[REWARDS are better behavior modifiers than punishment!]**

## Chaplain

Those fortunate institutions that have more than one chaplain should explore the possibility of decentralizing some of the activities sponsored and/or conducted by personnel in this department. This may involve no more than specifying which chaplain will be identified with which units for the purpose of establishing clearer lines of communication or each chaplain may undertake a much more extensive range of program endeavors. This may include interviewing new admissions, serving as the unit's religious counselor, providing counseling to inmates following referral by unit personnel, and so forth.

# Noninstitution Resources

## College/University Students

Often, correctional systems encourage students to enter the corrections field through the use of full- or part-time internships and the creation of collaborative practicum courses in joint sponsorship with a nearby college or university. Institutions (and/or individual units) should develop a strategy to recruit college students. Individuals selected to participate should receive an orientation to working in a correctional environment. At the unit level, the unit manager must ensure that an orientation-training session is provided along with formal supervision, the same as would be afforded to every new employee entering on duty.

A correctional setting is a complex and confusing situation for many students. Only mature individuals who responsibly can handle such a placement should be recruited. Consequently, screening interviews by unit staff are essential. They offer a means for assessing the stability and character of prospective interns. The potential student worker should be viewed in terms of whether this individual would be a likely candidate for career employment. Additionally, the screening sessions elicit information which should help in the design of an in-unit program that recognizes the students' capabilities and addresses their needs. Benefits from this type of program accrue for all involved. While students gain correctional experience, they contribute fresh ideas, which often improve a unit's correctional program.

### Volunteers

If the department of corrections' policies permit the use of volunteers, they can become a valuable resource for augmenting a unit's programs. Volunteers should be used to supplement, not replace, regular staff members.

Generally, unit managers have the responsibility for recruiting, orienting, and supervising the volunteers that service their unit. The chief of security and/or the shift commander may be asked to assist in the orientation process when such critical areas as contraband, inmate control, basic security procedures, and the fundamentals of staff/inmate relationships are being discussed.

A volunteer's services should support the unit's philosophy and its general programs. Therefore, clearly defined objectives are necessary and periodic monitoring by unit staff should be mandatory. For example, it should be made clear to the volunteer that excessive absenteeism will result in termination; what will be considered "excessive" and the procedure for reporting anticipated absences should be part of each volunteer's orientation training.

## Unit Management Issues

Twenty-five of the most frequently mentioned concerns are listed on page 43. Sixty-two participants involved in a week-long unit management training program sponsored by the North Carolina Division of Prisons (May 1997) indicated the five issues they would most like to have discussed. The number of endorsements/per item ranged from 21 (high) to 1 (low). Table 2.2 provides a list of their concerns (in rank order). The following section provides specific details on two major issues that unit management has generated. Scope of the unit's authority and female staff on male units (and vice-versa) are discussed in other chapters.

### "Turf" Battles

Conflicts between correctional versus unit staff are the single issue about which most participants (36 percent) were concerned. This is a perennial problem in unit management. It stems from the overlapping of security responsibilities that occurs in the unit. Traditionally, the correctional services staff oversees security functions throughout an institution. When unit management is implemented, security loses its total domain over this correctional function during the hours when the unit staff is on duty. Consequently, the likelihood of conflicts arising is high. There is a need for frequent communication. Hence, there is a requirement that both the unit managers and the chief of security report to the same administrator and that this individual hold weekly meetings at which these issues (among others) are discussed.

Additional suggestions for dealing with conflict between shift commanders and unit managers include: clearly defining everyone's areas of responsibility; coordinating within-unit security between the unit manager and the shift commander, with the unit manager having the final say; and having the shift commander control all off-unit security at all times.

At the 1988 National Conference on Unit Management, several of the participants commented on their experiences concerning "turf" issues. The federal system's representative stated that there always will be tension between security and unit staff, "such problems seem built into unit management." A representative from Virginia maintained that unit management will lead to fewer conflicts since both the custody and treatment staffs attend the same meetings and report to the same deputy warden; a major focus of unit management is specifying accountability, then "there is no turf problem whatsoever." The consensus seemed to be that turf battles, indeed, may occur in the wake of unit management implementation, and they should be dealt with forthrightly.

## Inconsistency Among Units

A concern voiced about unit management revolves around the fact that not all units are run the same (*see also* Within-unit Programs, page 71). This is also a reflection of unit management's flexibility. Since the type of inmate assigned to a particular unit may differ from those placed in another unit, perceived differences among units may reflect efforts to design a program that meets the particular needs of each offender type. While there should be similarity in program structure across units, variations within this "theme" are most desirable. They further a healthy, positive competition among units.

Such competition should not be permitted to degenerate into a negative situation. Rather, units can compete for the best sanitation with the winning unit for the week being rewarded with going to the dining hall first during the following week. Intramural competition can be initiated to find which unit has the best basketball team, or the champion checker player. The unit with the best average academic grades for the semester, or the fewest disciplinary reports for the month might win a special meal, for example, McDonald's hamburgers or a pizza party.

## Unit "Types"

As previously discussed, unit management deals with two "types" of units: general population and special program. Two characteristics distinguish between them: a special unit is smaller and has an in-unit program specifically designed for its population. However, a survey of participants at a National Institute of Corrections-

## TABLE 2.2: UNIT MANAGEMENT ISSUES+

[frequency of endorsement RANK—1 = highest ]

1. "Turf" battles—correctional versus unit staff — [1]*
2. Inconsistency among units — [2]*
3. Scope of unit's authority — [5.5]*
4. Female staff on male units (and vice versa) — [3]*
5. Unit correctional officers' inconsistency between day/evening shifts — [4]*
6. Where is unit management in chain of command? — [8]*
7. Unit manager's/staff's working hours — [8]*
8. Unit's level of responsibility — [8]*
9. Training needs of unit staff — [5.5]*
10. Distinguishing between duties of case manager and correctional counselor
11. Unit communication—staff/inmate; inmate/staff
12. What is unit management?
13. "Pulling" correctional officers off unit posts in nonemergencies
14. Unit manager's responsibility in an emergency?
15. Inmate orientation—is it happening?
16. Centralized versus decentralized inmate records
17. How is relief for unit staff provided?
18. For whom does unit correctional officer work?
19. Unit manager's rank in chain of command
20. What is the unit staff doing?
21. Unit's role in handling disciplinary reports
22. Assigning inmates to units
23. Inmates circumvent security, go to unit staff
24. Who monitors/supervises unit managers?
25. Inmates claim "no access" to unit manager

\+ Results of North Carolina's Unit Management training program, May 1997

* Ranking of results from a similar exercise held during a 1998 training session with North Carolina corrections personnel

## FIGURE 2.5 UNIT "TYPE" DECISION TREE

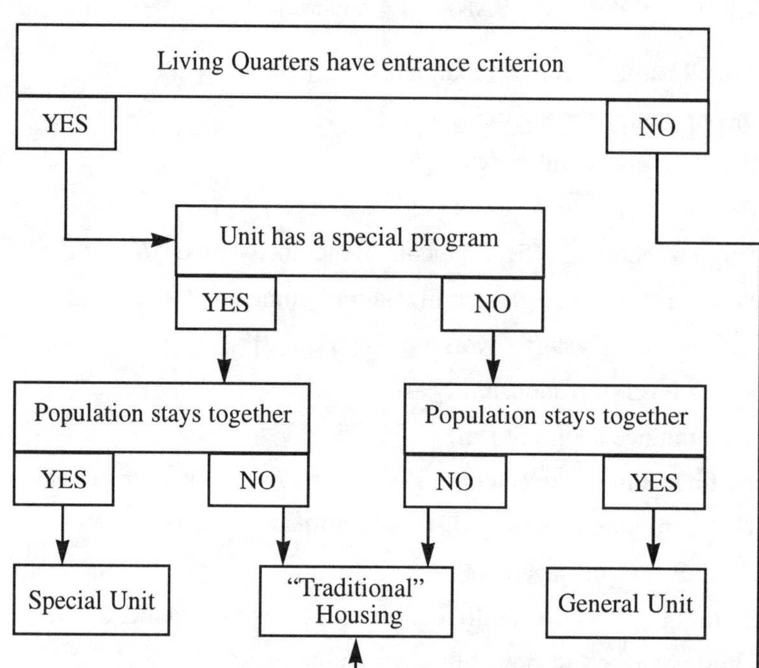


sponsored Workshop on Unit Management (1988) revealed many "different" kinds of units. Within a single system, the number of different unit types ranged from three to nine. All ten jurisdictions attending the meeting had general population units, but they also listed other kinds, many of which did not qualify as special units.

Figure 2.5 demonstrates that, in reality, there are three typical types of inmate living areas. When some criterion is used to restrict admission, for example, only inmates with histories of drug abuse are admitted to the unit, and there is a within-unit treatment program, then the living area qualifies as a special unit. If there is no within-unit program, but the inmates reside in the unit during their entire stay at the institution and the area meets the specifications listed on page 20, then the living area qualifies as a general unit. But, if the living area's population consists of, say, only disciplinary segregation inmates or only prison industry workers, then it is not a unit at all, but a traditional housing area.

Special units are program-intensive. Their populations have a demonstrated need for a specialized within-unit treatment regimen, for such issues as special needs—including alcoholism, drug abuse, geriatrics, mental health, mental retardation, physical disability, sex offenses, or for youthful offenders, and so forth. Special units are not job-based units—which, often, are established for the convenience of staff—nor custody-classification based, for example, minimum-custody inmates. Such nomenclature is a misapplication of the unit management concept since the resulting unit

**TABLE 2.3: TYPES OF LIVING AREAS**

| GENERAL | SPECIAL | TRADITIONAL |
|---|---|---|
| General inmate population in facilities at any security level (may include * inmates in "Traditional" column) | Special needs | Administrative control[1,2] |
| | Alcohol abusers | *Community program[1] |
| | Death row | *Early risers[1,2] |
| | Drug abusers | Forensic[1,2] |
| | Mental health program | *Industry[1,2] |
| | Mental retardation program | Jail detention[1,2] |
| | Typology-oriented program | *Late-shift workers[1,2] |
| | Youthful offenders | Male/female[1] |
| | | *Minimum custody[1,2] |
| | | Pre-trial/holdover[1,2] |
| | | Protective custody[1,2] |
| | | Reception[1,2] |
| | | Segregation[1,2] |
| | | Sentenced/unsentenced[1] |
| | | Special management[1] |
| | | Transfer[1,2] |
| | | *Work details[1] |

Not Special Because:
1 = no within-unit program

Not General Because:
2 = not assigned permanently

does not house inmates throughout their length of stay at the institution—a job change or a custody promotion/demotion results in a change in living quarters.

Traditional housing areas are not special units because they have no specifically designed in-house program. They are not general units because the inmates are not permanently assigned. These are living quarters that are being operated as housing areas were prior to the introduction of unit management. In other words, they are run in a traditional, centralized fashion.

Another example: a unit is set-up for early risers; is there a problem with describing this as an example of unit management? Yes, because as soon as prisoners get changed to the day or evening shift, they no longer will qualify and will have to move out. Therefore, "being an earlier riser" as an entrance criterion inevitably violates the unit management concept of being assigned to a single unit throughout the length of one's institutional stay. It disrupts positive staff/inmate relationships. It is a poor basis for making inmate assignments to units. In actuality, such housing is simply a traditional arrangement for holding a subsample of the facility's prisoners.

# Endnotes

1 In some institutions, this individual also serves as the case manager for long-term segregation inmates.

2 The New York City Department of Correction, which follows a "bid" system, resolved this issue by grouping together three correctional officers—a three-way mutual—each of whom wanted the morning, day, and evening shifts, respectively.

3 After a ninety-day trial, inmates can "opt-out" of Adult Basic Education. However, those who do not complete ABE, or who cannot demonstrate a 6.0 grade level of academic skill through preinstitution documentation, will be ineligible for certain institution jobs, for example, prison industry. Only inmates who have completed a GED or its equivalent should be considered for institution jobs at the department of corrections' top inmate-pay grade.

4 Professor Darrel Cheatwood, in a personal communication, reported that the Swedish prison system has set up a system whereby each correctional officer has three to four inmates assigned to him or her. If an inmate wants something, he has to go to his personal correctional officer, not to a treatment staff person. The most acceptance of this approach has come from the more secure institutions, where the officers feel the approach has made them and the facility a little more secure. Social workers are still in the prisons, but they only back-up the correctional officers and handle appeals. Their primary function has become counseling the officers on how to handle problems the inmates bring to the correctional officers' attention.

5 "In Missouri, because there are not enough psychologists to meet the requirements for unit management, whenever a person acts out, the unit staff makes a referral to the psychologist. The psychologist is called in as an expert—when requested—but is not assigned to the unit per se . . .

Yet, unit staff have received training in behavior management and know when to make a referral to the psychologist, who then may make a referral to the specialized mental health unit or call in the psychiatrist. All together the staff have preservice training of 160 hours," George Lombardi, director of adult institutions for the Missouri Department of Corrections told the ACA staff (September 1998).

6 "From the standpoint of psychology, there are many activities a Unit Manager can expect from the Psychologist attached to his [or her] team; for example: (1) Some initial psychological evaluation of each new resident; (2) Seeing team referrals promptly and pumping back relevant information to the team; (3) Participation in the weekly Unit Staff Meeting; (4) Actively participating in team staff training, particularly in counseling and in handling the more difficult residents; (5) Acquiring outside consultants for unit staff training in special counseling techniques (e.g., Transactional Analysis, Facilitative Counseling, etc.); (6) Assisting the team in evaluating their programs (especially, 'pre- and post-' testing of new programs); (7) Acting as a liaison with neighboring universities and bringing in graduate students to enhance programs in the unit; and (8) Actively participating in program development in the unit." Leo A. McCandlish, Ph.D., Regional Administrator, South Central Region, Federal Bureau of Prisons (Personal communication, July 7, 1975).

*. . . [Y]ou have laid out for us a potential which many people don't think exists. Because many of us are constantly faced with people saying you can't do anything in a prison, because it's such a large and intrinsically authoritarian place. . . . By formalizing this, all kinds of possibilities open up.*

—Hans Toch (1980)

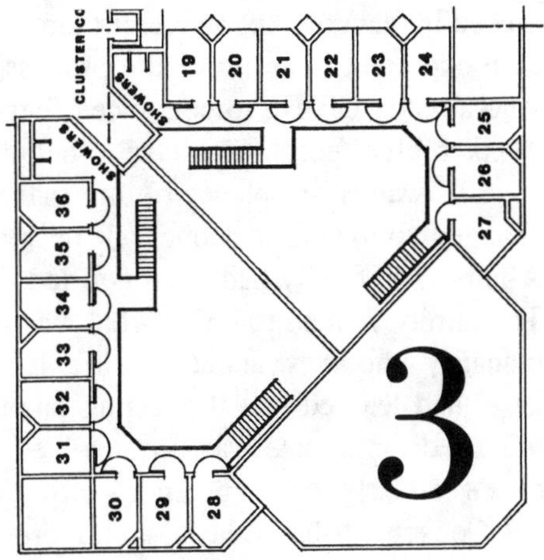


# Getting into Unit Management

## How Unit Management Starts

Sometimes it is the commissioner, but more often it is a warden who first proposes the idea of unit management. This person may have read or heard about it—frequently, at a training session sponsored by the National Institute of Corrections. However, most often, unit management starts in a department of corrections because of an inmate-initiated lawsuit in which a court has found the system's present conditions of confinement to be unconstitutional.

To meet stipulations in the judge's findings, or demands for action made by a court-appointed monitor, department of corrections' personnel may propose implementing unit management. Since the initiator often lacks a full understanding of what the concept is or entails, typically unit management is introduced at a single institution—"to see if it will work in our system."

Such caution, while realistic, also reflects the wariness many administrators have toward corrections' "fads." Many panaceas have come and gone. Some leave behind hefty price tags. Corrections officials want to be convinced that unit management is not another harebrained scheme dreamed up by some not-dry-behind-the-ears academic type. Also, change is tough!

We all like to think of ourselves as rational beings. Given that a difficult decision must be made—Should we go into unit management?—we collect what material we can: the experience of trusted others, the available research literature, information from attendance at relevant corrections' workshops, and so forth. There is also a less obvious factor: How open is one to new ideas?

Farberstein and Wener (1985) point out that the closed-minded cannot be convinced by data or experience. If there is at least some willingness to consider the idea, then experience can move the process forward. Data is mainly useful to help those who already believe to convince others. It is a variation of what has been called the "Tinkerbell effect"—you have to believe to make it happen.

Lukewarm acceptance of unit management by one North Carolina superintendent changed following a phone call he received from the Governor's Office of Citizen Affairs. The family had been notified that the prisoner tested positive for drug usage. The family wanted to know what was being done? The superintendent called the unit manager who knew about the case, having spoken to the inmate's case manager. The latter had learned that the testing laboratory had made a mistake and a reevaluation indicated the inmate was not involved in substance abuse. Following the superintendent's call back to the governor's office, unit management had gained a strong advocate.

Consultants have played an important role in the implementation of most unit management approaches in this country. We all have heard the many jokes about consultants: A consultant is someone who looks at your watch and then tells you what time it is, or anybody with an attache case who is fifty miles from home. However, if you are under a court order, consultants who know what they are doing regarding unit management can be a godsend. Nevertheless, consultants, alone, cannot make it happen.

Another vital ingredient, but one that is often overlooked, is the "friendly native." When advocating the implementation of a new idea, a consultant (who may be the most charismatic, charming, experienced, insightful, humorous, knowledgeable—pick your adjective) needs help. Sooner or later, the consultant goes home. Who then will have the commitment, or show the necessary initiative, to solve the myriad of little problems that inevitably arise? Lacking an in-house "friendly native" to make the repairs, the edifice will begin to crumble. Unit management and any other bright idea will survive only if someone in the system or institution takes "ownership" of it.

# Implementation

It is rare that an idea comes along that officials analyze, decide is "good," and put into practice. More often, change is a less rational process.[1] Frequently, it is a consequence of "progress by catastrophe." That is, a prison riot or an inmate lawsuit leads to court-imposed changes.

Less dramatic, but in the long run more integral changes originate within an organization. Someone, who understands how things are done, gets a bright idea. Because he or she really knows how the organization functions, that notion rather than withering is nurtured and grows. This was the case with unit management.

The unit management implementation process requires a series of planned steps (*see* the checklist, page 49). The rationale for the unit management implementation checklist activities was discussed briefly in the "Ten Commandments" section (pages 9-15). All twenty-five implementation steps are discussed more fully, in this section.

## Table 3.1: Unit Management Implementation Checklist

_____ 1. Obtain commitment from top administrator

_____ 2. Create unit management implementation task force

_____ 3. Set unit management start-up date

_____ 4. Modify chain of command to include unit managers

_____ 5. Identify units (inmate housing areas)

_____ 6. Select unit managers

_____ 7. Identify/hire unit secretaries

_____ 8. Select unit case managers

_____ 9. Select unit correctional counselors

_____ 10. Identify/create unit office space

_____ 11. Acquire unit equipment and supplies

_____ 12. Identify unit mental health staff

_____ 13. Identify unit education personnel

_____ 14. Identify unit recreation staff

_____ 15. Provide unit management orientation for all institution staff

_____ 16. Modify rotation schedule of unit correctional officers

_____ 17. Offer unit management training for unit personnel

_____ 18. Visit of staff to operating functional unit

_____ 19. Develop facilitywide unit management procedures (by unit management supervisor)

_____ 20. Write unit plans (by unit managers)

_____ 21. Classify inmates, if necessary

_____ 22. Orient inmates to unit management

_____ 23. Develop an institution-activation process

_____ 24. Initiate activation process

_____ 25. Conduct scheduled unit management assessment

## (1) Obtain commitment from top administrator

Getting a commitment from the top department of corrections' administrator is not only an essential first phase in the implementation process, it is also the first of unit management's "Ten Commandments." Without this commitment, there is no unit management. If the department of corrections' top administrator and the facility's warden do not publicly support it, unit management will fail.

Unit management should be an agency strategy rather than the personal philosophy of an individual warden. In the latter instance, a change in staff can undo years of effort. This lack of a firm foundation of support severely hampers the successful implementation of unit management. Corrections staff can masterfully play the "this-too-shall-pass" waiting game.

As mentioned, unit management involves a pervasive restructuring of an institution's operations, such as converting current positions, creating new job titles, and altering lines of authority. These frequently result in "turf" battles. Often subtle, and not so subtle, sabotage will undermine the unit management effort that has no clear statement of support.

In his opening remarks to the National Workshop on Unit Management (1988), Richard P. Seiter, then director of the Ohio Department of Rehabilitation and Correction, listed a number of reasons why unit management had his personal support (*see* Table 3.2).

### Table 3.2: Benefits of Unit Management

- Helps maintain control—by placing more personnel inside institutions, public/staff/inmate safety is heightened
- Increases staff morale—creates a new career ladder
- Improves staff relationships—multidisciplinary unit teams
- Inmates receive better services—better staff/inmate communication results in unit personnel being more knowledgeable about their inmates
- Reduces stress—responsibility is delegated and spread among a wider number of trained staff
- It does not cost much money*

—Richard P. Seiter, Former Director
Ohio Department of Rehabilitation and Correction

* In the early 1980s, Director Seiter learned that a new facility employing unit management concepts could be built for $13 million less than was estimated for the original (traditional) design of the Ross Correctional Institution. For example, a unit cell cost $15,476, compared to approximately $50,000, the average cost per cell in a modern correctional facility of similar security level (DeWitt, 1987). Additionally, staffing costs in the unitized institution would be reduced 21 percent—translating to more than $100 million in savings over thirty years.

## (2) Create implementation task force

A planning group needs to be established. This unit management implementation task force should be small (three-to-five members), interdisciplinary (include program and security staff), and consist of veteran personnel who have credibility among their peers.

The charge for the task force is to propose, in written form for approval by the commissioner and/or the facility's warden, plans and procedures for the implementation of unit management. To accomplish their function, the task force members will need to read material available on unit management, possibly visit an operating functional unit, and use a knowledgeable consultant. The implementation task force will develop the department of corrections' unit management "basics," and function as the system's initial unit management trainers.

## (3) Set start-up date

An early problem that those attempting to implement unit management will face involves delays. Many of these, initially, may appear to be realistic considerations. However, it soon will become evident—as the number of "reasons" to postpone proliferate—that "We're not ready!" is actually a form of resisting change. Staff frequently have "one last thing" they believe needs to be accomplished before unit management implementation can begin. The fact is that no system or facility ever will be 100 percent "ready."

Consequently, the commissioner (preferably) or the warden must set a starting date soon after the decision to get into unit management has been made. Past experience suggests:

- The date should be set nine-to-twelve months ahead.
- It should be announced in written form and widely disseminated among staff.
- Once communicated, the date should not be changed.[2]
- Only the official who declared the target date can modify it.

## (4) Modify chain of command

Another of unit management's "Ten Commandments" requires altering the traditional organizational table so that unit managers are at a department head level, and both the unit manager and the chief of security report to the same supervisor.

Unit managers are in charge of semiautonomous, mini-institutions: the functional units. They will be unsuccessful in carrying out their security, safety, sanitation, supervision, training, and programming responsibilities unless accorded sufficient authority in the chain of command. Unit managers must be able to deal with department heads—business office, education, industry, mental health, security, and others—on a parity status (*see* Figure 2.4, page 32).

Another set of potential "turf" battles can be avoided if central office and institutional directives clearly specify not only where unit management is in the chain of command, but "who is responsible for what." Differences of opinion will arise—you can count on it! For example, the perennial question, "Who is responsible for within-unit security?"

This issue comes to the warden in a variety of guises, unless both the unit managers and the chief of security report to the same supervisor. For example, in Ohio (National Workshop, 1988), each unit manager was a department head and at the same level as the major—who was responsible for all security; both positions reported to the same deputy superintendent.

Facilities currently operating within a unit management structure have found the following to be successful in resolving security/unit management conflicts:

- Clearly define everyone's area of responsibility
- The unit manager and major, together, attend weekly meetings, called by their immediate supervisor
- The major controls all off-unit security
- Within-unit security activities are coordinated between each unit manager and the major, with the unit manager having final control
- The role of unit correctional officers is to facilitate activities/programs developed by the unit staff

Unit manager/security tension is inherent in the unit management concept (National Workshop, 1988). However, in corrections, this type of conflict always has been the case, although often "below the surface." Unit management brings both "sides" together and provides mechanisms for dealing with these types of issues more forthrightly.

## (5) Identify units

Units are made up of one or more inmate housing areas. Depending upon their mission, units vary in size. General population units are larger (two caseloads) than special program units (usually one caseload). Unit size has grown over the years—from 50 (special) and 100 (general) to 100 and 250, respectively. Representatives from nine different states with unitized correctional systems and the federal prison system reported (National Workshop, 1988) that their units ranged from 72 to 450 inmates. The average was 160. They specified that their "ideal" unit would have 72 to 300 prisoners.

Since a unit may comprise more than one living area, a frequent question is, "How many units does institution XYZ have?" The answer: "Count the number of unit managers."

**[ Each unit manager has one unit! ]**

## (6) Select unit managers

Of course, you cannot have unit management without unit managers. Unit managers need to be identified early in the implementation process. What attributes should they have? As the litany of their responsibilities suggests (page 31), unit managers must be experienced corrections workers. They should come from all disciplines so that, as a group, each institution's set of unit managers will possess a wide range of expertise.

The work requires knowing how to manage, which includes an understanding of administrative, personnel, and financial practices, plus an in-depth knowledge of all aspects of case management and security operations. Individuals filling this position also need the ability to direct, coordinate, and supervise a staff—some of whom work on a rotational shift basis—who represent a variety of disciplines. Because of its varied demands and high level of delegated responsibility, the unit manager position has excellent career development potential for a department of corrections' future top-level administrator. Unit management can serve as a method for identifying a jurisdiction's future leaders.

## (7) Identify/hire unit secretaries

## (8) Select unit case managers

## (9) Select unit correctional counselors

Checklist items 7 through 9 deal with identifying and/or hiring other unit staff. Often institutions have too few secretaries to assign one to each unit. Consequently, activity should commence immediately to acquire these very important support staff in sufficient numbers—one per unit. Frequently, the necessary positions can be found in an institution's records office. These individuals should be reassigned to the units. Under unit management, the handling of inmate records should be on a computer so that authorized staff have access to them. In a facility without computerized records, the records should be decentralized—placed in a secure environment within each unit. Secretary "pools," one secretary for two units, and variations on share-the-front-office-secretary schemes all have failed in the past.

Each general unit should have two case managers (a minimum of one in a special unit). Where there are two case managers, at least one should be a well-trained, competent veteran. Unit managers should have input into selecting the staff for their unit.

The number of correctional counselors in each unit should match the number of case managers. They should be paired with the case manager with whom they share a caseload. The unit manager (with advice from the case managers) should have input into the correctional counselor selection process for their unit. Correctional counselors are selected from current correctional officers. These should be experienced correctional officers (at the sergeant level) who work well with inmates and are seen as having the potential for career advancement.

## (10) Identify/create unit office space

Once the number and types of unit staff have been decided, identifying and/or building needed office space and appropriately equipping these offices become central in the implementation process. Depending upon the age and design of the facility, this task may present some formidable problems.

Most newly constructed facilities have been designed around the unit management concept. In such instances, the requisite office space on the unit generally is available. It is a far more difficult task to convert a century-old prison into one which will support unit management.

In the latter instance, this situation—the difficult-to-modify architecture—often becomes another "reason" to delay and/or abandon implementation of the unit management concept.

**[ Architecture can help or hinder unit management, but it does not make or break it! ]**

Short of finding sufficient available space, some construction will be required. In an old institution like the Federal Penitentiary in Atlanta, Georgia, this meant using large, six- or eight-bed cells for offices. Other institutions combined two cells into one office by removing an intervening wall, such as at the South Dakota State Penitentiary. Ohio was forced to build offices in what formerly had been dayroom space for inmates—a bad solution.[3]

In a worst-case scenario, unit offices may have to be located adjacent to, rather than on, the unit. However, offices in the administration building and/or those separated from inmates by corridor grilles or sallyports are unacceptable since they defeat a major intent of the unit management concept, which is establishing easy access between staff and inmates.

Preferably, the unit manager's office will be large enough to hold unit team and unit classification meetings. If this is not the case, then private space of a size appropriate for these purposes should be available elsewhere on the unit. The unit secretary's office should be located close to the unit manager's and, if records are not completely on computer, the office should be designed to safely and securely hold the files of the unit's inmates. Unit case managers' offices and the office used by the mental health staff should provide the necessary privacy for one-on-one counseling/therapy sessions. Since much of the correctional counselors' time is spent out of the unit, they often do not have their own office; frequently, they share space with the case manager with whom they are paired.

## (11) Acquire unit equipment and supplies

All unit offices should be appropriately equipped with a desk, chairs, file cabinets, telephone, typewriter/computer, copying equipment, facsimile machine, and so forth, and provide an environment conducive to efficiency. This includes good lighting, appropriate heat and air conditioning, privacy, and the availability of necessary office supplies including paper, pencils, pens, and other items.

## (12) Identify unit mental health staff

In addition to the full-time staff that is assigned to each unit, there are also a number of part-time personnel who function as part of each unit team. Preferably, every unit should have its "own" unit psychologist; however, staff recruitment problems often make this impossible. Consequently, this is a requirement only for a special program unit. For general units, the psychologist becomes a half-time position. The psychologist splits his or her work hours between two units.

Unit staff, the chief psychologist, and unit inmates should understand which of the psychologist's days "belong" to which unit. This creates a sense of continuity, allowing the unit to schedule activities so that they coincide with the psychologist's availability.

## (13) Identify unit education personnel

## (14) Identify unit recreation staff

Similar conditions hold for both the education adviser and the recreation specialist. This means that staff and inmates should know who the adviser and specialist are and which specific days on the weekly schedule these individuals "belong" to which unit.

## (15) Provide unit management orientation for all institution staff

The widespread changes that result from introducing unit management affect all personnel, including those working outside of, as well as those assigned posts within, the units. Consequently, every institution staff member needs to receive a general orientation to the unit management concept.

In a currently operating institution, the inmate grapevine will blossom with rumors about this "new" procedure. Staff will be flooded with questions. They need to be able to make knowledgeable responses. In addition, change is stressful. Staff concerns about unit management will be reflected in many questions of their own:

- Will unit management work?
- Where do I "fit in" in unit management?
- What parts of my job will change?
- Is it going to make my job harder?

Orientation to unit management is equally important in a yet-to-be-opened facility. New—and often different—post orders will have to be drafted. Both new hires and veteran personnel will need to know the answers to issues. These, and similar questions, need to be addressed specifically during a series of training sessions.

If at all possible, the keynote speaker at the staff-orientation training should be the commissioner. This individual should clarify the department's confidence in this management style, and provide reasons why a move in this direction has been chosen.

The warden and other top-level institution personnel also should participate in these staff orientation sessions. Their remarks should address the on-the-job benefits staff can expect from a good-faith implementation effort. In addition to these speakers, members of the implementation task force should play an active role both in scheduling, and participating in, these orientation sessions—perhaps as a panel to answer questions, or as leaders of small discussion groups.

In general, the tone of the orientation training is to demystify unit management by providing knowledge and reducing stress. The opportunity for staff to ask questions and receive direct answers should occupy a significant portion of the time allotted for the training. Jurisdictions that are committed to unit management will incorporate the institution's orientation training (and experience) into a training module to be delivered at the department's training academy.

Several departments of corrections (Michigan, Ohio, Oklahoma, Tennessee, and the Federal Bureau of Prisons) provide special training in unit management for their staff. Ohio employees can receive specialty training throughout the year. Oklahoma's unit managers receive twelve days of training covering unit management skills, security, classification, programs, and basic unit management concepts. Before a recent change of governors and subsequent change in prison management, which resulted in the abolition of unit management, South Carolina had a four-week training course that included observing the actual functioning of staff in their positions at facilities that were using unit management.

## (16) Modify unit correctional officers' rotation schedule

It is important that unit staff and the inmates assigned to their unit have an opportunity to develop positive relationships. This principle underlies unit management "Commandment #5."

> Inmates and unit staff are permanently assigned to the unit; correctional officers are stationed for minimum of nine months.

Often, to meet correctional officer position-grade classification qualifications, it is required that correctional officers rotate among the different shifts (midnight, day, evening) and/or through different security posts.[4] It is not difficult to meet this condition under unit management. Officers can rotate among the midnight/day/evening shifts within one unit. After nine months (unless there are problems or potential problems for correctional officers), they can move to other types of correctional officer posts. There is no need to abrogate the important unit management principle of maintaining staff consistency and fostering the development of meaningful staff/inmate relationships.

Currently, in the Ohio Department of Rehabilitation and Correction, correctional officers are assigned to individual posts based on seniority with each facility having Permanent Pick-A-Post agreements with the local unions. The only time an officer would rotate out of a post is when he or she bids out to another post. The officers typically remain in the housing unit posts well in excess of nine months at a time (letter from Terry Tibbals to American Correctional Association staff, September, 1998).

## (17) Offer unit management training for unit personnel

As stated in item number fifteen, all staff need training regarding unit management concepts; however, the intensity of this training should vary—reflecting the differing levels at which staff members will function in unit management. The most concentrated training should be given to unit personnel.

Training objectives for each unit's personnel should include:

- Providing greater detailed information concerning the unit management concept
- Familiarizing staff with their new roles
- Helping alleviate "rookie" anxieties
- Beginning the development of a cooperative, mutually productive team spirit

## (18) Visit of staff to operating functional unit

The best way to reach all these training objectives is by an on-site visit. After some initial exposure to unit management information, unit managers should visit a well-functioning, long established, unitized institution—similar to their own. If possible, unit teams should make the visit.

These on-site trips differ from the typical "visiting fire fighters' walk-through." The visitors should view a unit's operation over an extended time period, including evening activities. Moreover, their schedule should include time when they can talk one-on-one with their counterparts about the daily "nitty-gritty" of functioning in a unit setting. An opportunity to talk with some inmates and learn about their views of unit management will provide the visitors with a perspective very important for the successful implementation of unit management at their home facility. A measure of the usefulness of the on-site trip will be the degree to which unit staff return with practical ideas and a readiness to write their own unit plan.

## (19) Develop facilitywide unit management procedures

The second of unit management's "Ten Commandments" concerns the requirement for a set of guidelines. An institution procedures manual (based on a Central Office Policy Statement; *see* Appendix 1) describes how this facility will implement headquarters' directives.

If unit management has been operative in the system, this implementation step will present few problems; however, having such a history is often not the case. Your facility may be the one that is pilot-testing unit management for the entire department of corrections. Therefore, there will be no in-house document to serve as a pattern for the unit management procedures manual; another jurisdiction will have to provide the model (*see* Appendix 1).

From a systems perspective, unit management implementation is often a bottom-up rather than a top-down process. That is, jurisdiction "A's" pilot program in unit management borrows documentation from department of corrections "B." It, then, modifies B's approach and develops its own—system/institution $A_1$—version of a unit management procedures manual. After the $A_1$ pilot project is deemed a success, jurisdiction A's central office policy statement on unit management gets written, incorporating the elements developed by pilot institution $A_1$. Subsequently, when other department of corrections' A facilities—$A_2$, $A_3$, and so forth—go into unit management, the central office policy statement is available to serve as their guide. Many of the unit management implementation checklist items become part of an institution's procedures manual.

## (20) Unit managers write their unit plan

The most basic document in the unit management concept is the unit plan. It is the foundation upon which all other aspects of unit management are built.

Within the guidelines specified in the department's unit management policy statement and the institution's unit management procedures manual, unit managers are required to write a description of how their own unit will operate. While each unit manager is responsible for creating a unit plan, often this becomes a team-building opportunity. Parts of the unit plan are "farmed out" to other unit personnel; their input becomes a focus for discussion: "Is this what (or how) we want to do XYZ in our unit?" The emerging consensus becomes a first draft of the unit plan (*see also* Appendix 2).

## (21) Classify inmates

The unit programs that are developed should recognize the humanness of the prisoners assigned to them. A well-managed unit will provide a safe, secure, and sanitary environment for its population. One way to facilitate this is through a systematic method of assigning inmates to units.

Unit management makes the use of an internal classification approach easier (Levinson, 1988). This process, which systematically assigns homogeneous subpopulations to housing quarters, repeatedly has demonstrated its ability to reduce incidents of violence (Quay, 1984). If such an approach is planned, then inmates need to be classified prior to assigning them to their quarters (*see* Part 5 on Internal Classification).[5]

Short of the adoption of an internal classification approach, inmates should be assigned to units on a random basis; that is, those with a register number ending in "1," "4," or "7" go into Unit X; Unit Y receives new arrivals with register numbers that have as a last digit "2," "5," or "8"; and, Unit Z gets inmates with numbers ending in "3," "6," or "9," while "zeroes" go to the unit with the lowest population. Assigning the latest arrival to the next open bed is not random assignment. It can result in placing a weak new admission beside (or in the same cell with) the facility's most aggressive inmate. It is the least desirable method for placing inmates into units.

## (22) Orient inmates

Long before unit management's start-up date, prisoners at the institution will have become aware of an impending change. Often, however, the inmate "grapevine" is inaccurate. Potentially disruptive rumors may become rampant. Therefore, it is highly important that the implementation task force plan ways by which the prison's population will receive accurate information fairly early during the process of converting to unit management.

Typically, and predictably ineffectual, a memo from the warden will be posted on one or more bulletin boards in the institution. Some inmate rips it off, and the rumors continue to proliferate. Communication channels, which have been useful in the past at some facilities, include:

- An article written by the warden for the institution's inmate newspaper
- A discussion of the upcoming change at meetings of the inmate council
- Case managers meet individually (or in small groups) with all inmates on their caseload to discuss how unit management will affect inmates

Regardless of the information dissemination methods used prior to the implementation of unit management, the first town hall meeting (*see* page 73) after unit management's start-up should deal with inmate questions concerning: "What does unit management mean for me?" Staff must know and be able to communicate the advantages of unit management in terms that have particular relevance for inmates. Information concerning unit management's many benefits (discussed in this volume) should help during the "kickoff" town hall meeting.

## (23) Develop an institution-activation plan

The implementation task force needs to pay explicit attention to the "how's" of moving into unit management. This will have particular importance when the implementation process involves many inmate moves.

As part of the implementation plan, the task force needs to develop a step-by-step plan (*see* suggestions in Bohn, Waszak, and Story, 1974) which will need approval by higher authorities. It spells out a series of procedures that will be used. Also, it includes a schedule of when every step is to occur, and who is responsible for overseeing each of them.

> Within the transition year . . . the [Federal Correctional Institution] at Tallahassee planned its move to Functional Unit Management, identified the resources and positions needed, identified the needed personnel and hired them, and moved from being a centralized institution to an institution housing residents within five smaller units.
>
> —Bohn, Waszak, and Story (1974)

It is critical that the inmates are made aware of the movement plans and told in advance that they will be allowed some choices in the process. That is, staff decides which prisoner goes where; however, inmates are permitted one change (provided it is consistent with the facility's unit management structure) during the two weeks following implementation—and none thereafter (Spieker and Pierson, 1989). For example, inmates may make one request and be permitted to move to a different bed, room, or cell within the unit, but not between units.

Several additional factors need to be considered and made part of the implementation plan when the sequence of inmate moves is established:

- Which prisoners move first
- What type housing for which prisoners
- The location (nearness to each other) of different types of housing areas
- Phase-in over time versus completion in one day

The potentially most disruptive inmates should be moved first. This prevents these individuals from attempting to take advantage of a time of high stress for both staff and other prisoners. It also demonstrates that the administration is clearly in control of the situation.

Prior to the actual physical relocation, identify the housing areas into which different types of inmates will move. The difficult-to-manage inmates should be housed in the facility's most secure (except for segregation) housing.

Additionally, the living quarters specified for these difficult-to-manage individuals should be located as far distant as the facility's architecture will permit from the housing planned for the institution's most easily victimized inmates. This "distancing" consideration also holds even when there are no differences among the security features of the inmate housing.

The issue of phased moves versus an all-in-one-day move often is resolved by recognizing that in crowded prisons a movement of this nature involves inmates exchanging beds—there is a ripple effect. Consequently, when facilities begin unit management, they avoid having some individuals move more than once by accomplishing all of the moves within one day, usually on a weekend. Thus, there is a need for a considerable amount of preplanning and paying close attention to logistical details.

Based on their own experience with unit management, the Missouri Department of Corrections offered the following implementation tips (Spieker and Pierson, 1989; pp. 29-34):

- Avoid scheduling the inmate relocation day when special events usually occur, such as mail, laundry distribution, and so forth.
- Have inmates notify visitors that visiting will be suspended during the relocation period.
- Coordinate moving day with other institution departments, for example, education and industry.
- Security may want to have additional officers on duty during the relocation day to discourage problems (and to have sufficient staff on hand to move inmates to segregation in case of refusals).

- Reschedule inmate counts so that they occur immediately before relocation begins and right after it ends.
- Food service might prepare sack lunches which inmates will eat in their housing unit after all moves have been completed.
- Work release and early-rise institution workers (such as food service) might be permitted to pack their belongings before other inmates, store these securely prior to leaving for work, and move into their new location when they return.
- Packing inmate belongings may require the availability of boxes.
- Transporting inmate belongings may require laundry carts, hand- or flatbed trucks.
- Four inmate rosters need to be prepared for every housing area, showing: (1) each area's population before relocation; (2) who moves out—grouped by destination; (3) who moves in—grouped by origin; and, (4) the unit's population after all moves have been completed.

An effective procedure for relocating inmates, when moving into unit management, involves having the staff concentrate on one housing area at a time. Missouri suggests beginning after breakfast on a weekend day. If the decision is to make the change to unit management during the week, then it should occur after work releasees leave for work and mandatory workers have reported to their assignments. All other inmates should be locked-down in their current housing area.

Start in the living area that will be used to house the more troublesome prisoners—Unit Z. Those not being moved should remain in their cells/rooms. Inmates listed on the roster as moving to Unit A carry their belongings and go—or are escorted—to Unit A. Unit A's inmates listed for Unit Z carry their belongings and move—or are escorted—to Unit Z. Then, Unit Z's inmates scheduled for Unit B are exchanged. This process continues until all of Unit Z's prisoners listed for relocation have moved out and have been replaced by Unit Z's new inmates from all the other housing areas. When Unit Z's population is "on board" and the count has been cleared using Unit Z's new roster, then the entire process is repeated for Unit A, then for Unit B, and so forth. An alternative phased-in approach to implementing unit management is described by Smith and Fenton (1978, pages 45-46) in which 1,500 penitentiary inmates made more than 1,200 housing changes during a two-month period.

## (24) Initiate activation process

Included in the previous section of developing an institution-activation plan, is the activation date. It should be the same day that was established initially by the commissioner (or warden) in item three (set start-up date). When the date arrives, activation is begun through the activation plan, and unit management ceases to be just an idea or a piece of paper—it becomes a reality.

> **Every organization needs a mountain to climb.**
> **—George Martin**

## (25) Conduct unit management assessment

The final assignment for the implementation task force is to schedule a formal, in-depth assessment of unit management. Good management and well-run programs generally are the result of closely tracking program activities and results. Making changes as they are needed and fine-tuning operations is largely what management is all about (Altschuler and Armstrong, 1995, page 162).

This evaluation is conducted by a knowledgeable regional (or central) office audit team (or person), twelve-to-fifteen months after the facility's start-up date. Subsequent audits should be completed annually.

The assessment visit is designed so that it extends over a sufficient period of time to allow the auditors to view both day and evening activities in all units. In addition to interviewing both staff and inmates, the reviewers should use a formal unit management audit checklist (*see* Appendix 3). The final event is a close-out meeting between the audit team and the warden (and his or her staff). Preliminary findings should be discussed so that the subsequent report contains no surprises. The intent of this process is to assess each unit's level of compliance with system policy and the institution's procedures manual.

Within two weeks following the on-site visit, the auditors send a written report to the warden (signed by the regional or central office unit management coordinator's supervisor). This initial report consists of two major sections: a summary of the results of the visit, and specific recommendations regarding areas in which the audit team found that the facility was currently out of compliance with the jurisdiction's unit management policy.

The facility has two weeks to prepare its response, namely, what it plans to do to come into compliance. That response, signed by the warden, is sent to the regional (and/or central) office.[6] All subsequent on-site unit management audit reports will contain a third section: a current assessment of the degree to which the facility's past out-of-compliance areas are now in conformity with the department's unit management policy statement.

# Endnotes

1 This has changed, to some degree, since 1979 when the American Correctional Association began the prison accreditation process (ACA, 1990).

2 It is not always possible to stay with this target since unforeseen situations do occur. However, frequent extensions of the start-up date are variations of the "not-yet-completely ready" syndrome.

3 At a North Carolina Department of Corrections' Unit Management Training Conference (1997), Gary C. Mohr, Warden, Correctional Reception Center, Orient, Ohio, indicated that all of Ohio's problems (following the introduction of unit management) have occurred in such retrofitted institutions.

4 If this is not a requirement in a particular system, then there is no problem.

5 Several approaches are available including, but not limited to, Quay's (1984) Adult Internal Management System; Megargee's (1979) MMPI-based method; using the number of "points" on an inmate's initial classification form—placing "high point total" new arrivals in a different housing area than those with point totals at the low end of the institution's range. *See also* Part 5, Internal Classification, page 75.

6 In systems which have regional and central offices, the facility's reply is sent to *both*.

*If you don't have a map, how will you know when you're there?*

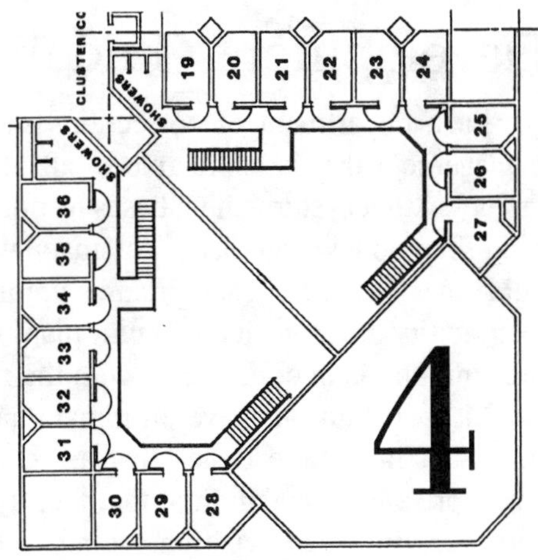


# Writing the Unit Plan

## Introduction

Every unit is required to develop its own unit plan. This, in essence, is a manual of within-unit operations. It covers items, issues, and procedures that affect both the staff and the inmates assigned to each unit. Unit plans, contained in three-ring binders or on computer disk, are intended to be "working documents." While a few sections of the plan are confidential—for example, memos to and from the unit manager—the plan should be written so that it can be disclosed to inmates and interested members of the public.

A unit plan describes the unit's purpose. It also clearly specifies (within the guidelines established by both central office policies and institution procedures) the operations by which that purpose will be achieved. The plan is the basic document which directs all other aspects of how each unit will be managed.

The unit plan is written by each unit manager, with input from other unit staff members. In its final form, it has the written approval of the unit manager's supervisor. The plan is reviewed and approved (signed and dated) annually, and updated, as necessary.

The intent of the unit plan is to provide a single place where interested parties can find a detailed description of how a particular unit will function. Requiring this to be a written document avoids having informal unit rules, which change at the whim of any individual staff member. Thus, in unit management there are no so-called "unwritten rules." Both staff and inmates are expected to abide by established operational procedures.

## Development Guidelines

Each department of corrections should develop a central office policy on unit management that is applicable to all of the institutions under its jurisdiction. Every facility in that system, then, bases its unit management procedures manual on this central office policy statement. The manual establishes an institution's unit management guidelines in light of each prison's unique characteristics. Subsequently, every unit in that facility develops its own unit plan. Each plan reflects the goals and objectives of that unit and is in compliance with the manual.

Most institutions have an inmate handbook. The inmate handbook should cover important items and issues that are germane for the daily living experience of the entire prisoner population at that facility. This should include such items as: sending and receiving mail, visiting, going to the commissary, arranging sick-call, setting work/program hours, and handling institutionwide program activities such as religious services, education, and others. These should be referred to, and do not need to be repeated in each unit plan.

**[ Authorship is ownership.**
**—Roy Gerard ]**

A sample unit plan is found in Appendix 2. Unit managers should use it as a model when writing their own plan. The following topical outline should be followed. All eleven sections must be addressed, and the numbered subitems should be included. Additions that reflect the uniqueness of each unit and that staff's intentions also need to be incorporated.

## Section 1 — Description of Unit

1. Brief narrative on the unit's mission or purpose
2. Unit description:
   a. Location
   b. Bed capacity
   c. Type of unit (general or special)
   d. Inmate selection criteria (if any)
   e. Within unit program approach (if any)
   f. Staffing

## Section 2 — Unit Objectives

Objectives should be specific to the unit and relate to its mission. Rather than statements of intent ("to give . . ." or "to provide . . ."), they should indicate, in quantifiable terms, anticipated outcomes. For example, if the unit houses inmates functioning below the fifth-grade level and requiring a remedial education program, one of its objectives may be to "increase ability to read and/or do fractions by 5 percent, as measured by final grades in reading and/or math;" a substance abuse program might have a focus of "improving self-esteem as shown by a 10 percent reduction in the number of unit inmates receiving minor disciplinary reports."

## Section 3 — Staffing

1. Positions and roles
   a. Unit manager
   b. Case manager(s)
   c. Correctional counselor(s)
   d. Secretary/clerk
   e. Other assigned staff
2. Current work-schedules—specified for all of the unit's full-time employees: duty hours (including evenings and weekends), days off, and so forth
3. Table of organization and line of authority
   a. Chain of command inside and outside the unit
   b. Performance evaluations—who completes them for whom?
   c. Leave approval
4. Unit team meetings—held when? Where? For how long? Who attends?
5. Staff training
   a. Staff training plans
   b. Staff meetings
   c. In-service training
   d. Reporting/documenting staff training
6. Interdepartmental coordination
   a. Administration
   b. Business office

c. Education/vocational training
d. Recreation
e. Food service
f. Industries
g. Maintenance department
h. Medical/mental health
i. Substance abuse
j. Records office
k. Religion
l. Security
m. Social services
n. Volunteers
o. Other unique services

[ **Maintenance gets done when the office that's flooded is yours.** ]

## Section 4 — Unit Rules and Regulations

The emphasis should be on those rules or regulations that are unique to the unit, such as personal property, room or cell assignments, intra-unit visiting, and so forth.

## Section 5 — In-Unit Routines and Schedules

a. Staff work-schedules
b. Unit activities schedule
c. Wake-up time
d. Showers
e. Counts
f. Disciplinary procedures
g. Quiet and leisure time
h. Television and radio procedures
i. Lights out

## Section 6 — In-Unit Activities and Programs

The unit manager will develop (and post in a glass-enclosed bulletin board) a schedule of unit programs, which will specify such details as time, place, frequency, and so forth. The unit plan includes descriptions of its programs or services that differ from the standard for the institution:

a. Unit admission and orientation programs

b. Classification and reclassification (procedures and schedules)

c. Group and individual counseling or therapy (procedures and schedules)

d. Substance abuse education or counseling (procedures and schedules)

e. Inmate advisory council (procedures and schedules)

f. Town hall (procedures and schedules)

g. Recreation (procedures and schedules)

h. Phone call procedures

i. Unique features (such as volunteer programs and special events)

j. Grievance procedures

k. Prerelease program

l. Release program

## Section 7 — Unit Fire Escape and Fire Drill Procedures

This section will include a schematic of the unit's fire escape plan. A copy of this should be posted conspicuously on each floor of the unit (in a glass-enclosed bulletin board).

## Section 8 — Unit Sanitation

The unit manager will organize a system whereby the highest levels of sanitation will be maintained. These procedures will be described thoroughly in this section, and will include:

a. Standards for unit sanitation

b. Unit sanitation supply requisition procedures

c. Method for assigning unit inmate orderlies

d. Description of unit orderly responsibilities

e. Staff responsibilities for sanitation inspection:
   - When (time of day) they occur
   - How often they occur (daily, weekly, monthly)

f. An explanation of how unit sanitation will be assessed

g. Description of a recognition or reward program based on unit sanitation

## Section 9 — Unit Services

Include those that occur on a daily, weekly, and/or monthly basis. These may include the following:

a. Medical or dental callout procedures

b. Meal scheduling (how it is determined when each unit goes to the mess hall)

c. Educational or vocational training activities

d. Mental health services (availability)

e. Social services (availability)

f. Religious program (availability)

g. Prison industry (qualifications and how assignments are made)

h. Work details inside and outside the unit (qualifications and how assignments are made)

i. Inmate advisory council (qualifications, length of term, and so forth)

j. Town hall (day and time of meetings, mandatory attendance)

k. Inmate organizations (names, how organized, and so forth)

l. Commissary (day, time, procedures, and so forth)

m. Clothing exchange (day, time, and procedures)

n. Laundry (procedures)

o. Barber/beauty shop (procedures)

p. Law and regular library (day, time, and procedures)

q. Visiting (legal, family) procedures

r. Special events

s. Receiving and sending mail and packages (procedures)

## Section 10 — Emergency Plans

a. Escape procedures

b. Homicide and suicide

c. Disturbance control

d. Hostage situation

e. Natural disaster

## Section 11 — Records, Data Collection, and Evaluation

a. Unit files

- Progress reports
- Classification reports
- Special incidents
- Parole reports
- Other

b. Unit files management

- Access
- Security
- Accountability (control)
- Records office monitoring

c. Unit reports

- Counts
- Sanitation
- Staff attendance
- Logs
- Daily, weekly, monthly, and/or annual reports

d. Research-related reports

# Within-unit Programs

One of the hallmarks of unit management is its flexibility. This is apparent from such a basic level as the campus-style site plan around which facilities designed for unit management are built (Webster, 1991). For example, the Federal Correctional Institution in Dublin, California, has housed both low-security and high-security (though not maximum-security) federal inmates, and housed all male, all female, and (on two occasions) coed populations.

Similar flexibility should be apparent among the programs established within an institution's units. That is, within a general framework, unit managers and their staff have the opportunity to develop programs that they feel are appropriate for their inmates. Every unit does not have to have the same program.

However, some consistency across units is also important to avoid having prisoners "whipsaw" the unit managers. That is, inmates in Unit A will complain about why they are not allowed to do something that the prisoners in Unit B can do. Maintaining a balance between "consistency" and "flexibility" requires frequent unit management coordination meetings.

Oklahoma found it very important to give their unit managers the flexibility to develop their own within-unit programs. A facility's unit managers get together "every now and then" (away from the institution) to share ideas. Virginia reported having a weekly unit managers' meeting for sharing ideas, and their unit managers are encouraged to visit other units to *see* how they do things.

One of the ways to achieve flexibility within a consistent framework involves the mix of in-unit programs. All units incorporate the following activities into their regular schedule: inmate participation in such services as undergoing orientation and classification, performing job/program assignment(s), taking part in recreation/leisure time activities, engaging in the unit's inmate advisory council, attending town hall meetings, and participating in a prerelease program and a release program. Staff duties include: classifying/reclassifying inmates, monitoring inmate monthly progress reports and the facility's incentive systems, processing inmate rule infractions, and providing direct input to the parole board, where parole is still an option. Although most of these have been touched upon, several require additional attention.

## Inmate Advisory Council

For many experienced correctional workers, inmate advisory councils have a highly negative aura. They remember how these sessions in the past quickly became a power-base for the institution's "toughs," or forums that prisoners used to verbally attack the administration and/or intimidate other inmates. This view, similar to that of the unskilled carpenter who blames his tools, reflects the unwillingness of staff to manage a valuable communication instrument.

Every unit should have its own inmate advisory council. Each tier, wing, ward, or cell block should elect an inmate representative by a secret ballot. The election process should be monitored by the unit staff. To be eligible to run for advisory council representative, each candidate must meet specific criteria stipulated by the unit staff, such as no major disciplinary reports for the past six months and no minor disciplinary reports for the past three months (plus any other conditions the unit may wish to establish). The term in office is short, not to exceed three months. Representatives can succeed themselves only once; then, they are eligible to run again after six months. Such regulations prevent any inmate from dominating these sessions.

A representative who is found guilty of a major disciplinary infraction is immediately removed from office, and a new election is held. A representative found guilty of a minor disciplinary infraction may or may not be removed from office (and a new election held). This latter determination is made by the unit disciplinary committee. Vacancies resulting from transfers, resignations, and so forth are filled by a new election.

Each inmate advisory council meets weekly with the unit staff, generally, before that unit manager's staff meeting. The advisory council has a twofold role: to advise the unit staff of concerns, wishes, ideas, and projects voiced by inmates in the unit, and to suggest topics for discussion during the unit's town hall meeting. By having unit staff establish the ground rules and monitor their functioning, no one is given the impression that inmates on the advisory council have too much influence.

## Town Hall

This is a large group meeting held in each unit, every other week (preferably weekly) that lasts sixty-to-ninety minutes. It is scheduled, generally, after the unit manager's staff meeting, at a time when all of the unit's staff and inmates can attend. The town hall is chaired by the unit manager. Its intent is to serve as a two-way communications channel: staff can inform inmates about new procedures and changes in unit operations. Inmates can bring up suggestions of their own and discuss ways to improve how the unit functions.

The purpose of the town hall is to develop ways by which both inmates and staff can "live together" better. Town hall is not the place for inmates to discuss issues that have only a personal relevance. Those type of items should be reviewed with the inmate's counselor or case manager. Topics that do not deal with general unit concerns should be ruled out of order.

It is important that the town hall meeting is held at the scheduled times, even when there does not appear to be any agenda items. It demonstrates that the unit does have structure that is accountable; that things, indeed, do happen when they are scheduled. Further, such an approach makes it more difficult for inmates to manipulate the situation. And, somebody just might bring up something. If nothing happens after five or ten minutes, the unit manager can recognize the fact that no one seems to have anything they want to talk about, and then the unit manager (not the inmates) ends the town hall session.Through the proper use of town hall meetings, staff can inform unit inmates about what is going to happen in the near future, and encourage them (by soliciting their ideas) to plan for and help make whatever it is run more smoothly.

## Prerelease/Release Program

Every unit should schedule its inmates (at least three months prior to their return to the free world) to participate in the institution's prerelease program. These types of programs incorporate such preparation-for-release activities as preparing a resume, learning job search techniques, budgeting, family planning, coping skills, and so forth.

In addition, each unit should develop its own release program. Such a program has two major components: transportation and intelligence.

(1) *Transportation.* This deals with how inmates released from the unit will get to a public means of transport that will take them home. The releasee's counselor or case manager should drive the releasee to the nearest appropriate common carrier (for example, bus or train). However, if the inmate's family and/or friends plan to come to the institution to meet him or her, then the need for this aspect of the program lessens.

(2) *Intelligence.* En route to taking the releasee to public transportation, the case manager/counselor should stop and treat the inmate to a soft drink and a burger. Since the inmate will not return to the facility, this provides an excellent opportunity to obtain information about what is really going on in the unit. However, when the releasee is to be met at the institution, his or her counselor or case manager should escort the inmate to the front gate (fifteen-to-twenty minutes before the scheduled pick-up time) and wait there until the relatives or friends arrive. Again, this is an excellent opportunity to learn who in the unit is doing what to whom, or who needs more attention from staff.

*We are all exceptional cases.*

—Camus

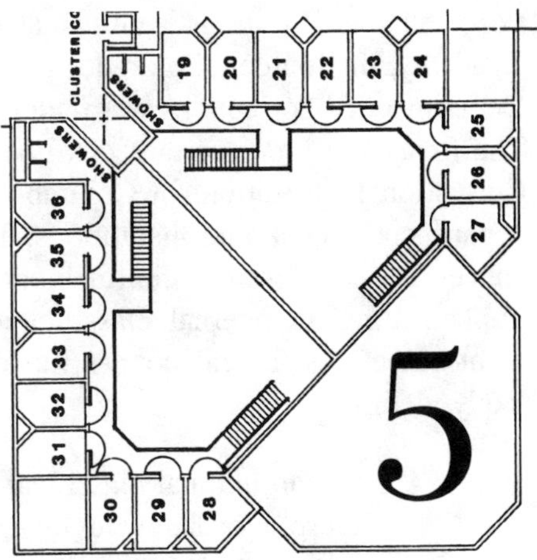


# 5

# Internal Classification and Unit Management*

## Introduction

The prime objectives of correctional management are to decrease the likelihood of prison disturbances, increase the prospect that released inmates will make a more successful return to free-world society, and enhance public safety. A key in achieving these desirable results is the approach that each prison system takes in classifying its inmate population. Accurately and objectively matching prisoners' security needs with the security features of the institutions available within a given prison system—a process known as external classification—is a cornerstone in such an endeavor.

An additional enhancement of this procedure concerns how inmates are assigned to housing quarters within an institution. This refinement, known as internal classification, consistently has demonstrated its ability to reduce inmates' problematic behavior. Moreover, internal classification allows a facility's prisoners to participate more fully in programs designed to increase the likelihood of their postrelease success.

* This chapter draws heavily from Herbert C. Quay's *Managing Adult Inmates*, American Correctional Association: Lanham, Maryland (1984) and was improved by editorial comments from Sammie D. Brown, Correctional Program Specialist with the National Institute of Corrections.

# Inmates

*Internal classification* was first coined as a term in corrections by the South Carolina Department of Corrections after Sammie D. Brown, then director of classification, attended a training seminar at the National Institute of Corrections Training Academy, in Boulder, Colorado. At that time (February, 1983), the South Carolina Department of Corrections was under two federal court orders, *Mattison* and *Nelson.*[1] The first court order pertained to the system's then end-of-the-line facility, Central Correctional Institution, in Columbia; while the second court order concerned the department's remaining institutions. To address constitutionally mandated standards concerning conditions of confinement, it was thought (correctly, as it turned out) that implementing an internal classification system at Central Correctional Institution would meet the federal court's mandate to separate predatory inmates from their likely victims:

> . . . an internal classification system would serve to identify those inmates who by their current institutional behavior have demonstrated the need for supervision and control. It would serve as a signal to staff to be alert to such potential acting-out behavior (South Carolina Department of Corrections, 1985).

The South Carolina Department of Corrections became the nation's first department of corrections to employ internal classification on a systemwide basis in its male[2] institutions. The Federal Bureau of Prisons was the first to use internal classification—Quay's Adult Internal Management System (AIMS) approach—in several of its facilities.

Initially, internal classification systems for adult prison inmates were developed from approaches created for juvenile delinquents, such as Warren (1969) and Quay and Parsons (1971). Quay expanded his dimensions of delinquency by employing a behaviorally oriented method (Quay 1979, 1984). He totally restandardized his earlier approach, using adult inmates. Other approaches also have been designed to accomplish the goals of internal classification with adult inmates, for example, by categorizing inmates using scores from psychological tests—Megargee's MMPI (Minnesota Multiphasic Inventory) method (1979). As indicated, the National Institute of Corrections is soon to release others.

Before internal classification can be achieved, there must be a proper external classification. The goal of external inmate classification is to appropriately house inmates according to their security needs in the least-restrictive environment. These security levels include: minimum prison camps, low, medium, high security and an administrative category that includes a variety of levels in such places as medical centers and pretrial centers. At intake, inmates are screened mentally and physically and separated according to security concerns based on background information.

At the Federal Bureau of Prisons, during admission and orientation, inmates are given a detailed overview of the institution and an overview of the everyday routine. They also are examined for medical and psychological problems, their educational status is assessed as is their substance abuse needs. Within four weeks of arrival, the inmate meets his or her unit team: the unit manager, case manager, counselors, secretary, and correctional officers, according to information provided to American Correctional Association staff by Delores Stephens, Assistant Administrator for Policy Development and Training at the Bureau of Prisons (1998).

During the initial external classification, the inmate and the unit team talk about program issues with representatives from education, drug treatment, and psychology. These personnel have had an opportunity to talk with the individual inmate. During this meeting, goals are set and programs are recommended. The inmate has an opportunity to request programming and ask questions. The decisions that are made are based on both the length of the inmate's sentence and the inmate's ability to pursue such programs. Later, during program reviews, these choices are revisited, modified, and/or dropped.

Custody level, initially, is based on the offense and institutional adjustment, including the degree of staff supervision required. Inmates needing special programs are put into appropriate units, including sex offenders and special needs inmates.

Currently, according to Terry Tibbals from the South Regional Office of the Ohio Department of Rehabilitation and Correction, Ohio's initial classification system includes six different variables: current detainer, current offense, time to release, prior incarceration, history of escape, and history of violence. Each offender's status, based on his or her initial classification, is reviewed on a regular basis. In addition, this review includes other factors: the percentage of time served, substance abuse history, stability to handle a lower level of security, disciplinary history, frequency of disciplinary reports, responsibilities, and family and community ties. Currently, this process is being reviewed and modified, Tibbals explained (Conversation with American Correctional Association staff, September, 1998).

# Definition

Basically, internal classification is an additional component of classification. As shown in Figure 5.1, internal classification is at the third level in the typical five-stage classification process (Levinson, 1982). Whereas "external" classification is the procedure for assigning inmates to an institution having the appropriate security features needed to control each prisoner's behavior, "internal" classification is an approach for systematically assigning inmates with similar behavior characteristics to housing units within an institution.

Internal classification does not deprive prisoners of their rights or privileges, nor does it change anyone's custody level. Rather, it houses together inmates with similar interests and behavior patterns, thereby separating likely predators from their victims and reducing the number of acts of inmate-on-inmate violence and exploitation. That is, all prisoners (regardless of their internal-classification category) remain eligible for any program or increase in privileges that they otherwise would be entitled to by virtue of their custody grade. In short, an internal classification system "separates the good guys from the bad guys when everybody is wearing a black hat" (Quay, 1984).

FIGURE 5.1 THE CLASSIFICATION PROCESS

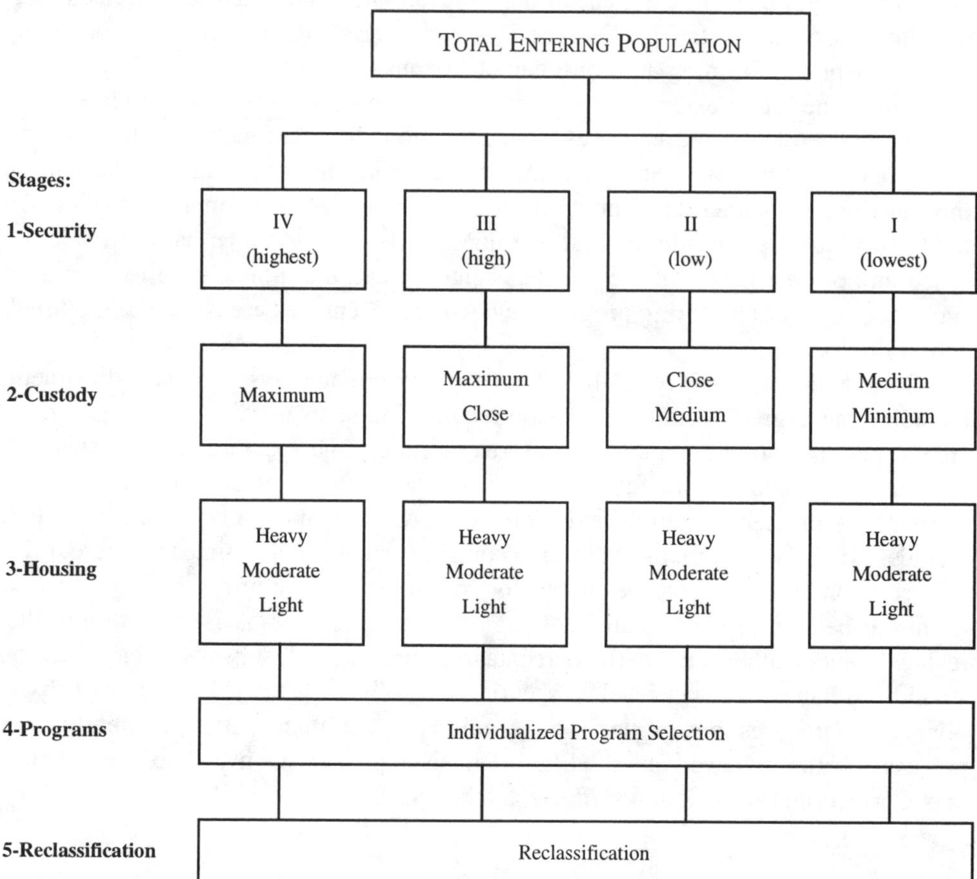


# Issues

All organizations exhibit a natural resistance toward change. Overcoming this when internal classification is introduced is helped substantially by ensuring that there is top-level administrative support for the initiative by the department's commissioner or the institution's warden. When such an individual does not "buy into" this concept or has his or her own ideas, the programs and plans that had been set in place may be derailed. However, the major issue in moving an entire corrections agency (or a particular institution) from its traditional method of operation into an internal classification approach is "the getting there." That is, implementing internal classification requires a comprehensive plan and then completing its sequence of steps.

*Resistance.* Resistance should be confronted by inviting the commissioner and other top-level officials from the jurisdiction to both "kickoff" and participate in an on-site training session. They should emphasize their support and the benefits for the staff that can be achieved by following this approach. Another method for overcoming resistance is to employ hands-on training exercises that include frequent question-and-answer discussion periods.

*Implementation.* The process of moving departments of corrections or institutions from their current operations into internal classification is the most difficult aspect of this undertaking. It involves anticipating untoward occurrences, making careful plans to cope with all contingencies, setting target dates, and sticking with them, and so forth. A major portion of any training session should be allocated to helping participants think through the "how-tos" of accomplishing this implementation process.

Since there are a number of different approaches to internal classification, a legitimate issue arises concerning selection. Why should a jurisdiction choose one system rather than some other one? This and other issues that must be dealt with when internal classification is being implemented include: labeling, mislabeling, changing labels, and so forth.

*Which approach?* Several different methods can be used as the basis for an internal classification system. As indicated earlier, the National Institute of Corrections anticipates developing a report on this topic, which should be available in 1999.[3] Internal classification may be based on psychological test scores, checklists of inmates' behavior, correctional classification factors, and others. However, making such a decision should not be a "seat-of-the-pants" operation. The National Institute of Corrections' publication *Prison Classification* (1981), based on Solomon's (1980) work, lists fourteen classification principles that also are important for internal classification. Megargee (1977) lists seven criteria for a good classification system. It should be complete, clear, reliable, valid, dynamic, economical, and have implications for treating offenders. An examination of these principles is part of the decision-making process regarding which internal classification approach a department of corrections will use.

As previously mentioned, Quay's (1984) Adult Internal Management System (AIMS) is an extension to adults of his earlier work with juveniles. Using separate factor analytic techniques, he developed two checklists: the first was based on data obtained through the observation of inmates' behavior in a correctional setting; the second used information from an offender's life (social) history obtained through an interview and a review of records pertaining to an individual's background. The two checklists are completed independently: the first by a correctional officer, the second by a case manager. Information from these two checklists is combined, and scores on five dimensions (the underlying factors) result: aggressive-psychopathic, manipulative, situational, immature-dependent, and neurotic-anxious.

Megargee's MMPI-based typology is based on the fourteen scales of the Minnesota Multiphasic Personality Inventory, the most widely used psychological test in corrections. Though a series of iterative analyses, ten personality types were identified, based on various configurations of the fourteen scale scores. Briefly, these are: Item—best adjusted; Easy—well adjusted, but underachievers; Baker—depressed, withdrawn; Able—self-confident, manipulative; George—poor self-image, submissive; Delta—psychopathic, hedonistic, amoral; Jupiter—introverted, impulsive; Foxtrot—hostile, immature; Charlie—bitter, suspicious; How—unstable, agitated, disturbed, ineffective.

According to the survey reports on internal offender classification by the National Council on Crime and Delinquency (Austin and Chan, 1994),[4] the majority of state correctional agencies are interested in participating in internal offender classification. A number of states indicated that they have a formal internal classification system. But in reviewing their classification manuals, it became clear that they do not have such a a system (in other words, an extra tier of internal classification in addition to the external system). Rather, their approach is a comprehensive system which "does it all," namely, institutional assignment, and unit housing assignment, which depends largely on program needs and work eligibility.

Moreover, most facilities have multisecurity- or multicustody-level housing units such as protective custody units and administrative segregation units. Placement into these "special" units is dependent largely on the results from the objective classification process, and to a smaller degree, on the professional judgment of prison staff. Therefore, some corrections personnel are under the impression that their objective classification also performs the job of an internal system.

Jurisdictions which claimed to have both formal external and internal classification systems are as follows:

1) *Federal Prison System*—The Adult Internal Management System (AIMS) developed by Dr. Herbert Quay has been implemented in a small number of facilities in the system. AIMS relies on two inventories to classify inmates: 1) the analysis of life history records, and 2) the correctional adjustment checklist.

2) *Georgia*—The AIMS system is used in all state correctional institutions.

3) *Illinois*—With the assistance of the National Council on Crime and Delinquency, the Illinois Department of Correction implemented a system in its four maximum-security facilities (Stateville, Joliet, Pontiac, and Menard). After an inmate is received at one of these facilities, the internal-classification system scoring instrument is used to determine the inmate's level of institutional aggression. Based on that score, the inmate is assigned to the appropriate housing, work, and program assignments. The instrument scores inmates on their level of aggression, largely determined by their disciplinary conduct and gang activities, but it also uses some of the same criteria found in the external classification system.

4) *Indiana*—In selected sites only, formal internal classification is being used to determine housing assignments. For example, in the Indiana State Reformatory, which is a maximum-security facility, all general population offenders were screened at intake to identify disruptive offenders. A second classification procedure also is required to process offenders for work assignments and housing assignments. Factors considered by classification staff are past conduct history, gang affiliations, and proofs of detrimental effect on the security of the facility and other inmates. Offenders are then housed in different cellblocks based on their levels of management risk and work eligibility.

5) *Louisiana*—The initial objective classification is an integrated system which determines institutional assignment, unit housing assignment, and also assesses programming needs.

6) *Missouri*—The Missouri Department of Corrections had been using the AIMS system since the late 1980s. It is now testing another system under auspices of the National Institute of Corrections. The system was in place at all of the department's secure facilities but was not used in the two community release centers or in the institutional treatment centers which provide specialized substance abuse programming. AIMS has never been used in female facilities.

7) *New Hampshire*—The state uses one comprehensive classification system which accomplishes most classification purposes. Its objective is to provide a profile of an inmate in these areas: security (public risk), custody (institutional risk), medical and health care needs, mental health needs, training/programming needs, education needs, vocational training needs, and work skills. Housing assignments within a designated facility are made based on a version of the Quay system.

8) *New Mexico*—In this state, classification is a comprehensive process which determines an inmate's custody level, institutional assignment, and programming assignments, which include: education; treatment; jobs; and decisions relating to family visits, furloughs, and good time awards. The initial custody classification determines institutional assignment and also recommends programs suitable for the inmates. Program recommendations at this point can be changed by the classification staff in the institution based on requests of the inmate or judgment of the staff. The department has a formal procedure for administrative segregation placement. Aside from that, it does not have a formal method for unit-housing placement within a facility. Basically, an inmate's custody level and program needs determine where the inmate will serve time.

9) *Ohio*—The Adult Internal Management System (AIMS or Quay) is used in a number of facilities.

10) *Oklahoma*—The Quay system is being used in a number of facilities.

11) *Pennsylvania*—This state has been using the Pennsylvania Additive Classification Tool (PACT) which was developed in conjunction with the National Council on Crime and Delinquency, to determine the custody levels of inmates since October 1992. PACT also contains a needs assessment. In addition to using the custody levels generated via PACT to assign inmates to facilities, the department also uses these custody levels to assign inmates to appropriate security level housing within the facility. Therefore, there is a degree of overlap in that the department uses PACT data as an external and as an internal classification to some extent.

12) *South Carolina*—The Adult Internal Management System (AIMS or Quay) had been implemented in all thirty-two facilities, but it is not currently being used.

13) *South Dakota*—The AIMS system has been implemented in a number of facilities.

14) *Texas*—This state uses an integrated classification system which determines both facility and housing unit assignments.

15) *Washington*—This state has implemented an internal classification system in one of its facilities. The system is Prison Management Classification (PMC), a personality-topology based system which classifies and segregates inmates according to their personality types. This system is being used only in the Callam Bay Corrections Center.

    In 1993, the Washington Department of Correction also implemented the Case Management System (the predecessor to Prison Management Classification) to match offender needs with appropriate placement and resources and to "have the right offender in the right bed at the right time."

16) *West Virginia*—The custody level scored by the inmates in the objective classification process determines in which facility they will reside. The custody level also determines to which housing area within a facility they will be assigned, for example, protective custody unit, dorm, segregation unit, and infirmary.

Thus, sixteen agencies[5] including the Bureau of Prisons have implemented formal internal classification systems (independent of the external system), and among these few, the most widely used system has been the Adult Internal Management System (AIMS).

Nevertheless, forty agencies have expressed interest in participating as a test site. The states most enthusiastic are Delaware, Hawaii, Indiana, Louisiana, Maine, Oklahoma, Oregon, Washington, and West Virginia.

Regardless of which approach is selected, all internal classification systems place inmates in one of several different categories which, in turn, are used to make housing (and, possibly, other) assignments. Critics of this type of "labeling" maintain that giving an inmate a label becomes a self-fulfilling prophesy. That is, because the inmate has been given a label, the individual is treated in a certain way which, then, increases the likelihood that the prisoner behaves in accord with the label. Whichever method is chosen, selection should result from a systematic process. The choice should be an approach that is designed to achieve better inmate management, one that can be outlined clearly so that it can be understood by the departments of corrections or the facility's staff.

*Labeling.* The question is sometimes raised: Does "labeling" inmates cause them to act like their labels? There is no evidence that this idea is valid. In an objective classification system, offenders must have histories documenting that they have engaged in the category's defining behavior. They also display such behavior during an observation period. While a wide variety of labels have been used, in general, internal classification systems identify three broad categories of inmates: Heavies—predators; Lights—victims; and Moderates—inmates who stand up to the former and do not abuse the latter (departments of corrections name their own inmate categories; *see* examples, Table 5.1, page 84).

*Changing labels.* Each system's classification staff should be clear about the positive and negative connotations of the labels they assign to each of the internal classification categories. No matter what an individual's category is, all inmates must have access to all programs and privileges for which they are eligible by virtue of their custody grade. There will be "good" and "bad" prisoners in every internal classification category. Further, inmates cannot change their classification label by good behavior. Since the internal classification process (by which the label is assigned) consists of an objective, valid, empirically based method, it cannot be altered by day-to-day variations in an individual's behavior.

*Mislabeling.* Sometimes it appears from an inmate's behavior that he or she has been placed in the "wrong" group. Consequently, there needs to be an explicit procedure for checking errors in the internal classification process before considering the possibility of changing an individual's internal classification category. Errors in the classification process may be due to the lack of current background information or be a consequence of insufficient time for staff to observe and evaluate an inmate. The reassessment procedure for internal classification should include using an impartial panel, rechecking and rescoring forms, and should be an exceedingly rare occurrence.

*"Faking."* It has been suggested that during the classification process, "con artist" inmates can disguise their true behavioral characteristics to qualify for a particular internal classification group. Experience in Missouri, South Carolina, Utah, and elsewhere has shown that this almost never happens. If, during an inmate orientation session, the AIMS program has been properly explained, there is no incentive for faking. Heavies, Lights, and Moderates all should be described in positive terms, such as the italicized terms in the following listing:

## Inmate Subgroup Characteristics

**Heavy** —*active in sports*, agitators, aggressive, *assertive*, *energetic*, hostile, *leadership abilities, quick decision-makers, shrewd, stands up for opinions, outgoing, thrill-seekers*, victimizers, violent

**Moderate** —*independent, family oriented*, little prior criminal history, *reliable*, minimal staff contact, *studious*, tend to remain uninvolved

**Light** —inattentive, *introspective, interacts with staff on a regular basis*, moody, passive, prefer nonphysical activities, *reflective*, rely on staff, self-absorbed, *sensitive to the needs of others*, short-fused, tense, withdrawn

Twenty-four-hour surveillance by veteran correctional officers (over a minimum of two weeks) will reveal the leaders and followers among new admissions in all groups, particularly by observing and being sensitive to the reactions of other inmates.

## TABLE 5.1 AIMS SUBGROUP: LABELS

<table>
<tr><th>SOURCE:</th><th>I</th><th>II</th><th>III</th><th>IV</th><th>V</th></tr>
<tr><td>QUAY</td><td>Aggressive</td><td>Manipulators</td><td>Situational</td><td>Inadequate</td><td>Neurotic</td></tr>
<tr><td>LEVINSON</td><td colspan="2">Heavy</td><td>Moderate</td><td colspan="2">Light</td></tr>
<tr><td>LEWISBURG</td><td colspan="2">MAB</td><td>SAN</td><td colspan="2">FAL</td></tr>
<tr><td>S. CAROLINA</td><td colspan="2">Alpha</td><td>Gamma</td><td colspan="2">Beta</td></tr>
<tr><td>UTAH</td><td colspan="2">Kappa</td><td>Omega</td><td colspan="2">Sigma</td></tr>
<tr><td>MISSOURI</td><td>High Alpha</td><td>Low Alpha</td><td>Kappa</td><td>Low Sigma</td><td>High Sigma</td></tr>
<tr><td>ALASKA</td><td>Spruce I</td><td>Spruce II</td><td>Birch</td><td colspan="2">Cottonwood</td></tr>
<tr><td>U.S. NAVY</td><td colspan="2">Alpha</td><td>Gamma</td><td colspan="2">Beta</td></tr>
<tr><td>D.C.</td><td colspan="2">Hawks</td><td>Eagles</td><td colspan="2">Orioles</td></tr>
<tr><td>S. DAKOTA</td><td>A</td><td>B</td><td>C</td><td>D</td><td>E</td></tr>
</table>

> "We work together, we rec together, we go to church together, we eat together, but we can't live with certain people! Who's kidding who? . . . The hell with Quay—stop putting labels on us!"
>
> "The new system tells me that the administration sees a need for a change, although this change may not be the best one at this time for CCI, . . . it is a step in the right direction."
>
> —Two inmates in South Carolina's Central Correctional Institution commenting following AIMS implementation

*Bed-space*. The number of inmates falling into each of the internal classification system's categories may not match the bed-space allocated to prisoners with that label. What happens when there is severe crowding in one housing unit and too few inmates in an area that houses a different category of inmates?

Quay (1984) identified five methods to adjust inmate numbers between housing units: (1) Moderates can fill vacancies in Heavy or Light units; (2) the number of units allotted to each category can be altered; (3) compatible smaller groups can be combined;

(4) nearly tied subcategory scores (such as those with one- or two-point differences can be treated as the same); and (5) the cutoff scores between subcategories can be modified, temporarily.

# Programmatic Separation

Programmatic separation is the practice of arranging prisoner assignments so that inmates most likely to be predators are kept separate from those most susceptiple to becoming their prey in nonunit programs (Levinson, 1991). In other words, predators and their victims are kept apart not only in the housing area but also in other portions of the facility. The Boonville Correctional Center in the Missouri Department of Corrections has had complete programmatic separation since 1987. Spieker and Pierson (1989) reported:

> Housing segregation is the most fundamental and essential separation since living quarters are the most common area for . . . victimization [to occur]. Lesser areas of victimization, which may also be separated are recreation, food service, and education . . . (page 10).

Missouri indicated that programmatic separation "further reduce[d] the possibility of [inmate victimization in areas other than housing units], such as the recreation yard, work, dining room . . . " (Spieker and Pierson, 1987).[6] The Missouri Department of Corrections strongly recommended recreation as the next area (after housing units) for programmatic separation. To achieve a highly sophisticated institution structure of this nature, careful scheduling is required so that every subgroup has equal access (not, necessarily, amount of time) to all the opportunities the facility offers through proportional time scheduling. For example, in a facility with 800 Heavies, 100 Lights, and 50 Moderates, it would be inappropriate to assign the same amount of in-gymnasium time to the 150 Lights and Moderates as for the 800 Heavies. Not only are the latter more numerous, but experience shows that they tend to have a higher gymnasium usage rate.

Missouri (Spieker and Pierson, 1987) reports that classroom attention and performance radically increase following separation by AIMS classification. Additionally, the type of academic instruction should be varied in line with Quay's (1984, p. 19) recommendations. That is, teaching may be more effective if self-paced workbooks are used with the Heavies while oral reading in small groups is used with the Lights (*see* Table 5.2).

Group separation in the vocational training and job assignment areas also helps reduce victimization. Missouri has found (Spieker and Pierson, 1987) that certain groups perform better in some institution jobs than in others. For example, Moderates are far superior to other inmates in clerk-type jobs, while Heavies have a good record in food service.

In general, an individualized, no-nonsense, behavioral contract approach that uses short-term goals and a system of prompt, tangible rewards and punishments, and incorporates nonrepetitive work (say autoshop rather than laundry) is effective with the Heavy group. A supportive, team approach using individualized verbal praise and encouragement and repetitive work appears more effective for the Light group.

# Benefits

Using an internal classification system allows staff to anticipate better where trouble is most likely to occur and frequently to forestall its occurrence. In regard to inmates, it permits them to be the following:

- Classified into behavior-relevant categories
- Housed in homogeneous groups
- Placed in units in which staff have been matched according to their interests and abilities to work with a particular type of inmate
- Assigned to appropriate programs identified with each behavioral category

> AIMS is designed to reduce conflicts between inmates and minimize management difficulties between prisoners and personnel.
>
> —Booneville (Missouri) Correctional Center Employee Handbook

Internal classification systems are designed to reduce conflicts between inmates and to minimize negative interactions between prisoners and personnel. This is accomplished by housing in the same housing area inmates having similar control requirements. The basic principle of internal classification systems is to separate the aggressive offenders from their most likely victims. The former are assigned to the facility's most secure housing and the latter to a unit that is as far away as the facility's site-plan will allow.

An additional benefit results from this type housing arrangement. Even among the Heavies, there is less conflict (than before AIMS implementation) since these inmates "respect" one another and a "stand-off" occurs.

Since the inmates are housed homogeneously, staff "matching" also can be employed. That is, staff who work best with a particular type of inmate can be assigned to the unit housing those individuals. Based on Quay's (1984) research, Table 5.2 displays the characteristics of the three broad categories of inmates and the most appropriate management approach for working successfully with each.

Each category of prisoners includes both "good guys" and "bad guys." Each group contains individuals with both positive and negative personality characteristics. For example (as shown in Figure 5.2) in South Carolina's end-of-the-line facility, over a fifteen-month period, 19 percent of the Heavies had no disciplinary reports, as did 39 percent of the Lights; while 58 percent of the Moderates had no disciplinary reports over this time frame—but 42 percent of the Moderates had one or more.

Moreover, 21 percent of the Heavy inmates amassed six or more disciplinary reports during this period compared to 9 percent for the Lights, and only 2 percent of

## TABLE 5.2: CHARACTERISTIC BEHAVIOR BY CLASSIFICATION CATEGORY

| HEAVY | MODERATE | LIGHT |
|---|---|---|
| • Aggressive/Sly | • Not excessively aggressive or dependent | • Dependent/afraid |
| • Directly or indirectly confrontational | • Reliable/cooperative | • Unreliable/anxious |
| • Easily bored/ Untrustworthy | • Industrious | • Passive/easily upset |
| • Hostile to authority | • Does not see self as being a criminal | • "Clinging"/seeks protection |
| • Disciplinaries: high-to-moderate rate | • Disciplinaries: low rate | • Disciplinaries: low-to-moderate rate |
| • Little concern for others/ Manipulators and "con artists" | • Concern for others | • Self-absorbed/explosive under stress |
| • Victimizers | • Avoids fights | • Easily victimized |

### DIFFERENTIAL PROGRAMMING BY CLASSIFICATION

| PROGRAM AREA: | HEAVY | MODERATE | LIGHT |
|---|---|---|---|
| EDUCATION | • Individualized<br>• Programmed learning | • Classroom lecture + research assignments | • Classroom lecture + individual tutoring |
| WORK | • Nonrepetitive<br>• Short-term goals | • High level of (supervised) responsibility | • Repetitive<br>• Team-oriented goals |
| COUNSELING | • Individualized (behavioral contracts) | • Group and individual (problem-oriented) | • Group and individual (personal orientation) |
| STAFF APPROACH | • By-the-book<br>• No-nonsense | • "Hands-off"<br>• Direct only as needed | • Highly verbal<br>• Supportive |

the Moderates; among the Heavies, 7 percent received eleven disciplinary reports or almost one serious report per month for fifteen months.

In addition to the benefits gained from staff "matching," other efficiencies result from the use of an internal classification approach with unit management. For example, the number and type of personnel can be varied by unit to obtain maximal efficiency. That is, with the Heavies, more correctional officers are needed who deal with inmates using a "top sergeant," by-the-book-type approach—because of the aggressiveness and hostility toward authority that inmates in this category have. The Lights require more case worker attention (because of their fears and tendencies to rely heavily on staff) and correctional officers who are willing to sit down and talk with inmates about the problems of living in a prison. The Moderates, who tend to be independent and not create management problems, need fewer staff to supervise them than the other two groups.

# Transition

The process of moving departments of corrections or institutions from their current operations into internal classification is the most difficult aspect of this undertaking. It involves anticipating untoward occurrences, making careful plans to cope with all contingencies, setting target dates and sticking with them, and so forth. A major portion of any training session should be allocated to helping participants think through the "how-to's" of accomplishing this implementation process.

Moving into an internal classification system has many similarities with the transition steps necessary when a system/institution changes from a traditional to a unit management structure. The first three of the fourteen steps for implementing an internal classification system are the same. Using Quay's (1984) AIMS approach for illustrative purposes, the eleven remaining implementation steps are as follows:

# AIMS Implementation

## Steps 4-14

Steps 1-3 see pages 50-51.

### (4) Training for AIMS Task Force

The Implementation Task Force (set up in Step 3) should: (1) read the material available concerning the internal classification approach the system plans to use, (2) visit an institution that is currently using that approach, and (3) seek advice from experienced people who are familiar with this approach and knowledgeable about implementing it in a corrections setting.

FIGURE 5.2 SERIOUS INCIDENT REPORTS X AIMS CATEGORY (15 MONTHS)*

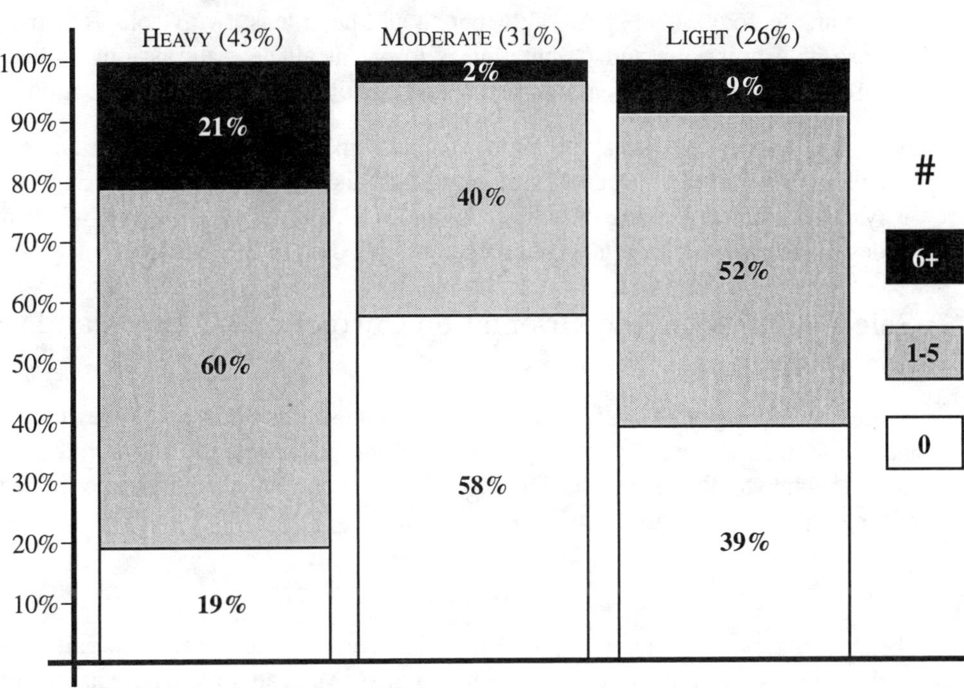


*Average Total Population = 1,113

## (5) AIMS Orientation for All Staff

(1) The AIMS task force proposes labels for the AIMS subgroups to the warden or commissioner, depending on whether this is an institution or systemwide implementation.

(2) The AIMS task force plans one (or more) staff training session(s) to present a general orientation on AIMS to all staff. The warden or commissioner is the opening speaker while other speakers include the task force members and the consultant.

(3) The focus of each training session is on the fact that the institution (system) is going into AIMS on [date]. There should be a thirty-to-forty-five minute explanation of what AIMS is and what it is not, a discussion of the advantages of AIMS in reducing violence and other inmate problems and its ability to improve service delivery, a discussion regarding how AIMS will affect current operations, and a question-and-answer session of at least fifteen minutes.

## (6) Modify Admissions Procedures

The specific sequence of events depends on whether the internal classification system is being implemented on an institution- or systemwide basis:

(1) If on an institutionwide basis, it will be necessary to create (if not already in existence) an Admissions and Orientation living area. The number of beds in this area depends on the average weekly intake. An inmate's length of stay in this area is four weeks, preferably, but should be at least two weeks. The purpose of Admissions and Orientation is to orient all new admissions, collect information for program assignments, and perform the AIMS classification.

(2) If on a systemwide basis, the need is to build-in the AIMS classification procedure as a part of the regular systemwide admission processing. Consequently, all inmates leaving Admissions and Orientation will arrive at their designated institution after having been assigned an AIMS category.

## (7) Select Admission and Orientation Corrections Officers and Case Managers

Veteran, knowledgeable staff should function in these positions, since they play a critical role in making the AIMS category assignments. If policy requires correctional officers to rotate to different posts, the frequency of such rotations should be slowed down; for example, three months on a post.

## (8) Train Admission and Orientation/Unit Staff

The AIMS task force should plan one intensive training session for all personnel directly involved in assigning inmates to an AIMS category. The warden (or commissioner) should be the opening speaker. The AIMS task force members and the consultant serve as trainers.

The intensive training should highlight the history of AIMS,[7] a discussion of how AIMS affects current practices, and training exercises. Training exercises include a sixty-to-ninety-minute hands-on session in which two-person teams AIMS-classify the same hypothetical case and perform an AIMS classification on at least one additional "live" case. This should be followed by a question-and-answer session that lasts a minimum of fifteen-to-thirty minutes.

## (9) Pilot-test (10 Percent Random Sample)

The purpose of doing this pilot-test is to determine the percentage of inmates in each AIMS category, to provide data for selecting living areas and the number of beds needed for each AIMS group, and to serve as a dry run to check for procedural problems before full implementation begins.

The procedure for choosing the random sample is to randomly select 10 percent of onboard prisoners (for example, use the last digit of an inmate's identification number). Then, after two-to-four weeks (longer is better), AIMS-trained correctional officers rate the randomly selected inmates using the AIMS Correctional Adjustment Checklist. They, next, give their completed forms to case managers. Then, based on a review of records and an individual interview, the case managers complete an AIMS Life History Checklist for each inmate in the randomly selected sample.

Case managers should score their own and the correctional officers' checklists to arrive at an AIMS classification for every randomly selected prisoner. They, then, send completed AIMS Classification Profile forms to the chair of the AIMS task force, who calculates the percentages of inmates in each of the AIMS categories. After this, based on the pilot-test data, the AIMS task force (in collaboration with the consultant) recommends specific living quarters for each AIMS group: the most secure areas for Heavies, a living area most distant from the Heavies for the Lights, and an area for Moderates between the Heavies and the Lights.

## (10) AIMS Task Force Should Develop Own Implementation Plan

(1) Identify correctional officers and case managers who will complete their respective checklists and the specific inmates (entire population) on whom they will complete them

(2) Establish a deadline for the completion of all forms

(3) Establish a deadline for case managers to tally scores and specify each inmate's final AIMS category

(4) Determine how inmates will move to the area housing their AIMS category (for example, one day, over a weekend, and so forth)

(5) Set the date on which the inmate moves will start

(6) Establish how and when (prior to move) both onboard and new inmates will be oriented to AIMS

(7) Decide how and when onboard inmates will be notified about their move to an AIMS unit. Emphasize that regardless of AIMS category, there will be no loss of any programming or promotion opportunities

(8) Move the Heavies first. Coordinate all planning with the security/operations staff

## (11) Activate the AIMS Implementation Plan

In other words, do what you said you were going to do, when you said you were going to do it.

## (12) Maintaining AIMS

*For new admissions and transfers:* All new admissions should be placed in the Admission and Orientation section and AIMS-classified. Transfers into the institution who arrive without an AIMS classification should be placed in Admission and Orientation and AIMS-classified. Transfers into a facility who arrive with an AIMS classification should be placed in the appropriate AIMS unit. If there is no room in the "correct" unit, then one of the methods specified on page 84 should be followed. The guiding theme is: new arrivals get preference over veterans for a "correct" unit placement.

*For internal moves:* When an inmate requests to make an internal move (for example, from one cell/room to a different cell/room), this request can be approved by the unit manager but only when the change takes place within the same AIMS classification.

## (13) Evaluation

In cooperation with the central office's research staff, the task force should plan an assessment of AIMS. They should collect baseline data (pre-AIMS implementation) on the number and type of disciplinary problems, and the number of program enrollments and completions. This same information should be collected by the task force after AIMS has been operational for one year.

Measures that can be used to see if there has been a reduction in violence or problems include: number, percent, and type of disciplinary reports; number, percent, and average length of time of segregation commitments; number and percent of disciplinary transfers; number, percent, and type of inmate grievances; number and percent of protective custody requests/lockups; number and percent of escapes or escape attempts; average number and percent of prisoners on sick-call; and number and percent of increases or decreases in the custody levels.

The task force should assess if the delivery of correctional services has improved. Among staff, what is the rate of turnovers, sick-leave, overtime, and promotions? How does this compare with what happened prior to the implementation of AIMS? Among inmates, what number and percent are enrolled and/or have completed their education or vocational training, and what social service types of courses or seminars have they been involved with or completed?

The task force and research office staff should analyze their findings relative to the amount of change occurring as a consequence of implementing AIMS. Copies of the report(s) should be sent to the commissioner, warden, department heads, and unit managers.

## (14) Internal Classification Results—In-house

Some studies have been done of the inmate populations in high-security prisons that use internal classification. Table 5.3 shows how these prisoners distribute themselves among the three broad internal classification categories: Heavy, Moderate, and Light.

An interesting contrast is revealed in the distribution by categories of AIMS-classified inmates confined in the Navy Brig System[8] where "approximately 80 percent of the prisoners are minimum or out custody: Heavy = 18 percent; Moderate = 64 percent; and Light = 18 percent."

Several state systems represented at the Unit Management National Workshop (1988) were using the AIMS classification. South Carolina reported that at its end-of-the-line penitentiary, Central Correctional Institution, 80 percent of the serious incidents involved the Heavy inmates and occurred on the living units housing this group. Additionally, South Carolina reported that serious incidents (for example, inmate assaults on staff or other inmates, escapes and escape attempts, destruction of property, disruptions of institutional operations, and suicides and attempts) had been reduced 18 percent. During the eighteen months their study lasted, the serious-incident rate per 1,000 inmates was cut in half—from sixteen to eight events per quarter.

At South Carolina's Perry institution, 88 percent of the serious incidents involved the Heavy inmates. As a consequence, South Carolina differentially assigned correctional officers to these units; that is, they assigned a greater number of correctional officers to the Heavy units and fewer were posted in the areas that housed Moderate inmates.

New Hampshire described a drop in the number of assaults, from ninety to thirty, one year after AIMS classification was implemented. Missouri's Boonville Correctional Center reported that following the introduction of AIMS "violence of all kinds has radically declined, and the protective custody population has been cut by 60 percent."

Silberman (1995) indicates that the use of functional units in conjunction with the AIMS reduced violence effectively at a high-security Pennsylvania prison. And Toch (1981) notes that social climate ratings improve both "for tougher and for more vulnerable inmates."

**Table 5.3: Distribution of AIMS Category Inmates by Security Level (in Percentages)**

| Department of Corrections | Heavy | Moderate | Light |
|---|---|---|---|
| Maximum Security: | | | |
| • Alaska | 66 | 11 | 23 |
| • South Carolina | 61 | 15 | 24 |
| • Virginia | 76 | 4 | 20 |
| (Average) | (68%) | (10%) | (22%) |
| Medium Security: | | | |
| • Bureau of Prisons | 47 | 27 | 27 |
| • District of Columbia | 64 | 21 | 15 |
| • Missouri | 66 | 14 | 20 |
| (Average) | (59%) | (21%) | (21%) |
| Minimum Security: | | | |
| • Bureau of Prisons | 35 | 35 | 30 |
| Overall Average | 54% | 22% | 24% |

Systems using an internal classification system in conjunction with unit management strongly endorsed the concept. For example, the Navy's Consolidated Brig in Charleston, South Carolina, reported: "While [unit management] has been operational for a relatively short time, the positive results . . . have been noted by both staff and prisoners. Exit interviews and follow-up questionnaires indicate prisoners considered their time spent at the brig productive. . . ." (Rucker, 1991).

Information concerning the reduction in prisoners' problematic behavior confirms data reported in the research literature; much of which is presented in Quay's (1984) monograph *Managing Adult Inmates*. Quay compared one federal penitentiary that tried AIMS with four similar institutions that continued their traditional program. Adjusting for population size, the target facility was expected to have 27 percent of the in-penitentiary, inmate-on-staff assaults. Pre-AIMS it had 33 percent; the average for four years post-AIMS was 11 percent (range 5-20 percent). Inmate-on-inmate assaults, also expected to be 27 percent of the total, were 18 percent before AIMS and averaged 12 percent (for the four years post-AIMS, the range was 9 to 21 percent) after AIMS was implemented. Thus, inmate assaults on staff were reduced two-thirds, and inmate-on-inmate assaults were reduced one-third.

On December 25, 1982, a major disturbance occurred between rival inmate factions in the dining room at the Federal Correctional Institution in Petersburg, Virginia. It resulted in the death of a correctional officer. Subsequent investigation revealed that a group of twenty inmates was primarily responsible for the disturbance. Of these, 85 percent were Heavies, while none were Moderates, or Lights—the remaining 15 percent were from a non-AIMS classified drug treatment unit. Institutionwide, Heavies represented 29 percent of the inmate population.

Results substantiating the Petersburg finding were reported for Alaska where the Heavies represented 66 percent of the population, but had 77 percent of the disciplinary reports; the Lights were 23 percent of the population and had 17 percent of the disciplinary reports, while the Moderates at 11 percent of the population, had 6 percent of the disciplinary reports.

Postrelease data was available on 220 cases in a federal random sample that had been in the community for two years (Quay, 1984). Clear differences were found among the AIMS groups, with the Heavies and the Moderates showing the greatest contrast. The former group, which represented 30.5 percent of the total follow-up sample, were responsible for 60 percent of the recorded violent offenses. Overall, the Heavies manifested greater crime involvement, poorer institutional adjustment, and a tendency toward violence both inside prison and postrelease. The Moderates were much less involved in crime, did not present serious management problems, and generally refrained from violence within the institution and following release.

# Endnotes

1 Unit management also was used to meet court-mandated remedies in Georgia: "Many of the developments described in this report have been effected by the implementation of unit management at Georgia State Prison" (*Guthrie v. Evans*, 1981).

2 The Quay system was developed for classification of male prisoners. A similar system for female inmates has not been developed.

3 "There are two issues in the discussion of unit management: one is unit management itself, and the other is internal classification. Missouri [which currently uses the Adult Internal Management System] is involved in [assessing] the prototypical internal classification system being sponsored by the National Institute of Corrections. . . . " George Lombardi, director, Division of Adult Institutions for the Missouri Department of Corrections told the American Correctional Association staff in September 1998. Missouri's concerns about AIMS echo similar apprehensions voiced by J. D. Williams, former assistant director of the Federal Bureau of Prisons; namely, the unrepresentative racial distribution of inmates when assigned to living units by AIMS groups.

A major intent of internal classification systems, such as AIMS, is to reduce assaultive/aggressive behavior among inmates and between inmates and staff. Racial identity is not part of the categorization process. An inmate's AIMS-assignment is based on his behavior—both current and past. Research studies (such as those cited in this volume) demonstrate that the use of internal classification systems indeed do reduce the incidence of problematic behavior.

4 Austin and Chann (1994), Survey Report on Interim Report.

5 Alaska and Utah, both of which use AIMS, should be added to this list.

6 See endnote 3 (above).

7 Use R. B. Levinson (1988) "Developments in the Classification Process: Quay's AIMS Approach," *Criminal Justice and Behavior.* (15) 1, pp. 24-38, and/or H.C. Quay's *Managing Adult Inmates*. 1984. American Correctional Association.

8 Information supplied by Michael R. Rucker, correctional programs officer, Naval Consolidated Brig, Charleston, South Carolina.

*People claim they believe only what they see; the problem is that they are better at believing than they are at seeing.*

—Anonymous

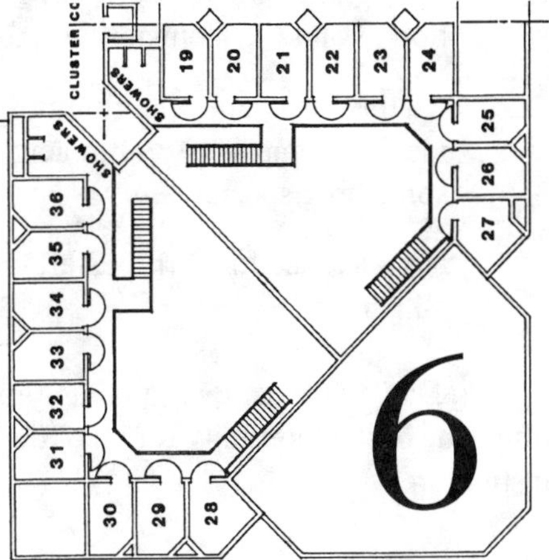


# Does Unit Management Work?

## Introduction

How does one decide whether a particular correctional program "works"? Typically, testimonials and research results are used to indicate that a new program is more effective in achieving a desirable goal than either the current approach or alternative innovations. Presented below are examples of both types of "evidence" as it relates to unit management.

## Successful Correctional Programs

During his keynote presentation at the National Institute of Corrections-funded National Workshop on Unit Management (1988), Dean Sherman Day of Georgia State University—and the National Institute of Corrections' first director—spoke about the characteristics of successful programs in correctional institutions. Gleaned from this nation's 200-plus-year history with prisons, Dr. Day listed eight characteristics:

1. Strong visible leadership; it must be clear that government is in charge
2. Emphasis is on safety and security for both staff and inmates
3. Clean, orderly institutions in which discipline is evident

4. Clear expectations of staff concerning goals, procedures, and methods
5. Clear expectations of inmates concerning behavior, goals, and procedures
6. Collegiality among staff—ownership of program at all levels and an appreciation of and the inclusion of line staff in meaningful ways
7. Quality program opportunities that encompass a belief in the rehabilitation ideal; an emphasis on literacy; the expectation of work; and being known for something special
8. No tolerance for corrupt staff—fair, honest models of law-abiding behavior by all personnel

Dr. Day's summary was that unit management is a proven organizational plan that offers the best opportunity for all of these characteristics to be present in a correctional institution.

## When Things Go Wrong—At the State Level

At the American Federation of State, County, and Municipal Employees' founding Congress of AFSCME Corrections United, Mr. Gerald W. McEntee, International President, American Federation of State, County, and Municipal Employees, AFL-CIO, spoke to the 600 attendees during the opening ceremonies. He stated: "No correctional officer ever asked for a unit system, but we have to live under it and die under it!"

Mr. McEntee was referring to the riot that had occurred at the Southern Ohio Correctional Facility, in Lucasville, Ohio, in which one staff member and ten inmates died, and property damage of $91 million occurred.[1] According to Gary C. Mohr,[2] who headed the team that investigated the causes of the 1993 riot, there were several significant obstacles to a successful unit management operation at Lucasville:

1. *Lack of communication.* Unit staff reported that shift supervisors routinely reassigned unit correctional officers and correctional counselors to other duties outside of their units, without the approval or knowledge of the unit manager. [Unit managers should have the final say regarding their correctional counselors and should be included in the decision-making process concerning the correctional officers in their unit.]

There was a similar lack of communication between units; they operated independently of each other, with only limited interaction. [There should be a weekly unit managers' meeting (chaired by the deputy warden) in which these type of issues are discussed.] This became a source of confusion for the correctional officers, counselors, and inmates who were assigned and transferred between the units. Occasional inconsistent responses to, or resolutions of, inmate concerns by unit staff and officers resulted in misunderstandings with the prisoner population. Staff also reported that the lines of communication between unit management and security had to improve.

2. *Lack of trust.* Unit staff reported during the board of inquiry interviews that they and security staff conducted investigations into the same incidents independent of one another and without any communication or sharing of results. [When unit staff

are on duty, within-unit security is the responsibility of the unit manager.] Staff also indicated that unit management and security needed to develop a more respectful, trustful, and cooperative relationship.

3. *Lack of a shared mission.* Interviews with both unit staff and security personnel indicated that the historic power struggle of treatment versus custody had been replaced at Lucasville by a power struggle between security and unit management. The board of inquiry interviews showed that correctional counselors were hired or promoted as sergeants and not specifically as counselors, which is the case at other Ohio facilities. Seventy-five percent of the counselors had goals for advancement in areas other than unit management.

In regard to training, not all of the unit management staff at Lucasville had completed the approved curriculum for unit management: while all nine unit managers had completed the training; ten out of fifteen (67 percent) of the case managers, twelve out of sixteen (75 percent) of the correctional counselors; and four out of eight (50 percent) of the unit secretaries—overall, 27 percent—had not completed the training. [Unit management training for unit staff is mandatory and compliance with this policy should be monitored by the warden and the head of the unit management section at the regional or central office level.] Of the thirty-five trained unit management staff, only fourteen (40 percent) had completed the revised unit management training.

4. *Limited inmate access to staff.* In-unit restrictions had a negative impact on staff accessibility at Lucasville. All units reported an inmate-initiated "kite system"—letters or messages—which were used to start formal contacts with the unit staff. Generally, the transmission of messages was controlled by the correctional officers on duty. Inmates who wanted to talk to staff members would notify the correctional officer who, then, would advise the staff member of the request. [Apparently, the offices for unit management staff were not in the living quarters, violating the requirement for easy access to staff by inmates.]

This riot occurred in 1993 and the deployment of women in prisons has undergone a profound change since then. However, at the time, 50 percent of the female case managers reported they did not go onto the cell block ranges to conduct inmate interviews unless they were escorted by a male staff member. All male case managers reported they could go on the ranges as they wished. Additionally, all but one female case manager reported they were not permitted to conduct formal office interviews with inmates or conduct in-unit programming unless a male staff member was present in the area. If a male staff member were not available, groups had to be rescheduled or were canceled.

Michigan reported (at the National Workshop, 1988) that in the past, the career ladder for females working in corrections stopped short due to system-imposed restrictions. The women sued the state and won. As of 1997, 60 percent of Michigan's correctional employees are male and 40 percent are female.

In Virginia, unit management has opened positions for all staff, especially females. The most secure unit in the state is the segregation building at Mecklenburg. Its unit management team consists of a female lieutenant, a male sergeant, and a female counselor. "It is functioning the best that it ever has. Having the women on the unit team seems to have a calming effect on the inmates in the unit." In fact, recent research by Criminal and Juvenile Justice International revealed that male officers were assaulted 3.6 times more often than female officers, and assaults on female officers have declined by 47 percent since 1992 (Rowan, 1996).

5. *Unit classification decisions overruled at central office.* One-third of the case managers, interviewed during the Lucasville inquiry, reported a lack of direction and support of their efforts (by the programs deputy and the director of social services) to develop and provide effective programming. Time intervals when programming could be conducted conflicted with inmate work schedules and with the periods set aside for prisoner recreation. [Unit managers should set the activity schedules for inmates in their unit.]

Overall, 79 percent of Lucasville's unit staff felt that unit management could function successfully in a maximum-security setting. Eighty percent (thirty-six out of forty-five) of the unit staff had a positive view of the leadership and direction they received from their superiors. Within the units, 78 percent of those interviewed stated that they received good leadership and direction from their unit managers.

## When Things Go Wrong—Federal Bureau of Prisons

In October, 1995, the Federal Bureau of Prisons initiated a nationwide lockdown—inmates in 85 federal institutions were locked into their cells after several prison disturbances occurred. According to John Vanyur, former researcher and current warden at the Federal Institution in Butner, North Carolina, "an after-action review found that while the BOP did an outstanding job in emergency response, the agency concluded that managing disturbances is 95 percent prevention and 5 percent training and preparing for disturbances." He stated that "unit management plays a key role in that prevention."

A board of inquiry found among other slippages of standards that emergency preparedness accounted for 95 percent of training and prevention for only 5 percent—exactly opposite of the "right mix." During a June, 1996 interview, Kathleen M. Hawk-Sawyer, the current Director of the Federal Bureau of Prisons (since 1992), was asked about any changes that were planned in light of the disturbances that had "flared-up at BOP institutions across the country." In addition to other plans, she replied: "We are also working on improvements in our unit management system to better communicate with and supervise inmates. . . ." Unit staff resumed working weekends; inmate counts were scheduled more frequently; unit teams held classification meetings in the evenings; unit disciplinary committees (as opposed to a single hearing officer) were reinstated; paperwork was reduced so case managers could spend more time interviewing and counseling inmates; the role of the correctional counselor was defined more explicitly; inmate attendance at classification and reclassification meetings resumed being mandatory—their attendance had become optional; and, more attention was paid to having case managers and correctional counselors holding group meetings.

# Research Findings

The following sections report on research studies conducted on unit management internationally, and at the federal, state, and local (jail) jurisdictional levels. These projects differ from previously mentioned assessments in that they do not deal with the degree to which unit management operations are in compliance with unit management standards. Rather, they focus on the degree to which the implementation of a unit management approach has realized anticipated beneficial results.

An effective evaluation program requires the establishment of objectives, which break down program goals into measurable, discrete activities. Accomplishing these objectives—the anticipated beneficial results—is indicative of the level of success of unit management.

## International

**Australia.** Borallon Correctional Centre was one of the first institutions in Australia to practice unit management. The success of this approach is attributed to the ability of the staff to adopt a unit management style on a continuous basis.

> In most modern facilities, the design concept has provided for direct supervision, by removing many of the traditional physical barriers of catwalks, barred gates, security glazing and other mechanical separators between officer and prisoner. The living units have been redesigned into community configurations rather than linear and remote, and many custodial officers appear to believe that this itself constitutes unit management. In fact it does not (Dickson, 1994).

Robson (1989) found that the physical and social environment provided by unit management at Bathurst Jail in New South Wales, Australia was "conducive to efficient management. . . [and] is cost effective." He reported that unit management reduces tension, increases inmate participation, improves inmate/officer relationships, improves inmate morale, and encourages custodial officers to see themselves as "change agents." According to Robson, unit management requires "officers who are committed to inmate rehabilitation and willing to practice dynamic versus static security (the former involving active continuous contact with inmates, the latter involves watching inmates from guard towers or control rooms)."

Benefits likely to arise for both officers and inmates, include:

- officers developing a more favorable attitude towards inmates
- officers becoming responsible for rehabilitative outcomes
- decreasing incidences of security breaches

- deriving a more satisfying and professional occupational experience for officers
- professionalizing the correctional officer's role by involving them in case planning decisions.

In Victoria, Australia, the state government developed a coordinated approach to effectively tackle the problem of violent crime, a component of which included unit management in its correctional facilities (Harmsworth, 1991).

Dr. Barry Ellem, senior lecturer at Monash University (Victoria, Australia), Centre for Police and Justice Studies, reported (Ellem, 1995) that the cost of locking up offenders dropped by about 35 percent during the past five years since innovative new management styles were introduced in the prison system. At the same time, the number of violent incidents within prisons also fell about a third.

The success of the new model hinged on "placing prisoners into small groups, known as unit management, and assigning individual case managers to prisoners within those units." According to Dr. Ellem, this results in "more positive interaction between prisoners and prison officers," which reduces a climate of friction and hostility and "forces prisoners to use their time more productively." There are positive indications that "the new, proactive approach to prisoner management is helping to break the cycle of offending behavior; for instance, there has been a reduction in the recidivism rate, and the types of crimes [for those who have been released and reoffended] have not been as serious as before."

Dr. Ellem states that these "developments within Victoria prisons . . . placed the state at the forefront of prison management both nationally and overseas." In 1991, based on information available from practical experience, a corrections review committee said that unit management should operate in all Australian custodial institutions.

In 1995, the Queensland (Australia) Corrective Services Commission reported:

> [Correctional Officers] with more positive correctional orientation expressed greater support for Unit Management, were more likely to endorse CSC objectives, felt more empowered on the job, experienced a greater sense of physical security on the job, and were more satisfied with their career development and most recent performance evaluation (Lariviera and Robinson, 1995).

**Canada.** In 1986, the Correctional Service of Canada decided to establish unit management to integrate security and rehabilitation in correctional insitutions and to increase interactions between staff and inmates, improve career development for correctional staff, delegate authority, and provide accountability at all levels (Correctional Service of Canada, 1990). They adopted nine principles for correctional operations that are applied in every institutions. These included:

- meaningful interaction between teams of staff members and groups of inmates
- an integration of case management, program functions, and security

- staff participation in the facility's decision-making process
- individuals and groups being held responsible for their decisions

Unit management is intended to effectively standardize the management of inmates and provide a focus for correctional practices. It

> is the organizational and operational standard for all institutions of the Correctional Service of Canada. It ensures the integration of the key elements of case management, programs, and security functions while emphasizing the promotion of positive staff/inmate association through mutual, open communications; staff teamwork; the delegation of decision-making authority to the lowest level possible; accountability on the part of both staff and inmates; and consistency of operations for all institutions" (*Interactive Corrections*, March, 1997).

**New Zealand.** The Honorable Minister of Corrections for New Zealand, Paul East, cited unit management as a "significant development" contributing to the considerable improvements that have occurred in the way prisons are managed (press release, 1997).

# Historical Federal Research

The following information summarizes a series of unit management studies or projects conducted in institutions of the Federal Prison System. This information was originally collected and organized by Howard L. Kitchener, director of research, Bureau of Prisons (Bureau of Prisons, 1975).

## Demonstration Counseling Project

The first systematic research effort to evaluate the effects of the unit management approach occurred during the Demonstration Counseling Project begun in 1961 at the National Training School for Boys in Washington, D.C. The results of that project are summarized in a report published by the Bureau of Prisons, entitled *Rational Innovation* (1964).

When the Demonstration Counseling Project began, the National Training School used a traditional organizational approach. The initial objective of the Demonstration Counseling Project was to investigate what could be done in one cottage—unit—with an increase in staff and the initiation of an interdisciplinary program effort. Three correctional officers/counselors were added to the unit staff, which also included a clinical psychologist, a group social worker, and twenty-four-hour coverage by correctional officers. An intensive counseling and recreation program was established.

From the in-resident population, seventy-five delinquents were selected randomly and assigned to the Experimental (Demonstration Counseling Project) Group. A second group of seventy-five inmates also was selected randomly and placed in a control group (a traditionally organized cottage at the National Training School for Boys). A secondary control group, composed of randomly selected delinquents in the National Training School's other cottages, was identified later; they remained scattered throughout the institution. During a twenty-one-month period, these three groups were compared on measures of institutional adjustment, interinmate relationships, psychological changes, and release follow-up data.

The experimental group was released by the parole board significantly sooner than the delinquents in the control group, suggesting their generally better institutional adjustment. Moreover, the experimental group ranked first in intercottage competitions, was rated higher (as a group) in academic training, earned (on average) higher inmate merit pay, received fewer misconduct reports, and spent less time in segregation.

Interinmate relations were much more positive in the experimental unit, which had fewer sick-call complaints, and fewer disciplinary offenses. An examination of clique structure found differences in that associations in the experimental unit were more prosocial.

With regard to psychological changes, the experimental group had more positive scores on the Edwards Personal Preference Schedule and on an adjective checklist. The Semantic Differential test demonstrated that the experimental group became more like noninstitutionalized youth and less like a prison group after exposure to the Demonstration Counseling Project program.

In terms of recidivism rates, an examination of follow-up data found no statistically significant differences between the experimental and control groups. However, compared to the control group, the delinquents exposed to the Demonstration Counseling Project program remained in the community for a significantly longer period of time before failing, and committed less serious offenses.

Results from the Demonstration Counseling Project led to the restructuring of the entire National Training School for Boys along functional unit management lines. Each cottage (unit) had its own interdisciplinary staff.

It was clear that the unit management approach had a significantly positive impact on the delinquents' institutional adjustment and the climate within the training school. Although the recidivism rates of the experimental and control groups did not differ at a statistically significant level, the former had a more positive community adjustment than the latter as reflected in their longer postrelease length of stay and less serious recommitment offenses. Positive within-institution results may have been limited postrelease by factors in the community over which the Demonstration Counseling Project had no control.

In *The Effectiveness of Correctional Treatment* (1974), Robert Martinson cited the Demonstration Counseling Project as being "well designed" and of "high quality." This program was among the few in his study that showed a favorable postrelease outcome.

## Kennedy Youth Center, West Virginia

The Robert F. Kennedy Youth Center in Morgantown, West Virginia, was opened by the Bureau of Prisons in January 1969 (Gerard, et al., 1970). Both its architecture and program—which incorporated a differential treatment approach for each inmate type (Quay, 1971)—were designed around a unit management concept. Dr. Robert

Vintner, from the Graduate School of Social Work at the University of Michigan conducted an evaluation of the Kennedy Youth Center program.

In addition to periodic on-site observation, the Vintner study included the use of anonymously completed questionnaires intended to measure staff and offender attitudes and perceptions regarding the Kennedy Youth Center. These were refined versions of similar surveys developed earlier for use in six state and private correctional facilities.

Kennedy Youth Center offenders were positive in their assessment of the staff and the program. Comparisons with a similar offender population at the more traditional—at that time nonunitized—Federal Youth Center, Englewood, Colorado, found that at the Kennedy Youth Center, offenders reported "more frequent contacts with staff [who were] more often perceived to be friendly, accessible, committed, and able to help." Offenders at the Kennedy Youth Center also were more likely than the Englewood population to rate both their living quarters and their counseling program as "good" or "very good" (82 percent versus 31 percent, and 72 percent versus 40 percent). Vintner's results support the conclusion that Kennedy Youth Center staff were successful in establishing a positive institutional climate and that unit management played an important role in that effort.

## Kennedy Youth Center Recidivism

To test the effectiveness of the Kennedy Youth Center's differential treatment/unit management program, a long-term outcome study was conducted. Releasees from the Kennedy Youth Center were compared with a group released from the Federal Youth Center, Ashland Kentucky, which had a traditional, centralized program. A two-year follow-up was done on 278 Kennedy Youth Center and 297 Ashland releasees.

The two groups were divided into Quay's (1971) four juvenile behavioral categories and compared on rates of in-program failures and recidivism. Recidivism was defined as a parole violation or conviction resulting in a new commitment of sixty days or more. Measures were taken at six, twelve, eighteen, and twenty-four months. When the Kennedy Youth Center and Ashland populations were equated in terms of their background differences, by use of the U.S. Parole Board's Salient Factor scores, releasees from the Kennedy Youth Center were found to have succeeded at a statistically significant higher rate than the Ashland releasees.

## The CONSAD Study

While the purpose of this evaluation was for the CONSAD Research Corporation, Pittsburgh, Pennsylvania, to study the Narcotic Addict Rehabilitation Act programs in the Danbury, Connecticut and Terminal Island, California, Federal Correctional Institutions, their findings have relevance for unit management.

CONSAD's contract interviewers contacted and collected data on four groups: (1) 75 Narcotic Addict Rehabilitation Act program graduates who had been released from aftercare; (2) 200 Narcotic Addict Rehabilitation Act releasees—still in aftercare or returned to prison; (3) 100 study group inmates—rejected as not appropriate for the Narcotic Addict Rehabilitation Act treatment program; and (4) a contrast group of 100 drug abusers who were not evaluated for placement in the Narcotic Addict Rehabilitation Act treatment program.

CONSAD stated, ". . . we find all groups reporting change in the direction of reduced drug use and criminality with the least change reported by the members of the contrast group." For example, 79 percent of the graduate group reported daily heroin use before incarceration, while 13 percent reported daily use after incarceration. For releasees from Danbury, the respective figures were 81 percent and 17 percent; while Terminal Island's releasees reported 80 percent and 31 percent. For the contrast group, 51 percent reported daily use before incarceration, while 33 percent so reported after incarceration. Generally, inmates exposed to the Narcotic Addict Rehabilitation Act program had higher drug usage rates before incarceration and lower usage postrelease; their degree of positive change was much greater than for the non-Narcotic Addict Rehabilitation Act group. Similar positive results were found for changes in daily habit cost, daily drug sales, illegal income, average criminality, legal income, and reported arrests.

The CONSAD study provided good evidence that the Narcotic Addict Rehabilitation Act programs had a positive effect on outcome as assessed by several community adjustment measures. The fact that the study depended upon self-report measures does not reduce its validity since any errors in data collection would have been distributed equally among the various groups. Additionally, the CONSAD findings support the unit management concept since the better performing inmates were in units while the less well performing subjects were from centralized, nonunitized institutions.

## Federal Youth Center, Ashland, Kentucky

The Federal Youth Center in Ashland, Kentucky was assessed (Karacki and Prather, 1974) on two occasions, using a research questionnaire similar to the one employed in Vintner's study of the Kennedy Youth Center. The first data collection occurred in 1972, prior to Ashland's initiation of unit management, while the second assessment took place in 1974, after functional unit management had been implemented partially.

Comparison data revealed that "staff perceived more of an emphasis on treatment and training, particularly in the living areas but also in the school area." There also were indications that "staff [in 1974] were now more receptive to program changes than before."

On items specifically designed to measure reaction to the unit management system, staff response was fairly positive:

> Seventy percent of staff thought the unit manager system increased staff interaction, 51 percent responded that they now knew more about the residents in their unit, 39.5 percent said they had greater input into the development of programs, and 45 percent said their attitude toward their job had improved. On the other hand, 43 percent agreed that the unit management system had created more paperwork for them.

Compared with prisoner results on the 1972 survey, Ashland's 1974 findings indicated that inmates were more likely to rate their living unit as "good" or "very good," to report more contact with counselors, and to view counselors as having more influence than before. Thus, the Ashland study found that both staff and resident responses suggest positive changes as a consequence of implementing unit management. These changes (which were greater for staff) suggest that unit management had more positive impact for personnel than for inmates.

## Federal Correctional Institution, Milan, Michigan

The Vintner questionnaire was administered at Milan both prior to, and some nine months after the facility's shift to unit management. In addition, Moos' (1975) Correctional Institution Environment Scale also was given to Milan's staff and inmates. The Correctional Institution Environment Scale provides a measure of the social climate of a correctional institution by generating profiles of its various living units (and of the institution as a whole), based on independent staff and inmate perceptions. Nine dimensions are assessed: three pertain to the nature and intensity of relationships (involvement, support, and expressiveness), three reflect a living unit's type of treatment (autonomy, practical, and personal-problem orientation), and three are system maintenance dimensions (order and organization, clarity, and staff control).

Vintner reported:

> . . . compared with the October 1973 findings, the survey results for November 1974 appear to show an institution which has undergone a fair amount of change as perceived by both staff and residents. [S]taff . . . are now more involved in decision-making than before, that maintaining order and providing role models for inmates are now more important, and that there is now a more active involvement with the outside community. . . .
>
> Residents reported more contact with staff and contact of a more positive nature than was the case in 1973 . . . [T]hey now saw more of their living unit staff and now found staff to be fairer, more concerned, friendlier, and less inclined to talk down to residents than before. [Inmates] also rated the counseling program and living unit conditions as being better than before. Lastly, there is some indication that the impact of the program changes at Milan is beginning to have a more direct positive effect on residents in such areas as whether they feel they have been treated fairly and the help they have received in preparing for a future job.

On the Correctional Institution Environment Scale, both staff and inmates were more positive in their assessment of Milan's social climate in 1974, following the shift to unit management. For personnel and prisoners, six of the nine dimensions showed an improvement of five or more points.

The Vintner survey results and the Correctional Institution Environment Scale data strongly support the position that substantial positive change in Milan's social climate had occurred since the introduction of unit management. An additional indication of positive change is revealed in Milan's furlough[3] figures. Between July 1973 and January 1974, the institution's centralized Warden's Review Committee approved 341 inmate furloughs for which the escape rate was 2.3 percent. In July 1974, the institution's furlough policy was liberalized, and the unit management staff were delegated decision-making responsibility. Between July 1974 and January 1975, the units granted nearly three times as many furloughs (905), while the furlough failure rate decreased to 1.7 percent. This finding suggests that decision-making by unit staff who are familiar with inmates in their units has considerable value over the former traditional, centralized procedures.

## Federal Correctional Institution, Seagoville, Texas

The study conducted at the Federal Correctional Institution in Seagoville, Texas (Karacki and Prather, 1975b), was very similar to the Milan research using the Correctional Institution Environment Scale. At Seagoville, the Correctional Institution Environment Scale was administered on four occasions—twice before and twice after the introduction of unit management. The two early profiles ($E_1$ and $E_2$) are similar to each other as are the two later profiles ($L_1$ and $L_2$). The difference is that the "Ls" are substantially more positive than the "Es" on virtually all nine Correctional Institution Environment Scale dimensions. This reflects a positive impact on Seagoville's social climate resulting from the introduction of unit management.

The Georgia State Prison Policy Statement on unit management (1982) cites another Seagoville study that reported a 17 percent increase in inmate program involvement and a 70 percent increase in inmate programs completed, following the latter facility's implementation of unit management.

## Federal Reformatory, Petersburg, Virginia

In June 1975, two similar units at the Petersburg, Virginia, Federal Reformatory were compared using the Correctional Institution Environment Scale. The Drug Abuse Program unit was a special intensive program for offenders with histories of drug abuse, while E West was a general population unit. The staff-to-inmate ratio in the Drug Abuse Program was one-to-five (including unit manager, case managers, and correctional counselors); in E West it was one-to-thirty. Both units (which were in the same building) had around-the-clock correctional officers and access to all other institutional resources; in other words, the living conditions in these two units were quite similar.

Study results showed the Drug Abuse Program unit with much more desirable Correctional Institution Environment Scale scores than E West; on eight of the nine scales, the differences in the scores were statistically significant beyond the $p = .01$ level. These findings suggest that increasing program staff and program activities lead to significantly improving a unit's social climate.

## Federal Correctional Institution, Tallahassee, Florida

A Correctional Institution Environment Scale study done at the Federal Correctional Institution in Tallahassee Florida (1975a), found that 61 percent of the staff "agreed" or "strongly agreed" that functional unit management was more effective than the facility's prior, traditional program; 62 percent believed it increased staff interaction. However, only 23 percent of the staff believed unit management decreased the need for security. Thirty percent of Tallahassee's staff indicated that unit management created more work for them. With regard to employee development, 64 percent of the staff thought that improvements had been made in training programs, while 71 percent indicated unit management increased opportunities for promotion.

It is notable that a majority of Tallahassee's staff "agreed" or "strongly agreed" that unit management better met residents' needs and increased staff interaction, two very important goals of correctional management. Both staff and inmates thought that functional unit management improved an institution's interpersonal climate.

## Federal Correctional Institution, Alderson, West Virginia

This Federal prison for women showed a 31 percent decrease in negative-incident reports during the six-month period following the implementation of unit management, when compared with the number six months prior to its implementation, as cited in the Georgia State Prison Policy Statement on Unit Management (1982).

## Federal Correctional Institution, Otisville, New York

As mentioned in Farbstein and Wener (1985), this federal prison, although following a unit management concept, was designed harder and tighter—to serve as a "new Leavenworth" for the worst federal inmates. Although 50 to 60 percent overcrowded, during its first five years, Otisville did not have any attempted escapes, only two minor inmate assaults on staff, and one inmate-on-inmate assault.

## Federal Prison Camp, Safford, Arizona

This Federal Prison Camp had an 18 percent increase in program enrollments and completions, and the number of its major disciplinary reports was cut almost in half—from 4.07/week to 2.16/week—over a 24-month period after the implementation of unit management, as cited in the *Georgia State Prison Policy Statement on Unit Management* (1982).

## U.S. Navy, Corrections Branch

> In summary, the experience gained at the Norfolk Correctional Center in implementing a FUM [Functional Unit Management] program had indicated three major keys to success: Interdisciplinary cooperation, open and effective communication, and continuous supervision. (Butler, n.d.)

At a meeting on October 10, 1985, at the National Institute of Corrections, Aaron Brown and Jay Farbstein discussed developing a report dealing with a comparison of direct supervision and indirect supervision jails (*see also* Part 7—Unit Management and Jails). Case study examples were suggested to show the development of the direct supervision approach in jails. Navy corrections was cited as an example of a system that abandoned its old-style facilities and built new institutions incorporating unit management (Farbstein and Wener, 1985).

## Summary

These studies provide a great deal of evidence that the unit management approach to managing inmates in a wide variety of institutions leads to a better facility or interpersonal climate—one which is safe, humane, and minimizes the detrimental effects of confinement for both staff and inmates. The Vintner studies at Ashland and Milan, and the Correctional Institution Environment Scale studies at Milan and Seagoville demonstrate this finding through the differences found between measures obtained before and after unit management was implemented. These results are further corroborated by the Kennedy Youth Center and the Tallahassee results. All of these findings show that both staff and inmates have more positive attitudes about working and living with unit management (*see also* Jesness, 1975).

Unit management's positive effect on residents' institutional and personal adjustment was shown in the National Training School for Boys' data. Petersburg's results demonstrated that more staff and program activities improve social climate. This is important because such resources are major variables affecting the effectiveness of unit management. The National Training School for Boys, the Kennedy Youth Center, and CONSAD's Narcotic Addict Rehabilitation Act program results all suggest that postrelease community adjustment can be affected favorably by functional unit programs.

# State Research

In a recent book on riots and disturbances (Montgomery and Crews, 1998) the authors state ". . . many of the institutions designed for unit management have fewer violent incidents than . . . [traditional] facilities."

**Arkansas.** The Central Office of the Arkansas Department of Corrections, in a letter to the National Institute of Corrections requesting Technical Assistance (September 3, 1993), stated:

> As have most departments of correction, [the Arkansas Department of Corrections] has experienced unprecedented growth in the past decade. As the inmate population has increased, it has become increasingly clear that the linear system of management, directing all problems to the top, has become inefficient and overloads upper- and mid-level management. Problems not quickly resolved become crises and administrators find themselves in a management-by-crisis mode. Grievances have multiplied and clogged the system,

> leading to reducing the ability of staff to respond, leading to use of external channels and lawsuits to resolve what often started out as minor problems.
>
> We believe that a more distributed system of management can resolve many problems promptly and while they are small. We hope that unit management can do this for us. We feel that this must be a systemwide effort with strong command emphasis in order to succeed.

**Massachusetts.** A report on Walpole Prison after the introduction of unit management indicated that "a 10-year history of violence, cost overruns, and general administrative turmoil" came to an end (Herrick, 1989); (*see also* Love and Ingram, 1982). A multidisciplinary unit management approach achieved major goals at Walpole, such as: having inmates live safely and without fear, giving correctional staff a say in the classification process, creating a safe working environment while maintaining greater control over inmates, and providing nonsecurity staff with more information about, and giving them more consistent contact with, inmates (Farmer, 1988).

Farmer (n.d.) also studied the effects of unit management on two state prisons in Massachusetts—one had unit management in all of its housing units and another used unit management in only one section. Results suggest that flattening an organizational structure without decentralizing authority seems to have negative effects on staff supervisory relations and job satisfaction. Inmates reported a better quality of life and more effective staff response under unit management.

**Missouri.** As part of a series in a *Corrections Today* theme issue devoted to unit management (Pierson, 1991), the Missouri Department of Corrections stated:

> What have been the benefits to [the Missouri Department of Corrections] from its Functional Unit Management System?
>
> - Closer interaction with inmates had improved security.
> - The classic custody versus treatment rivalry has been greatly ameliorated, if not eliminated. The experience of working in tandem (aided by the "hybrid" [Correctional Classification Assistant] position) breaks down mistrust.
> - New career ladders have been created [that] . . . provide promotion opportunities for both custody and nonsecurity personnel. In addition to an important positive effect on staff morale, it also encourages staff to view corrections as a career. This yields . . . a decrease in turnover rate, growing interest in further training, cultivating in-house expertise, etc.

- Unit management has freed-up time for top management to engage in long-range planning and other macro-level activities (e.g., improving the inmate transportation system, evaluating alternative medical care providers, etc.).

**Ohio.** Farbstein and Wener (1985) cited Ohio as an example of "how a new director, who was committed to [unit management, turned] around a system." A 1987 report from Ohio's Ross Correctional Institution (1,051 inmates) indicated that "a direct supervision management approach will save 21 percent in manpower," when each housing unit functions as an independent unit with a manager and support staff.

Ohio reported in their 1991 *Unit Management: Inspection and Evaluation Report*, which compares five years *before* with five years *after* the introduction of unit management:

> Since the transition to unit management [in 1986], we have observed a marked improvement in the overall operation of our institutions. Although it is difficult to fully attribute operation improvement success to unit management alone, it undoubtedly has been a major contributing factor.
>
> - Escapes have been significantly reduced since the inception of unit management. In 1981, there was a rate of 3.04 escapes per 1,000 inmates. This was reduced to 0.25 per 1,000 in 1991 [during which time the population more than doubled—from 13,482 to 32,155].
>
> - A reduction [occurred] in the number of recorded assaults on staff by inmates. In 1986 there were 398 assaults on staff. In 1990, this number was reduced to 153. . . [from 1 per 52 inmates to 1 per 198 inmates, while the population doubled].
>
> - Multidisciplinary staff positions were placed on-site in the inmate living areas, increasing staff-to-inmate ratios in these areas [average 1 to 30.8 before unit management to 1 to 20.8 after].
>
> Over recent years, Ohio's population has escalated at an unprecedented pace. This increase has surpassed bed-capacity . . . . [Nevertheless] our inmate escape rate and assaults on staff have diminished. The overall quality of life in the prisons has improved. For these reasons, the adoption of unit management has been extremely beneficial (also cited in Houston and Stefanovic, 1996).

In a 1998 letter from the South Regional Office of the Ohio Department of Rehabilitation and Correction to the American Correctional Association, Terry Tibbals writes that Ohio's mission statement for unit management is as follows:

> Unit management enhances accountability, security and communication by dividing large groups of offenders into smaller groups supervised by teams of trained staff located in close proximity to inmate living areas; correctional services delivery is improved through early problem resolution and mediation by staff familiar with assigned caseloads.

As a correctional counselor from Ohio's Orient Correctional Institution commented: "It [unit management] solves small problems before they can become big ones."

**Pennsylvania.** The report of the Senate Judiciary Committee of Pennsylvania, following riots at their Camp Hill facility, recommended administrative action that included "a department-wide transition to Unit Management" (cited in *Ohio's Unit Management Inspection and Evaluation Report*, 1991).

**South Carolina.** As part of a pilot-test to assess unit management, South Carolina examined the number of serious incident reports that inmates received at a maximum security facility during an eighteen-month period before and after the introduction of unit management. Data was collected for six three-month periods. The rate of serious incident reports per 1,000 inmates was cut in half—from 16 during the study's first quarter to 8 during the last quarter. Farbstein and Wener (1985) cite South Carolina as an example of a system that "bought into unit management and then objective classification," and they explain how this drove the design of the facilities they subsequently built.[4]

## National Survey

On May 30, 1996, the Wisconsin Department of Corrections released the results of a national survey they conducted on unit management. Michael J. Sullivan, Secretary, Wisconsin Department of Corrections sent survey forms to fifty-one jurisdictions ("to all states and the Federal Bureau of Prisons") and received replies from forty-one agencies—an 80 percent response rate.

- Twenty-seven jurisdictions (66 percent) were using unit management.
- Twenty of these jurisdictions (74 percent) had used unit management for five years or more (see figure 6.1).

Additionally, Wisconsin's national survey revealed:

- In twenty-one jurisdictions (78 percent), security staff on the units report directly to the unit manger; in all department of corrections, security staff take direction from unit managers.

## FIGURE 6.1 NUMBER OF INSTITUTIONS IN WHICH UNIT MANAGEMENT IS OPERATIONAL

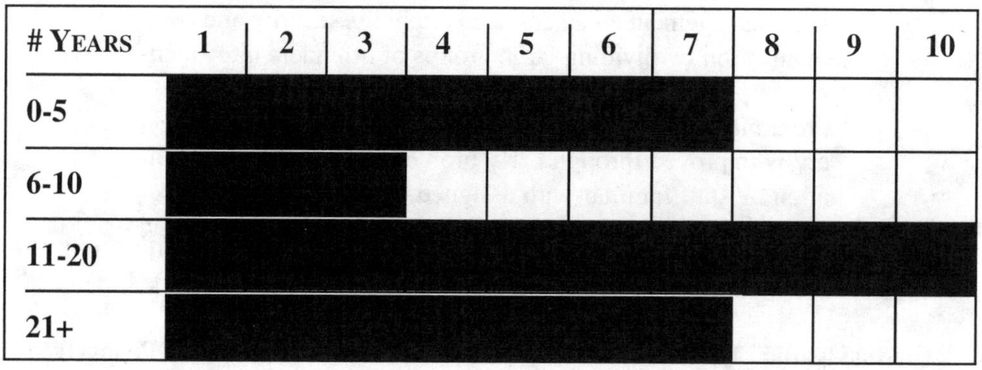

| # YEARS | 1 | 2 | 3 | 4 | 5 | 6 | 7 | 8 | 9 | 10 |
|---|---|---|---|---|---|---|---|---|---|---|
| 0-5 | ■ | ■ | ■ | ■ | ■ | ■ | ■ | | | |
| 6-10 | ■ | ■ | ■ | | | | | | | |
| 11-20 | ■ | ■ | ■ | ■ | ■ | ■ | ■ | ■ | ■ | ■ |
| 21+ | ■ | ■ | ■ | ■ | ■ | ■ | ■ | | | |

- In virtually every case, unit managers were responsible for all aspects of unit operation, which included security, programming, and basic functions.
- Several agencies have modified their approach to unit management, with most expanding the unit manager's authority and responsibilities.
- Staff reactions to unit management, particularly among security personnel, have been mixed but with more experience, they have shown improvement.
- Ninety-six percent of the jurisdictions using unit management plan to continue its use; with 89 percent indicating it will be used in new facilities as they are brought on line.
- Administrators consistently evaluate unit management positively, and indicate that relative to the traditional model, unit management improves security, safety, programming, control, operations, planning, communication, information-sharing, interaction, and teamwork. "In short, it enhances the institution's ability to meet its goals and objectives" (Wisconsin Department of Corrections, 1996).

Replies by twenty-eight of the responding jurisdictions included an answer to the question: How would you describe the effectiveness of this model in terms of correctional goals and outcomes?

**Alaska**—Very effective.

**California**—The unit management model has been applied to all California state prisons for approximately twenty years and has become a standard mode of operation that is accepted by staff and management. It has especially proven its worth during the past twelve years of escalating prison populations.

**Colorado**—It allows for more familiarity between staff/staff and staff/inmates. Consistency of policy is a plus.

**Connecticut**—(1) Handles issues with the unit - very effective. (2) Excellent - high accountability and performance. (3) Very effective services to inmates; i.e., classification, programming, parole eligibility, etc. have become more efficient compared to a central institutionwide system. (4) Unit management has been tremendously successful. Security aspects of inmate management have been improved and can be directly linked with the decrease in overall facility incidents. (5) A facility that specializes in managing mental health and security-risk group populations has staff with specific skills and training to handle these groups effectively. Unit management works very efficiently. (6) Staff intensive—costly.

**Federal Bureau of Prisons**—Extremely effective.

**Hawaii**—Not effective because it has not been fully implemented.

**Idaho**—Unit management appears to contribute to increased security, as the constant interaction between staff and inmates keeps both informed of issues or potential problems. Inmates are better prepared for release, through the monitoring of program participation.

**Illinois**—Good.

**Indiana—**Fair.

**Kansas**—The effectiveness is contingent upon the level of implementation and support of facility management teams and wardens. It can be efficient. The KDOC supports the unit team concept, believes it is of value, and will continue its use.

**Kentucky**—The Department of Corrections believes the unit management concept not only provides more personalized supervision but a safer environment as well.

**Louisiana**—It works well. You should try it!

**Michigan**—No data to answer this question.

**Minnesota**—This seems to be a very efficient way to manage an institution. The chain-of-command is used more often. Inmates get answers more quickly. Responsiveness has increased. Staff seem to appreciate having proprietary responsibilities.

**Nebraska**—Unit management far exceeds the traditional case management model. All aspects of operations/management within the housing unit are the responsibility of the unit staff, including safety/sanitation, classification, discipline, work, programming, etc.

**New Hampshire**—The best way to operate a prison. I could not imagine going back to the traditional, centralized model.

**New Mexico**—Outside of the obvious expense, we have been so used to the traditional model, that a great deal of training would be needed to break old habits and instill new responsibilities.

**North Dakota**—Inmate contact by staff has drastically increased, resulting in early identification and resolution of problem issues. Interdepartmental communication and relationships have improved greatly due to multidisciplinary staffings and daily communications. Inmate case plans now coordinate needs and services from intake through probation.

**Ohio**—Excellent - Reduced problems, reduced violence, increased programming, reduced idleness, increased security.

**Oklahoma**—Has put more staff on the unit with direct involvement with the inmate population; is meeting their immediate programmatic/education needs, and readily addresses the small issues.

**Pennsylvania**—Better knowledge of inmate population, "mood," and problems on the unit. Helps all staff work toward common goals.

**South Dakota**—Effectively places decision-making process with the unit team who knows the inmate best.

**Tennessee**—Tennessee Department of Corrections has found that unit management is in concert with its goals, and the goals of facility supervision in general.

**Vermont**—Too early to answer with our experience. However, if done right, it should work.

**Washington**—Very effective.

**West Virginia**—Excellent. Unit management working well at present.

**Wisconsin**—Excellent. Enhances institution's ability to meet its mission and goals.

**Unidentified**—It is our belief that unit management has been effective in improving operations within our facilities. It focuses more attention onto housing units, and, as a result, it has reduced the incidents of violence.

An earlier report by Farbstein and Associates (1989) was based on 52 responses (78 percent) of the mail surveys they sent out across the nation to 47 prisons and 20 jails. Administrators rated direct supervision (unit management) significantly higher on measures of safety, reporting less violence than at indirect (nonunitized) supervision facilities—13 incidents versus 32 during a 12-month period.

Additionally, from 612 inmate questionnaires completed at seven sites, significant differences on selected dimensions were reported, *see* Table 6.1.

Inmates in unitized facilities reported more contacts between officers and said that the contact was more pleasant and less hostile than reported by prisoners in nonunitized facilities. They also stated there was less personal stress and few acts of

**TABLE 6.1: SIGNIFICANT DIFFERENCES BETWEEN NONUNITIZED AND UNITIZED INSTITUTIONS—INMATE DATA**

| FACTOR | NONUNITIZED | UNITS |
|---|---|---|
| INTERACTION | CO/inmate contact less businesslike | CO counsels inmates more often<br>CO/inmate contacts less hostile |
| PRIVACY | | More privacy in conversations |
| SAFETY | Feels less danger of inmate-on-inmate attack<br>Feels less danger of sexual assault | Feels less danger of CO/inmate attacks<br>COs respond quicker to emergencies<br>CO/inmate fights less often |
| STRESS | | Less somatic stress |

vandalism. However, unitized facilities reportedly take more effort and commitment to plan, train for, and manage.

In June 1998, officials from the Maryland Division of Correction visted the Federal Correctional Institution in Cumberland, Maryland to review its unit management operations. The state is planning to introduce unit management in all of its institutions. The interest of prison systems in this management approach continues.

## Local (Jail) Research

**New York City.** New York's Adolescent Reception and Detention Center (ARDC) houses approximately 1,800 inmates, split evenly between adults and adolescents. "Throughout 1984 and 1985, ARDC consistently had a level of violence that was two to three times higher than the average throughout the City's other jails. . . ."

The Adolescent Reception and Detention Center was separated into two "mirror images"; that is, comparable adolescent and adult populations. Half of the facility was run in the traditional manner; the other side was split into two 400- to 500-bed units—both of which consisted of dormitories and cell blocks. Throughout the seven-month project, information was collected by the Adolescent Reception and Detention Center staff and forwarded to the system's Central Office for analysis. The data—Table 6.2—showed a clear reduction in violence (assaults/attempts on staff with/without weapons, assaults on other inmates with/without weapons, and sexual assaults).

One of the Adolescent Reception and Detention Center's top-level managers stated: "Nobody thought it [unit management] would work. The institution's architecture was against it working; so was the idea of trying it on adolescents. Now even the bad

**Table 6.2: Violent Infractions per 100 Inmates (Average)**

| | Traditional | Units |
|---|---|---|
| Adolescents | 14.8 | 11.5 |
| Adults | 5.6 | 3.5 |

inmates want it. They see it as being fairer. Among the staff there is less 'ducking and hiding' which was the traditional way of handling problems. . . . The good guys won."

# Endnotes

1 When Kirkland (South Carolina) had a riot several years after unit management began, according to Warden George Martin, inmates protected staff and no correctional officers were injured.

2 Currently, Warden, Chillicothe Correctional Institute, Chillicothe, Ohio.

3 An unescorted visit at the inmate's home extending over at least one night.

4 South Carolina and Oklahoma were ranked (for 1994 and 1995) among the seven most economically run state prison systems in the country.

*A jail is not a prison!*

—Ken Kerle

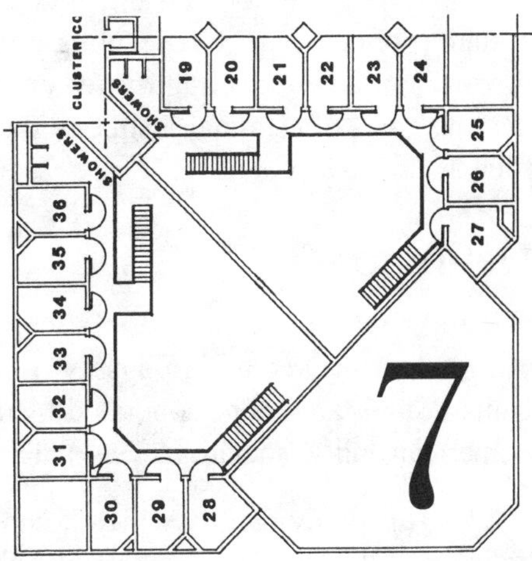


# Unit Management and Jails*

## Introduction

Jails are not prisons! Prisons are not jails! The general public, as well as a good many practitioners who work in both type of settings (at all levels of government) often cannot articulate the difference between these two entities. Some of this confusion is due to the media of this country, which frequently uses the terms "jails" and "prisons" interchangeably. Much information from both print and electronic media about corrections tends to be negative and sensational, leaving citizens with inadequate and inaccurate perceptions (Freeman, 1996).

## Differences between Jails and Prisons

The Bureau of Justice Statistics noted (U.S. Department of Justice, March 6, 1997) that there are almost thirty times as many admissions to local jails as new court commitments to state and federal prisons. In one year, more than 11 million people were booked into local jails and another 11 million released, almost comparable to the combined populations of Ohio and Illinois (*U.S. Bureau of the Census*, 1996). This mass of humanity moving in and out of jails on a fairly constant basis presents prob-

---

* Written by Kenneth E. Kerle, Ph.D., Managing Editor, *American Jails*

lems of a different magnitude than found in long-term correctional institutions—particularly in the areas of suicide, handling mental illness, and providing medical procedures (Kerle, 1998).

Many jails are not well integrated with other components of the criminal justice system (police, courts, prosecuting attorneys, and community corrections). The public pays a price for this fragmented criminal justice system, often failing to understand that the goals of criminal justice in the community extend beyond simplistic slogans such as *law and order*.

## Definitions

With rare exceptions, people who end up in the state or federal prison systems started their incarceration odyssey in jail. The vast majority of the 3,272 jails in the United States are county-operated facilities; there are only about 300 municipal jails (American Jail Association, 1994). There are other distinctions, as well.

*Lockup*—Any facility which holds prisoners for periods of less than seventy-two hours; usually found in large metropolitan police precincts. Eventually, many of the prisoners who start out in police lockups get transferred to a jail if they cannot be released. There seem to be no accurate figures on the total number of lockups in the United States.

*Jail*—Traditionally, jails hold two types of individuals: persons arrested (pretrial) and those sentenced to less than a year. Unfortunately, continued crowding at state and federal prisons has resulted in a number of states incarcerating individuals with longer sentences at local jails. Categories of prisoners in jail include the following:

- People arrested and held in jail pending arraignment, trial, conviction, or sentencing
- Readmitted probation, parole, and bail-bond violators, and absconders
- Temporarily detained juveniles pending transfer to juvenile authorities—unless waived to be tried as adults in adult court
- Mentally disturbed people held pending their movement to appropriate health facilities
- Individuals held for the military, for protective custody, for contempt, and as witnesses for the courts
- Inmates held prior to their transfer to federal, state, or other authorities
- Inmates housed for federal, state, or other facilities due to crowding
- Temporary detainees held in custody for juvenile and medical authorities
- Individuals from community-based electronic monitoring (or other types of supervision) programs (Perkins, Stephan, and Beck, 1995)

*Direct Supervision*—This is the unit management concept (as used in a jail setting) that allows staff to control a housing unit rather than just supervise it from the outside. Services are brought to the inmate. This reduces inmate movement and operational and staffing costs (Hurlbert 1996).

## Organizational Structure

More than sixty years ago, the Wickersham Commission recommended that the states assume responsibility for county jails. This recommendation was repeated by the President's Commission on Law Enforcement and the Administration of Justice in 1967 and again by the National Advisory Commission on Criminal Justice Standards and Goals in 1973. For the most part, it never happened. Only six states in the United States have combined jail and prison systems (Schafer, 1994).

The Federal Bureau of Prisons and the fifty state prison systems in the United States have unified command and hierarchal structures culminating with a top-level director or commissioner of corrections. Seventy-five percent of the county jails, however, are operated by elected sheriffs; the others are operated by appointed jail administrators who are answerable to an elected county board. Not only is the sheriff the chief correctional person in the county, this individual is also the chief police figure directing road patrols and often detective divisions. In addition, the sheriff functions as an arm of the court providing courtroom security and serving warrants issued by the courts.

Sheriffs and jail administrators range from excellent to mediocre in their ability to run jails. This explains why one frequently finds well run and poorly run jails within the same state. Elected sheriffs may possess a background in criminal justice or may have been employed in a local garage. They get placed in office for the first time by voters who judged them on qualities other than administrative or management skills.

Moreover, fifteen states lack mandatory state jail inspection standards; they require no mandatory training for new jail officers. In some of these jurisdictions, large megajails (systems which house more than 1,000 inmates) operate their own training academies. At the other extreme, nearly two-thirds of the nation's jails have rated capacities of fifty inmates or less (American Jail Association, 1994). Most of these smaller jails will not be candidates for the transition to direct supervision management.

## Metropolitan Correctional Centers

The Federal Bureau of Prisons introduced ideas developed from its corrections experience with unit management into jail facilities when it constructed the first three metropolitan correctional centers; *see* page 3. As previously stated, unit management as applied to jails is known as direct supervision.

### The Metropolitan Correctional Center, Chicago, Illinois

In 1975, W. Raymond Nelson, a veteran Federal Bureau of Prisons warden opened one of the first three metropolitan correctional centers (MCCs) in Chicago, Illinois—the other two were located in New York City and San Diego, California. These facilities were built in compliance with a 1969 presidential directive indicating a need to improve the conditions under which federal prisoners were being housed in local jails.

The plan for unit management (as implemented in a metropolitan correctional center) involved staffing each facility's general jail population housing units with only one officer. This staff member was to be placed *inside* each pod—the unit (a term coined by Warden Ray Nelson at the Chicago Metropolitan Correctional Center)—with its inmates.[1]

The idea was to see if these federal jails could operate effectively following ideas based on the Bureau of Prisons' unit management approach used successfully with federal prisons. Warden Nelson did not feel confident at the prospect. For example, his new jail had commercial grade chairs and tables and carpets to help reduce noise, and vitreous china toilets and sinks. Nelson believed that inmates normally housed in institutions with vandal-proof fixtures would make short shrift of such soft furnishings. This type of normalized environment was advocated by Fred Moyer and his colleagues at the National Clearinghouse for Criminal Justice Architecture, headquartered at the University of Illinois in Champaign-Urbana. Much to the surprise of many, the furniture in this more civilized environment survived; the anticipated destructive behavior of unruly inmates did not occur.

Additionally, the warden and many of his staff felt disaster was in the making when they learned that there were more conditions to be met:

> My anxiety was further heightened by the news that, as the result of the passage of the Equal Employment Opportunity Act of 1974, we could expect that 20 percent of our new correctional officers would be women. Admittedly, this was male chauvinist fear that [now] may not be fully appreciated. . . . But in 1975 we were pioneers. We had to convince young female recruits that they could safely manage a housing unit of 44 male felons by themselves, not to mention convincing their male supervisors, all of whom were veterans of maximum security facilities (Nelson, 1988).

Nelson has since written that his Chicago Metropolitan Correctional Center's experience proved to be the most satisfying institutional event of his career. The soft-furnishing and use-of-female-officers-to-supervise-male-inmates calamities never materialized. Twenty-two beds reserved in segregation were never filled and not one general population unit was ever locked down. Inmates chose to comply with the rules in this new institutional environment. Officers in the pods experienced a high degree of safety: "Officers suffered more assaults in the community during their off-duty hours than at work on their units" (Nelson, 1988).

A well-known architect pointed out that a podular design can increase direct supervision of inmates without expanding the number of jail personnel (Atlas, 1989). This has the additional benefit of enhancing the quality of life inside these institutions and, as a consequence, reducing the motivation of prisoners to commit suicide—a major area of concern for jail administrators.

## DIRECT SUPERVISION

According to James Kessler, AIA, of HOK Architects, "direct supervision is a management approach that improves the effectiveness of the correctional officer in influencing inmate behavior. An officer in a control room is limited to observing inmates and activities. When officers are located in the space, they have the opportunity to become proactive about the demeanor of inmates in the dayroom. The physical design of direct supervision pods affords architectural opportunities unavailable in the design of indirect supervision pods. The strict geometry required for sight lines from a control room to multiple housing pods often results in a configuration that requires excess space. Direct supervision pods, not linked to a control room, give priority to influences of constructability and practicality.

"Direct supervision and the extensive use of dry cell pods (housing units with centralized toilet facilities as opposed to locating toilets in each cell) fosters a normalized environment and saves money in construction and equipment costs. In these areas, inmates generally are allowed free access from their cells to the dayroom and toilet facilities. The pod officer establishes the dayroom schedule and maintains the ability to lock down inmates. Cost is saved in the elimination of security doors, plumbing fixtures, and special chases. The inmate retains privacy and personal territory."

According to James Kessler, AIA, of HOK Architects, direct supervision is illustrated by the following key points in dayroom design (numbers 1-5 correspond to the numbers on the design, *see* page 126):

1. **Visibility.** Visibility is the basis of control. The design should promote visibility from wherever the officer is in the dayroom. Correctional officers act like police on the beat or teachers in a classroom and know what is going on throughout their area.

2. **Information.** Correctional officers, through the use of computers can supply inmates with information about activities such as visiting, court dates, and commissary. This establishes, not only a relationship of authority between the officer and the inmate, but allows the fruits of a cooperative relationship to be reinforced.

3. **Outdoor recreation.** Outdoor recreation at the pod can allow natural light to enter the dayroom. It also provides continual access to outdoor activities at the discretion of the pod officer. This means the outdoor recreation area can be open all day or shut down, depending on the degree of cooperation received from the inmates.

4. **Acoustical control.** Acoustical ceilings and wall panels reduce noise and help the dayroom officer establish control by letting his or her voice be heard.

## MECKLENBURG COUNTY JAIL CENTRAL

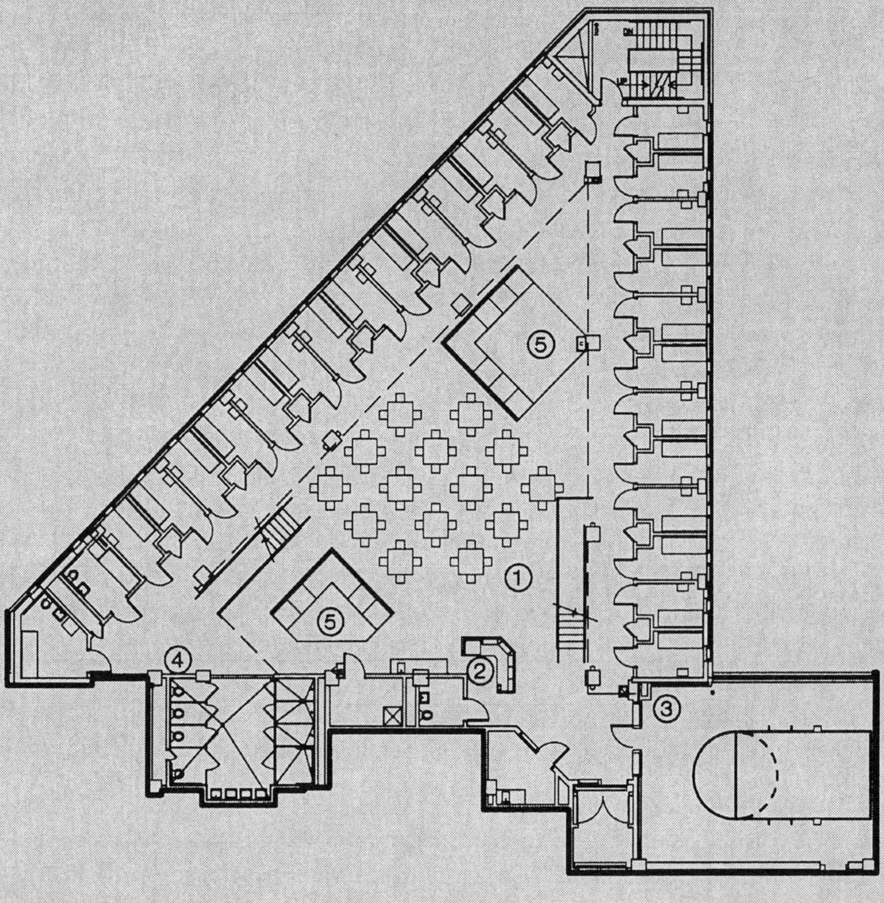

ARCHITECTS

*LITTLE/HOK JOINT VENTURE*

DRAWING

*HOK ARCHITECTS*

5. **Comfortable furniture.** Comfortable furniture is an amenity that can be withdrawn from uncooperative inmates.

6. **Immediate sanction.** Immediate sanction reinforces the authority of the correctional officer. Housing units devoid of dayroom amenities and controlled indirectly must be available without delay for noncooperative inmates.

*Photo by Rick Alexander, courtesy of Little/HOK Joint Venture architects.*

## Mecklenburg Dayroom

*The "inmates" in the picture are really architects in jail uniforms who tested out the facility before turning it over to its owner, the Mecklenburg County Jail in Charlotte, North Carolina.*

In podular design, cells are positioned on the perimeter of a central, common area. This common area and the surrounding inmate cells contain more "normal" furniture and fixtures. Proponents of podular designs believe that such an environment sends the message that prisoners are expected to behave (Nelson, 1988). The increased surveillance made possible by podular architecture also facilitates interaction between officers and inmates. Such interactions make detainees feel less isolated and, thereby, reduces the likelihood of self-harm.

This concept has gained increasing acceptance over the years to the point that the American Correctional Association's *Guidelines for the Development of Policies and Procedures: Adult Local Detention Facilities* (1992) assume that institutions follow a direct contact philosophy and that a unit management system is in place.

# Evolution of Direct Supervision Architecture

Two jail management architecture designs preceded the metropolitan correctional center podular (unit) direct supervision style. The older, "linear remote surveillance," lined up cells in rows and had officers looking into them as they patrolled the catwalks or corridors in front of each cellblock. This intermittent viewing of inmate activity provided only occasional opportunities for officers to communicate with prisoners. The next generation architecture was dubbed the "indirect surveillance" model. It began in the 1960s when cells became rooms and bars were replaced by solid doors. In this modification, cells surrounded an open dayroom space for television viewing and other activities. Officers sat in secure, glass-enclosed control booths from which they observed what went on; personal contact with inmates was minimal.

A third architectural generation, called "direct supervision," consisted of jails that incorporated the indirect surveillance model but made greater use of softer materials and, most important, stationed an officer inside the pod with the inmates. This placed a premium on the officer's ability to use interpersonal communication, crisis intervention, and counseling. The spatial change required that the officer actively supervise and manage the inmates (Billy, 1989).

# Management Principles of Direct Supervision

Basic principles of direct supervision, identified by the National Institute of Corrections, consist of the following eight guidelines.[2]

1. *Effective Control.* The officers/managers must be in total control of the jail at all times. There cannot be areas under *de facto* inmate control.

2. *Effective Supervision.* The staff must be in direct contact with prisoners and rely heavily on personal interaction for inmate supervision. Manageable staff-inmate ratios are critical for effective supervision.

3. *Competent Staff.* Recruitment, training, and leadership by management are necessary for direct supervision to operate as intended.

4. *Safety of Staff and Inmates*. The basic mission of a jail is to keep inmates safe and secure without exposing staff to undue risk.

5. *Manageable and Cost-effective Operations*. Running a less dangerous institution allows for more architectural options, at reduced cost, and provides an incentive for inmates to maintain acceptable standards of behavior.

6. *Effective Communications*. Frequent communication between staff and inmates is critical.

7. *Classification and Orientation*. Inmates should be observed closely during the first forty-eight hours of confinement (when the suicide risk is greatest) and oriented to the operations of the facility. A key to positive inmate behavior is identifying and isolating individuals who will not conform to the behavioral norms of the living unit.

8. *Justice and Fairness*. Conditions of confinement must respect the inmates' constitutional rights. Prisoners must believe that they will be treated fairly and that there are administrative remedies for disputes (National Institute of Corrections Jails Division, 1993).

In 1992, the American Jail Association added a ninth principle of direct supervision called *Ownership of Operations*. This required all persons working in the jail (from the line officer to the top administrator) to develop a possessiveness about their job and its associated tasks. In such an environment, personnel are empowered by management, innovation is welcomed, line staff support policies and procedures, and the employees understand that the jail belongs to them—not to the inmates (Perroncello, 1995).

## Direct Supervision—Nonfederal Jails

Ray Nelson became the Chief of the National Institute of Corrections—Jails Division in 1981. He was surprised to learn that not a single large jail at the local level had adopted the direct supervision model. Many local jail officials expressed doubt that such a concept—requiring a single officer to be inside a unit for an entire shift—could work.

One deputy stated that he had arrested many of these inmates on the streets. If placed in a unit to manage and supervise these same individuals, he believed (based on his interpersonal communication skills) he would not last ten minutes. Others expressed opinions that federal inmates were easier to manage than the local homegrown variety who were, supposedly, the most mean and vicious in the country. Many of these erroneous beliefs border on the mythical. Jail personnel had a hard time accepting that a correctional worker placed inside a unit to "rub shoulders" with a bunch of prisoners actually could survive and be accepted as the boss of the pod.

### Contra Costa County, California

When the Contra Costa facility opened in January 1981 as the first direct supervision county jail, changes from the Chicago Metropolitan Correctional Center design were evident. A lounge area was included at the booking station. This allowed newly arrived inmates to watch television. Each living unit had an adjacent outdoor recreation area, eliminating the necessity for moving prisoners to a common exercise yard. Instead of a being multistory jail, it had a low-rise configuration. Unit management's flexibility had appeared in a jail configuration.

This new jail operation hummed along; it worked fine. But many unbelievers asserted the familiar—Contra Costa jail inmates differed from other county jail inmates across the country (Nelson, 1988).

### Best Practices

As described in *Best Practices: Excellence in Corrections* (American Correctional Association, 1998), when it came time to build a new jail for Licking County, Ohio, the sheriff—Gerry D. Billy—decided on a 162-bed podular direct-supervision facility. Subsequently, he reported that the jail's more normalized setting has resulted in fewer medical complaints by inmates, reduced sick leave use by staff, and an absence of vandalism. In addition, podular direct supervision jails are less expensive to build, easier to maintain, improve employee morale and productivity, and reduce prisoner stress and violence, the sheriff explained.

Despite some modifications, the National Institute of Corrections' Advisory Committee endorsed direct supervision in 1983. Within a few years, direct supervision had received the "seal of approval" from the American Jail Association (AJA), the American Correctional Association, and the Committee on Architecture for Justice of the American Institute of Architects.

The National Institute of Corrections Jails Division did much to educate local jail personnel about the idea that direct supervision was a viable concept. At the American Jail Association training conference in Seattle (in 1986), it sponsored a direct supervision symposium where interested individuals could exchange information concerning this new approach to jail management. In 1995, the National Institute of Corrections issued a volume which listed 200 direct supervision jails—in whole or in part—with a total rated capacity of roughly 94,000 beds (National Institute of Corrections Jails Division, 1995).

The American Jail Association ultimately became the sponsor of this approach. In 1998 in Cincinnati, Ohio, the American Jail Association held its thirteenth Annual Direct Supervision Symposium. *American Jails* magazine has published more than thirty-five articles on direct supervision jails since 1987. Clearly, the direct supervision concept has been accepted by an increasing number of jail practitioners, sheriffs, and county governing officials.

## Direct Supervision Housing—Continued Growth and Design Change

Jails have not escaped from the crowding that has resulted from new laws implementing such concepts as "mandatory minimums," "truth in sentencing," and "three strikes and you're out." The following chart (Gilliard and Beck, 1998) illustrates this escalating growth.

| TABLE 7.1: AVERAGE DAILY JAIL POPULATION | |
|---|---|
| 1985 | 256,615 |
| 1990 | 405,320 |
| 1995 | 507,044 |
| 1997 | 567,079 |

This surge in population has put pressures on jail architects to design pods that hold more inmates. For example, the Federal Bureau of Prisons responded (in 1983) by building units at the Los Angeles Metropolitan Detention Center that house from sixty-four to seventy-two individuals. Officials recognized the crowding in the older metropolitan correctional centers (such as in New York and San Diego) and realized that the original units—designed for forty-four to forty-eight inmates—no longer would be adequate (Nelson and Davis, 1995). The number of prisoners in federal custody had increased from 35,781 in 1985 to 99,175 as of June 30, 1997 (Gilliard and Beck, 1998).[3]

By 1994, housing pods in direct supervision jails were being designed for seventy and seventy-two inmates; for example, Plymouth County, Massachusetts, and Alachua County, Florida. Other changes introduced included:

- Developing double-occupancy cells with glass fronts—the Horizon Facility in Orange County, Orlando, Florida
- Reducing construction costs by using drywall between cells and replacing wet-cells with dry-cells (the unit has gang-toilet facilities)—the West County Facility in Contra Costa County, California, which opened in 1993
- Experimenting with dorms, which reduce inmate privacy but also are considerably cheaper to construct. Some pod officers indicated a preference for dorms claiming it gave them improved visibility of the sleeping areas.

The open lounge area which had started at Contra Costa has come full circle. The Hillsborough County Central Booking Unit in Tampa, Florida, which has 43,000 admissions a year, built its intake processing services so that they surrounded this seating area. Only about 3 percent of those admitted require a more controlled environment; they are placed in secure holding cells (Nelson and Davis, 1995).

## Arlington County, Virginia, Detention Facility

In *Best Practices: Excellence in Corrections* (American Correctional Association, 1998) there is a report on the development of a high-rise urban jail to replace an "existing facility . . . of a linear design with limited inmate-management flexibility." The final design was based on a mini-jail concept first used to transform New York City's Tombs into a modern correctional facility. "The building was divided into a stack of three autonomous units, each managed separately . . . ." Except for the law library, specialized medical services, and visitation, all other services are provided within each mini-jail.

> The twelve-story [Arlington County] detention center is organized into five two-story "mini-jails" served by three stories of support space located in the base of the building. Each mini-jail operates as a semi-autonomous grouping. Service delivery is maximized while inmate movement is minimized (page 222).

Data calculated from Arlington County's average daily population show a rise in the number of disciplinary reports due to an increase in the level of staff supervision and accountability of inmates. There also was a decrease in the number of assaults suggesting that the facility was safer. "Most notable is the increase in the percentage of inmates participating in activities, which reduces idle time and provides tools for successful reintegration back to the community." This latest variation on the unit management theme allowed the "Arlington County Detention Facility to expand its operation, and more specifically the programming for its inmates, while enhancing security" within the institution.

## Undermining Direct Supervision

Direct supervision will be unsuccessful if staff is not thoroughly indoctrinated in its principles and there is no commitment to these principles from top jail management. Unfortunately, the National Institute of Correction's funding for training direct supervision staff in transition procedures and in the development of interpersonal communication skills has been virtually eliminated (Nelson and Davis, 1995). Counties have only limited funding for training. The result has been that a number of jails have opened in a direct supervision mode without their personnel having a thorough understanding of what direct supervision really is. It is not uncommon to discover transition training programs in which five times as many training hours are allocated to the operation of the jail's computer system as were earmarked for learning to manage inmate behavior through direct supervision. The unfortunate consequences have been:

- Jails in which inmate disturbances resulted in the loss of control over two general population housing pods
- An inmate suicide in a direct supervision jail that was not discovered for forty-eight hours
- An assault on a module officer that resulted in significant injury and the escape of seven inmates from a general population unit

Though the jail facilities involved in these incidents differed in design, similar circumstances contributed to each of these episodes.

1. Managers had received only an orientation course in direct supervision
2. There was significant pressure to open the facilities early, despite warnings that the building was not ready and transition planning had not been complete.
3. Module officers were unsure how direct supervision principles were to be applied
4. Training officers had been given no formal instruction in how to train others in direct supervision methods and principles
5. There were no problem-solving experiences in the training course to encourage the examination of problems in the context of direct supervision principles
6. The lack of continuity in officer assignments resulted in inconsistencies and no sense of ownership by the officers assigned to each module (Nelson and Davis, 1995)

Dennis R. Liebert (1996) addressed the shortcomings of direct supervision. He indicated that the jail leadership often did not buy into the concept. This lack of leadership engendered a minimal understanding of the problems and issues of direct supervision. For example, politics in one community caused the removal of commercial television sets from the jail's dayrooms without any comprehension of the impact that this would have on the housing officers and their ability to control inmate behavior. Jail administrators were replaced with people who had neither jail experience nor direct supervision training.

Liebert also cited: the greater noise levels in the dayrooms; an increased ratio of inmates to staff; dayrooms too crowded for circulation, seating for meals, and television watching; shower-to-inmate ratios no longer in compliance with standards; some cells double- and triple-bunked; and, disciplinary segregation units becoming crowded. These, in turn, generated other problems which resulted in:

- Officers having less opportunity to communicate with the inmates
- Officers supervising each housing unit facing more difficulties because of the greater number of inmates
- Officers' opportunity to take a more proactive stance in managing the unit becoming more difficult because of the number of inmates
- Administrators' ability to properly classify and segregate inmates as originally planned being negatively affected
- Inmates being locked down for long periods of time to relieve crowding in the dayrooms
- General housing units that were not designed as overflow disciplinary units being used for that purpose, and as a result, not having proper security

In addition, county boards frequently do not increase jail staff commensurate with the rise in the number of inmates. This means that some jails are understaffed with officers attempting to supervise too many prisoners. Cell searches no longer are conducted on a regular basis because of personnel shortages. Having more than one officer in the dayroom pod changes the dynamics that direct supervision was originally intended to implement. Training is significantly reduced, other direct supervision jails are not toured, and many of the trainers in these jails have only a limited knowledge of direct supervision. Often, according to Liebert (1996), an attempt is made to compensate for the lack of training by on-the-job field experience. This gives the officer the skills to do the job (supposedly), but without any understanding of the whys and wherefores.

A basic part of the direct supervision philosophy is inmate programs. Liebert observed that inmate programs are "politically incorrect" in some jurisdictions, that crowding causes pressure on available program spaces, and that staff shortages and budget cuts eliminate some programs resulting in inmates spending more time in lockdown status (Liebert, 1996).

## Research on Direct Supervision Jails

Linda Zupan, who wrote the first book on direct supervision (Zupan, 1991), stated that the jury is still out on this concept—more research and systematic evaluation needs to be done (Zupan, 1993). Michael O'Toole, former head of the National Institute of Corrections Jails Division, disagrees. Although some researchers continue to state that no empirical research has been completed on direct supervision jails (for example, Senese, Wilson, Evans, Aguirre, and Kalinich, 1992), O'Toole contends that when evaluating the significance of incremental differences, while methodology and statistical techniques are important, these techniques are superfluous when differences are so large as to be readily apparent to even the casual observer. He notes that if one travels from the North Pole to the equator, it is not necessary to have temperature tables with means and standard deviations to know conclusively that it is a lot warmer at the latter than at the former (O'Toole, 1993).

In a study of podular, direct-supervision jails (Farbstein, et al., 1996), the authors reported that "when compared with indirect-supervision jails, the direct supervision jails were . . . rated as safer . . . despite greater crowding. . . . [T]his suggested that direct-supervision jails were more manageable [than indirect-supervision jails] . . . ."

# Summary

Direct supervision is a dynamic new and improved way of managing jail inmates, but only if the people involved at all levels of local government make the necessary pledge to stand by its supervision and management principles. These principles require strong support from the jail administrators and the leaders in government who finance jail operations. Much more is involved than architectural design and construction. Successful jails that operate in the direct supervision mode have leaders who understand the direct supervision philosophy and who make the necessary commitment to themselves and their staffs to see that everybody in the jail environment lives by this philosophy.

# Endnotes

1 In addition to general housing units, each metropolitan correctional center had additional units designed for medical services, protective custody, and administrative/punitive segregation.

2 These principles were expanded later to include seven behavioral dimensions of direct supervision (Zupan, Menke, Lovrich, and Manning, 1986).

3 The inmate population housed in federal institutions reached more than 105,000 in May, 1998.

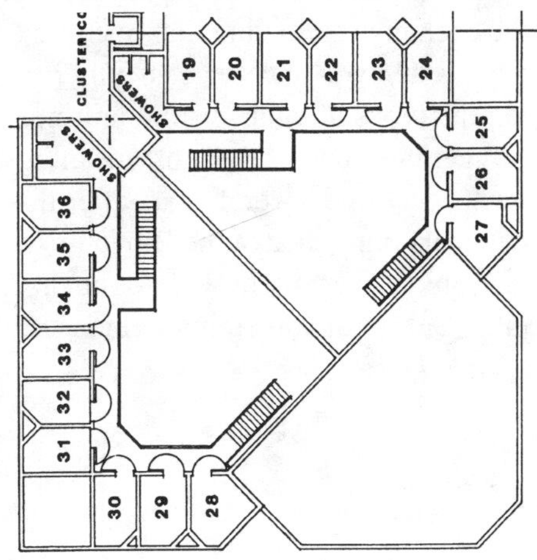

# Epilog

Begun in the sixties, blossomed in the seventies, and a corrections fixture by the eighties, unit management's progress has been onward and upward; nevertheless, valleys have been encountered. An often-asked question is: Has unit management ever failed?

To the best of my knowledge, no system that started unit management has stopped it—except one. In that jurisdiction, following a change of governors, the director of the department of corrections was replaced. The newcomer—from out of state—had different priorities. More than a decade of effort was undone. Disenheartened staff and several inmate disturbances resulted.

As has befallen many other venues, the formerly new and innovative eventually becomes just how-we-do-things and old-hat. We begin to take for granted the progress that has been made. Pioneers retire and are replaced by individuals who assume the procedures they find always have been there—that's what "everybody does." A snip here results in a little change there, and standards begin to slip. Pretty soon, we have another unfortunate example of the consequences of not knowing our own history.

But rather than ending this volume on a dispiriting note, one last "war story."

"You are ruining the Bureau of Prisons!" The voice belonged to the highly regarded, long-experienced Assistant Director for Correctional Services—the highest ranked security official in the Federal Prison System. It was directed at Roy Gerard and this author: the subject was unit management.

This was the beginning of a loud discussion at the Bureau's regular Monday morning executive staff meeting in the Washington, D.C. central office. The director, Norman Carlson was out of town this particular day; therefore, the meeting was somewhat less structured than typically would have been the case. However, the nature of the exchange following that opening accusation was more than a little out of the ordinary. When you have successfully run prisons for more than twenty-five years, accepting the types of changes that unit management advocates "ain't easy."

Perhaps, one of the most meaningful indicators of unit management's accomplishments occurred several years after this incident. That same outspoken gentleman, at a national conference of the Bureau's wardens stood up and said that he had been wrong.

Unit management will not be the last innovation that comes down the corrections pike. But, until something demonstrably better comes along, it is the way to go.

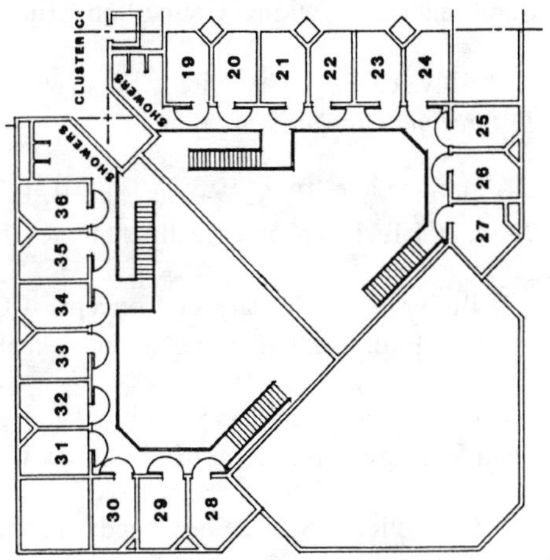


# References

Altschuler, D. M., and T. L. Armstrong. 1995. Managing Aftercare Servicers for Delinquents. In B. Glick and A. P. Goldstein, eds.: *Managing Delinquency Programs that Work.* Lanham, Maryland: American Correctional Association. 137-170.

Alwin, Lawrence F. 1996. *A Report on Prison Unit Cost Comparison.* No. 97-015. Texas Department of Criminal Justice. Office of the State Auditor. Available from the National Institute of Corrections, Longmont, Colorado.

American Correctional Association. 1983. *Design Guide for Secure Adult Correctional Facilities.* Lanham, Maryland: American Correctional Association.

———. 1992. *Guidelines for the Development of Policies and Procedures: Adult Local Detention Facilities.* Lanham, Maryland: American Correctional Association.

_______. 1998. Best Practices: Excellence in Corrections. Lanham, Maryland: American Correctional Association.

American Federation of State, County, and Municipal Employees. 1993. Technical Assistance Report (for the National Institute of Corrections). Columbus, Ohio.

American Jail Association. 1994. *Who's Who in Jail Management, 2nd Edition.* Hagerstown, Maryland: American Jail Association.

Arkansas Department of Corrections. 1993. Letter to National Institute of Corrections.

Atlas, R. 1989. Reducing the Opportunity for Inmate Suicide—A Design Guide. *Psychiatric Quarterly*. Summer, 60 (2): 161.

Austin, J. and L. Chan. 1994. *Survey Report on Internal Offender Classification System.* San Francisco: National Council on Crime and Delinquency.

Billy, G. D. 1989. Direct Supervision—A New Ball Game in Local Corrections. *Law Enforcement Technology*. June.

Bohn, M. J., R. A. Waszak, and B. R. Story. 1974. *Transition to Functional Units: 1973-1974*. FCI Technical and Treatment Notes. Federal Correctional Institution, Tallahassee, Florida.

Butler, T. F. No date. A Concept of Correctional Institution Organization and Management, as Implemented at the Norfolk Naval Station Correctional Center. Norfolk, Virginia.

Cavior, H. E. and A. Schmidt. 1978. A Test of the Effectiveness of a Differential Treatment Strategy at the Robert F. Kennedy Center. *Criminal Justice and Behavior*. 5, 131-139.

Correctional Service of Canada. 1985. *Orientation Training for Living Unit Officers and Case Management Officers*. Psychological Services Division, Offender Programs Branch. Ottawa, Ontario: Correctional Service of Canada.

———. 1986. *Unit Management. Offender Policy and Program Development*. Ottawa, Ontario: Correctional Service of Canada.

———. 1990a. *Meeting the Challenges of Unit Management Implementation*: "What Works." Ottawa, Ontario: Correctional Service of Canada.

———. 1990b. *Unit Management Principles of Correctional Operations—A Discussion Paper*. Ottawa,Ontario: Correctional Service of Canada.

———. 1990c. *Unit Management Stanards for Correctional Service of Canada Institutions*. Offender Management Division. Ottawa, Ontario: Correctional Service of Canada.

———. 1992. *Case Management Session Sessions I and II: Information Modules for Correctional Operations*. Correctional Service of Canada. Ottawa. Canada.

———. 1997. *Interactive Corrections*. Correctional Services of Canada—Community Operations, March. Ottawa, Ontario.

DeWitt, C. B. 1990. *Building on Experience: A Case Study of Advanced Construction and Financing Methods for Correction.* Washington, D. C.: Department of Justice.

Drapkin, M. 1996. *Developing Policies and Procedures for Jails.* Lanham, Maryland: American Correctional Association.

East, P. 1997. Prison Officer's Presentation. Press Release: New Zealand Government.

Ellem, B. 1995. Breaking the Cycle. Monash University Home Page.

Farbstein and Associates. 1989. Mimeo.

Farbstein, J., D. Liebert, and H. Sigurdson. 1996. *Audits of Podular Direct-Supervision Jails*. Longmont, Colorado: National Institute of Corrections.

Farbstein, J. and R. Wener. 1985. Evaluation of Direct vs. Indirect Supervision Correctional Facilities. Mimeo. Brooklyn, New York: Jay Farbstein and Associates.

Farmer, J. F. n.d. *Effects of Unit Management on Inmates' Quality of Life in Two State Prisons*. NCJRS Abstracts Database: Document Number 141601.

———. 1994. Decentralized Management in Prison: A Comparative Case Study. *Journal of Offender Rehabilitation*. 20:3-4, 117-130.

———. 1998. Case Study in Regaining Control of a Violent State Prison. *Federal Probation*. March, 52(1), 41-47.

Freeman, R. M. 1996. Correctional Staff as the Villain and the Inmate as Hero: The Problem is Bigger than Hollywood. *American Jails*. July/August.

Friedman, S. B., G. L. Horvat, and R. B. Levinson. 1982. The Narcotic Addict Rehabilitation Act: Its Impact on Federal Prisons. *Contemporary Drug Problems*. 11(1), Spring.

Georgia State Prison. 1982. Unit Management, Policy Statement 910.1.

Gerard, R. E. 1970. Institutional Innovations in Juvenile Corrections. *Federal Probation*. 30:37-44.

———. 1991. The Ten Commandments of Unit Management. *Corrections Today*. April, 53 (2): 32-36.

Gerard, R. E., R. B. Levinson, and G. R. Mote. 1988. National Workshop on Unit Management. Columbus, Ohio: National Institute of Corrections.

Gerard, R. E., R. B. Levinson, and H. C. Quay. 1970. *Differential Treatment: A Way to Begin*. Washington, D.C.: U.S. Bureau of Prisons.

Gilliard, D. K. and A. Beck. 1998. *Prison and Jail Inmates at Midyear 1997*, NCJ 167247. Washington, D.C.: Bureau of Justice Statistics.

Harmsworth, P. 1991. Managing Violent Offenders in the Correctional Setting: A Coordinated Approach. In S. A. Gerull and W. Lucas, eds.: *Serious Violent Offenders: Sentencing, Psychiatry, and Law Reform*. Canberra, Australia: Australian Institute of Corrections.

Herrick, E. 1989. The Surprising Direction of Violence in Prison. *Corrections Compendium*. 14(6): 4-17.

Houston, J. 1995. *Correctional Management: Functions, Skills, and Systems*. Chicago: Nelson-Hall.

———. 1997. Unit Management and the Search for Excellence. In T. Alleman, and R. Gido, eds. *Turnstile Justice: Contemporary Issues in American Corrections*. Englewood Cliffs, New Jersey: Prentice-Hall, Inc.

Houston, J. and D. Stafanovic. 1996. "Corrections in a New Light: Developing a Prison System for a Democratic Society." College of Police and Security Studies, Slovenia, National Criminal Justice Reference Service Home Page.

Hurlburt, L. 1996. Integrus Architecture. Seattle. *Journal of Commerce*.

Ingram, G. L. 1968. *Project R.E.A.D.Y.* Washington, D.C.: U.S. Bureau of Prisons.

Ingram, G. L., R. B. Levinson, H. C. Quay, and R. E. Gerard. 1970. An Experimental Program for the Psychopathic Delinquent. *Journal of Research In Crime and Delinquency.*

Jesness, C. 1972. Comparative Effectiveness of Two Institutional Treatment Programs for Delinquents. *Child Care Quarterly*. 1:119-130.

Johnson, R. 1996. *Hard Time: Understanding and Reforming the Prison, Second Edition.* Belmont, California: Wadsworth Publishing.

Karacki, L. 1991. Era of Change: Evolving Strategies of Control in the Bureau of Prisons. *Federal Prisons Journal.* Summer, 2(3): 24-32.

Karacki, L and J. Prather. 1974. *Vintner Questionnaire Results for Ashland.* Washington, D.C.: Federal Bureau of Prisons.

———. 1975a. *Vintner Questionnaire Results for Tallahassee.* Washington, D.C.: Federal Bureau of Prisons.

———. 1975b. *CIES Profiles for Seagoville—December 1974.* Washington, D.C.: Federal Bureau of Prisons.

———. 1975c. *CIES Profiles for Milan—October 1975.* Washington, D.C.: Federal Bureau of Prisons.

———. 1975d. *Preliminary Vintner Questionnaire Results for Milan—October 1975.* Washington, D.C.: Federal Bureau of Prisons.

Kerle, K. E. 1998. *American Jails: Looking to the Future.* Woburn, Massachusetts: Butterworth-Heinemann.

Knox County Sheriffs Department Corrections Division. 1984. *Direct Supervision Training Manual For Line Officers.* Knox County, Tennessee. Available from the National Institute of Corrections Information Center, Washington, DC.

Lansing, D., J. B. Bogan, and L. Karacki. 1977. Unit Management: Implementing a Different Correctional Approach. *Federal Probation.* March.

Lariviera, M. and D. Robinson. 1995. Attitudes of Federal Correctional Officers towards Offenders, Executive Summary. Queensland, Australia: Corrective Services Commission.

Levinson, R. B. 1972. Dimensions of Delinquent Behavior. *Proceedings: XXth International Congress of Psychology*. Tokyo, Japan, August.

———. 1980. TC or Not TCS. In H. Toch, ed. *Therapeutic Communities in Corrections.* New York, New York: Praeger.

———. 1982a. A Clarification of Classification, Guest Editorial. *Criminal Justice and Behavior*. 9(2), June.

———. 1982b. Try Softer. In R. Johnson and H. Toch, eds. *The Pain of Imprisonment.* Beverly Hills, California: Sage.

———. 1984. Differential Treatment: An Adult Typology. In I. Jacks and S. G. Cox, eds. *Psychological Approaches to Crime and Its Correction: Theory, Research, and Practice.* Chicago, Illinois: Nelson-Hall.

———. 1988. Developments in the Classification Process: Quay's AIMS Approach. *Criminal Justice and Behavior*. 15(1):24-38.

———. 1991a. Unit Management: The Concept that Changed Corrections. Introduction to the theme issue on unit management. *Corrections Today*. April, 53(2): 6.

———. 1991b. Unit Management: The Future. *Corrections Today*. April, 53(2): 44-48.

Levinson, R. B. and R. E. Gerard. 1973. Functional Units: A Different Correctional Approach. *Federal Probation*. XXXVII, No. 4: 8-15. Also in P. Killinger and P. Cromwell, eds. 1976. *Issues in Correctional Administration.* St. Paul, Minnesota: West Publishing.

———. 1986. Classifying Institutions. *Crime and Delinquency*. 32(3): 291-301.

Levinson, R. B. and J. J. Greene. In Press. "New Boys' on the Block: Under-18-year-olds in Adult Prisons," *Corrections Today.*

Levinson, R. B. and H. L. Kitchener. 1963. The Demonstration Counseling Project. *Progress Report*. Washington, D.C.: Federal Bureau of Prisons.

———. 1964. *Rational Innovation*. Washington, D.C.: Federal Bureau of Prisons.

———. 1966. Treatment of Delinquents: Comparison of Four Methods for Assigning Inmates to Counselors. *Journal of Consulting Psychology*. Vol. 10.

Levinson, R. B. and J. D. Williams. 1979. Inmate Classification: Security/Custody Considerations. *Federal Probation*. March.

Liebert, D. R. 1996. Direct Supervision Jails—The Second Decade: The Pitfalls. *American Jails*.

Love, C. T. and G. L. Ingram. 1982. Prison Disturbances: Suggestions for Future Solutions. *New England Journal on Prison Law*. 8:2: 393-426.

Marshall, J. 1990. *Unit Management: Principles of Correctional Operations, Linkages to the Mission Document of the Correctional Service of Canada*. Ottawa, Ontario: Correctional Service of Canada.

McMillen, M. J. and J. Hill. 1998. "Jadults and Adulniles: Housing the New Breed of Youthful Offender." *Corrections Today*. April. 100-104.

Megargee, E. I. 1977. A New Classification System for Offenders. *Criminal Justice and Behavior. 4:107-116.*

Megargee, E. I. and M. J. Bohn. 1979. *Classifying Criminal Offenders: A New System Based on the MMPI*. Beverly Hills, California: Sage.

Montgomery, R. H. and G. A. Crews. 1998. *A History of Correctional Violence: An Examination of Reported Causes of Riots and Disturbances*. Lanham, Maryland: American Correctional Association.

Moos, R. 1975. *Evaluating Correctional and Community Settings*. New York City: John Wiley.

Mote, G. R. 1988. Lecture at National Workshop on Unit Management, Columbus Ohio.

National Institute of Corrections—Jails Division. 1993. *Podular, Direct Supervision Jails Information Packe*t. Longmont, Colorado: National Institute of Corrections.

———. 1995. *Podular Direct Supervision 1995 Directory*. Longmont, Colorado: National Institute of Corrections.

Nelson, W. R. 1988. The Origins of the Podular Direct Supervision Concept: An Eyewitness Account. *American Jails*. Spring:10.

Nelson, W. R. and R. M. Davis. 1995. Podular Direct Supervision—The First Twenty Years. *American Jails*. July/August:14.

North Carolina Division of Prisons Training Conference. 1997. Appalachian State College, Boone, North Carolina. Personal notes.

O'Toole, M. 1993. Evaluating New Generation Jails. Class in Correctional Administration. Denver, Colorado: University of Colorado.

Perkins, C. A., J. J. Stephan, and A. J. Beck. 1995. Jails and Jail Inmates 1993-94. *Bureau of Justice Statistics Bulletin*, April.

Peroncello, Peter. 1995. Toward a New Direct Supervision Paradigm. *American Jails*. July/August-September/October.

Pierson, T. A. 1991. One State's Success with Unit Management. *Corrections Today*. April: 24-32.

Prison Service of United Kingdom. 1984. Managing the Long-Term Prison System. Penal Lexicon Home Page.

Quay, H. C. 1974. *The Differential Behavior Classification of the Juvenile Offender*. Washington, D.C.: Department of Justice.

———. 1984. *Managing Adult Inmates.* Lanham, Maryland: American Correctional Association.

Quay, H. C. and R. B. Levinson. 1967. *Prediction of the Institutional Adjustment of Four Sub-Groups of Delinquent Boys.* Washington, D.C.: Federal Bureau of Prisons.

Quay, H. C. and L. B. Parsons. 1971. *The Differential Behavioral Classification of the Juvenile Offender.* Washington, D.C.: Federal Bureau of Prisons.

Roberts, J. 1997. *Reform and Retribution: An Illustrated History of American Prisons.* Lanham, Maryland: American Correctional Association.

Robson, R. 1989. Managing the Long Term Prisoner: A Report on an Australian Innovation in Unit Management. *Howard Journal.* 28:187-203.

Rowan, J. 1996. Who is Safer in Male Maximum Security Prisons? *Corrections Today.* April 2, 58(2): 186-189.

Rowe, R., E. Foster, K. Byerly, N. Laird, and J. Prather. 1987. *The Impact of Functional Unit Management on Indices of Inmate Incidents.* Washington, D.C.: Federal Bureau of Prisons.

Rucker, M. R. 1991. Unit Management in the Navy Brig System. Paper presented at the Annual Congress of Correction, American Correctional Association, Minneapolis, Minnesota.

Schafer, N. E. 1994. State Operated Jails: How and Why. *American Jails.* September/October: 35-44.

Scott, R. J., J. Pasquale, and J. J. Cosgrove. 1980. *Functional Unit Management in Missouri—Evaluation of an Innovative Prison Management Model—Final Report.* Washington, D. C.: U.S. Department of Justice Law Enforcement Assistance Administration, National Institute of Justice. Grant #80-EF-Z1-MU04.

Senese, J. D., J. Wilson, A. O. Evans, R. Aguirre, and D. B. Kalinich. 1992. Evaluating Jail Reform: Inmate Infractions and Disciplinary Response in a Traditional and a Podular/Direct Supervision Jail. *American Jails.* September/October.

Silberman, M. 1995. *A World of Violence: Corrections in America.* Belmont, California: Wadsworth.

Smith, W. A. and C. E. Fenton. 1978. Unit Management in a Penitentiary: A Practical Experience. *Federal Probation.* September: 40-46.

Solomon, L. 1980. Developing an Empirically based Model for Classification Decision-making. *Prison Law Monitor.* 2:217: 234-237.

South Carolina Department of Corrections. 1985. *Objective Classification Plan.* Mimeo

Spieker, D. J. and T. A. Pierson. 1987. *Adult Internal Management System (AIMS): Implementation Manual.* Jefferson City, Missouri: Missouri Department of Corrections and Human Resources.

Toch, H. 1980. *Therapeutic Communities in Corrections.* New York, New York: Praeger.

———. 1992. Functional Unit Management. *Federal Prison Journal.* Winter, 2(4): 15- 19.

———. 1997. *Corrections: A Humanistic Approach.* Guilderland, New York: Harrow and Heston.

United States Bureau of the Census. 1996. *Statistical Abstract of the United States, 1996.* Washington, D.C.: U.S. Bureau of the Census.

United States Bureau of Prisons. 1964. *Rational Innovation: The Cottage Life Intervention Program.* Washington, D.C.: Department of Justice.

———. 1975. *Preliminary Evaluation of the Functional Unit Approach to Correctional Management.* Washington, D.C.: Department of Justice. Mimeo

———. 1979. *Security Designation and Custody Classification System.* Program Statement 5100.1. Washington, D.C.: Department of Justice. Mimeo.

———. 1990. *Unit Management Manual.* Program Statement 5321.4. Washington, D.C.: Department of Justice. Mimeo.

———. 1992. *Program Review Guidelines for Correctional Programs Institutions.* Operations Memorandum 170-95 (5300). Washington, D.C.: Department of Justice. Mimeo.

United States Department of Justice. 1983. Audit of the Bureau of Prisons' Unit Management System, October. Washington, D.C.: Department of Justice.

Van Voorhis, P. 1994. *Psychological Classification of the Adult Male Prison Inmate.* Albany, New York: State University of New York Press.

Warren, M. Q. 1969. The Case for Differential Treatment of Delinquents. *Annuals of the American Academy of Politics and Social Science.* 381:37-59.

Webster, J. H. 1991. Designing Facilities for Effective Unit Management. *Corrections Today.* April: 38-44.

Wisconsin Department of Corrections. 1996. Survey. Madison, Wisconsin: Wisconsin Department of Corrections.

Zupan, L. 1991. *Jails, Reform and the New Generation Philosophy.* Cincinnati, Ohio: Anderson Publishing Co.

———. 1993. This Jail for Rent: Anatomy of a Deal Too Good to Be True. *American Jails.* January/February.

Zupan, L., B. Menke, N. Lovrich, and D. Manning. 1986. *Model Personnel Selection Process for Podular, Direct Supervision Jails.* Longmont, Colorado: National Institute of Corrections.

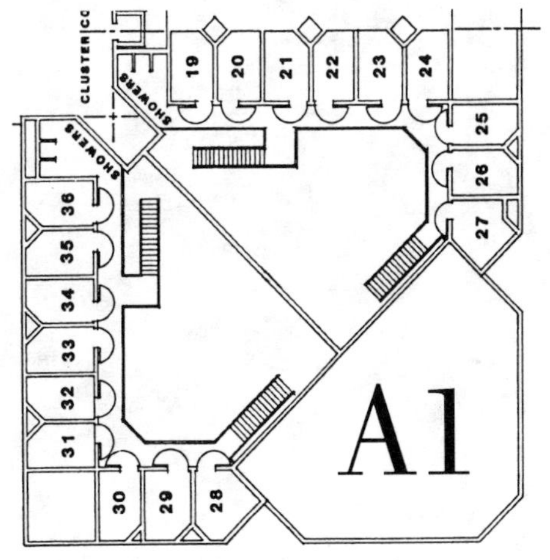


# Appendix 1

*Prepared for the South Dakota Department of Corrections*

## Sample Unit Management Manual: Institution Procedures

December, 1992.

This material is adapted by each facility to meet its specific needs.

Robert B. Levinson, Ph.D.

# Appendix 1—Table of Contents

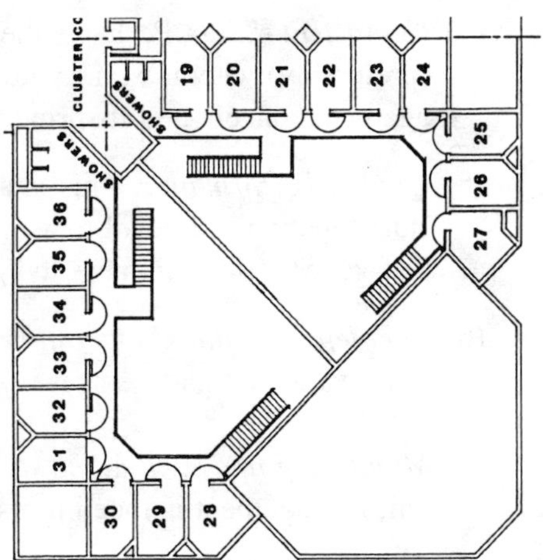


# Appendix 1

## Overview

Unit management is a method for managing inmates that emphasizes decentralization and delegates decision-making authority to a unit team. An institution functioning under unit management subdivides its housing areas into several units. Each unit houses a subgroup of the institution's inmate population. The unit is managed by a semi-autonomous unit team whose offices are located on (or proximate to) the prisoners' living quarters.

A unit's staff consists of: a unit manager (who heads the team), case managers, correctional counselors, a unit secretary, correctional officers, and part-time education and psychology services advisers. All of these individuals function together in an effort to manage the delivery of programs to "their" group of inmates more effectively.

Eight principles essential to the success of unit management, are as follows:

(1) *Leadership from the central office, institution, and unit levels.* This means having a commitment to the concept and the willingness to examine and change "traditional" procedures.

(2) *Unit Plan.* Each unit must have a written plan that details its mission and operational procedures.

(3) *Adequate Resources.* There must be staff, money, time, and material necessary to meet the Department of Corrections' written policy expectations for unit management.

(4) *Competent Staff.* Perhaps the most critical component is a well-trained, (preferably) veteran staff, who have a personal commitment to the unit management concept and its principles.

(5) *Quality Performance.* This is a component of staff competence. It means the staff function at a level that meets high professional standards and reflects a self-generated willingness to "go the extra mile."

(6) *Interdepartmental Cooperation.* Cooperation and assistance among an institution's various departments is imperative; unit management will fail in a vacuum.

(7) *Monitoring and Evaluation.* A systematic assessment of the degree to which unit management is meeting its established goals is necessary.

(8) *Analysis and Refinement.* A periodic determination, based on evaluation data, yields specific recommendations designed to maximize unit management's overall effectiveness.

# Major Objectives

Society incarcerates individuals found guilty of law violations for one or more of the following reasons: punishment, incapacitation, deterrence, or rehabilitation. It is the responsibility of departments of corrections to care for, control, and correct offenders sentenced to periods of confinement. Unit management provides a balanced approach towards accomplishing society's objectives and fulfilling corrections' mandate.

Unit management achieves its objectives by enhancing the quality of relationships between staff and inmates. It accomplishes this by:

- eliminating interunit transfer of inmates
- assigning staff to a unit on a permanent basis. However, for correctional officers this means they are assigned to a unit for a minimum of nine months, although they may rotate through the morning, day, and evening shifts
- providing better observation of inmates
- increasing the amount of contact between staff and inmates
- holding inmates accountable for their own behavior
- giving unit staff specified decision-making authority
- individualizing inmate program plans
- allowing units to develop different treatment strategies

As a consequence of the unit management approach, problems are identified and dealt with earlier. This reduces the likelihood that small issues will be neglected and/or permitted to become major conflicts.

# Staffing

Staffing standards establish a basis for quality control, which is an aspect of unit management's eight essential principles. Chart A lists the personnel requirements for a typical general population unit.

### Chart A: Staffing Standards—General Unit

| Position | Standard |
|---|---|
| Unit Manager | one (1) per unit* |
| Case Manager | at least one (1) per 125 inmates |
| Correctional Counselor | at least one (1) per 125 inmates |
| Unit Secretary | one (1) per unit |
| Education Adviser** | part-time |
| Unit Psychologist** | part-time*** |
| Correctional Officers | at least one, 24-hours every day |

* = Unit's size should not exceed 250 general-population inmates.

** = Each unit must have an Education and Psychologist Adviser assigned, but both may function on more than one unit.

*** = Full-time position on special population unit.

Special units, however, have different characteristics:

- smaller—in other words, less than 125 inmates
- more staff intensive—in other words, a full-time mental health person
- recruits inmates with a specific program need—for example, drug abuse counseling
- provides a specialized within-unit program to meet this need

# Staff Roles

## Central Office

One person at the central office level should be assigned the responsibility for monitoring the operation of unit management throughout the Department of Corrections. Among the duties of this individual are to do the following:

- develop Department of Corrections policy statements for unit management

- monitor the degree to which units implement these policies
- represent the budgetary interests of unit management
- manage/conduct training for new unit managers
- coordinate in-service training for all unit staff
- conduct annual on-site audits of unit management
- coordinate evaluation efforts related to unit management
- provide technical assistance to local correctional agencies

# Institution

In a nonunitized facility, decision-making is centralized or made by department heads. The implementation of unit management results in much decision-making authority being delegated to unit managers. Ensuring that this delegation of authority actually occurs is the most difficult step to accomplish when an already functioning facility moves into unit management.

## Administration

*Warden*—Under unit management, the chief executive officer of the facility retains final authority and responsibility for all matters occurring within the institution. However, unit management will not succeed unless the warden, as final arbiter, ensures that appropriate delegation of authority to the unit managers does occur. An explicit objective of unit management is to have semi-autonomous units functioning in all of the Department of Corrections' institutions; it is not merely the redistribution of staff among a facility's housing areas.

*Deputy Wardens*—Wardens usually delegate supervisory and monitoring responsibilities for unit management to one of their deputy wardens. It is essential that unit managers and correctional services (security) both report to the same deputy (*see* Chart B, page 153).

The deputy warden for programs monitors unit procedures to ensure conformity with central office policy. He or she will ascertain that the authority and responsibility delegated to the units are being managed effectively.

Establishing guidelines within which the units are to function is also part of the leadership responsibilities of the deputy warden for programs. This means allowing some within-unit flexibility while maintaining cross-unit consistency in critical areas. Frequent interaction (such as a weekly meeting) between the unit managers and the deputy warden for programs is a critical factor in assuring success.

The deputy warden for programs shall ensure that each unit manager is assigned a cost center to permit the independent purchase/management of minor unit supplies and program equipment. In general, the deputy warden for programs conveys to unit management staff the Department of Corrections' philosophy—an amalgam of the department's policies and the mission of the institution.

## Chart B: Institution Chain-of-Command

WARDEN

EXECUTIVE OFFICE
- Executive Assistant
- Warden's Secretary
- Public Information

DEPUTY WARDEN (PROGRAMS)
- Chaplaincy Services
- Education/VT/Recreation
- Psychology Services
- Security Services
- **Unit Management**

CASE MANAGEMENT COORDINATOR

SUPERINTENDENT OF INDUSTRIES

DEPUTY WARDEN (OPERATIONS)
- Administrative System
- Business Office
- Food Service
- Maintenance Services
- Medical/Dental Services
- Personnel Department
- Records Office
- Safety and Sanitation

## Unit Management Personnel

*Unit Manager*—The unit manager is an administrator, supervisor, coordinator, and monitor of a multidisciplinary team of staff members who are assigned to work in his or her unit. As a department head, the unit manager will be called upon to perform other institution-related functions as well, for example, serve on institution committees and promotion boards, serve as institution duty officer, and meet regularly with the deputy warden for programs and with other unit managers to coordinate and improve management functions throughout the facility.

At the unit level, a unit manager is responsible for the overall operation of all phases of his or her unit in regard to both staff and inmates. For staff, this includes: providing orientation and direction, scheduling, training, supervising, and doing performance evaluations, and creating a unit plan. Regarding inmates, the unit manager will develop in-unit programming and, in collaboration with unit staff, will have decision-making authority regarding: classification and reclassification, program and job assignments, program reviews, and the handling of minor disciplinary reports.

The unit manager is a generalist with broad administrative responsibilities regarding unit staff. This includes supervisory authority over the unit's case managers, correctional counselors, secretary, and the day and evening shift correctional officers. In exercising this authority, the unit manager will make use of the expertise of other department heads, for example, the chief of the records office in regard to the unit secretary, and the major in regard to the unit's correctional officers. Accordingly, the unit manager will foster good communications and working relationships with other institutional department heads.

More explicitly, unit managers have responsibilities in the following areas:

**A. Administrative**

_____ accreditation

_____ duty officer

_____ collateral duties

_____ unit operational reviews

_____ staff work-schedules

_____ within-unit activities schedule

_____ special assignments/task forces/committees, and so forth

_____ designate an acting unit manager

**B. Security**

_____ contraband control

_____ inmate personal property

_____ unit security inspections

_____ security of inmate files, computers

_____ key control

_____ emergency plans

_____ unit disciplinary panel

**C. Safety, Sanitation, and Facilities Maintenance**

_____ fire drills

_____ unit emergency equipment/exits

_____ unit sanitation inspections

_____ facility maintenance

_____ emergency repairs

**D. Unit Program Responsibilities**

_____ unit orientation for inmates

_____ group/individual counseling/therapy

_____ on-unit work details, such as sanitation

_____ special on-unit programs, such as disabled inmates

_____ leisure time/recreation activities

_____ wellness program

_____ unit pre-release/release programs

**E. Human Resource Development**

_____ recruiting/interviewing prospective staff

_____ unit staff career development

— mentoring

— in-service and off-site training

— staff retention activities

_____ unit retreats

_____ unit staff annual performance evaluations

**F. Supervision**

_____ ensure accessibility/availability of unit staff to inmates

_____ unit staff's responsiveness to inmates, nonunit personnel, other agencies, and to the public

_____ timeliness of decisions, paperwork, reports

_____ input into unit correctional officer selection/evaluation

_____ staff attendance/lateness records

**G. Quality Control**

_____ correspondence with outside agencies/public

_____ interdepartmental referrals

_____ unit plan development/updating

_____ unit admission and orientation program

_____ inmate files

_____ classification/reclassification procedures

_____ court recommendations follow-through

_____ unit-based programs

_____ disciplinary procedures/comments

_____ grievance procedures

_____ furlough/pre-release/release programs

**H. Financial Responsibilities**

_____ repair/replace unit equipment

_____ professional manuals/reports for unit staff

_____ unit sanitation supplies

_____ unit program materials

_____ unit recreation supplies

_____ miscellaneous unit costs, such as for planning materials, retreat needs

_____ overall management of unit budget

**I. Strategic Planning**

_____ participate in devising institution's strategic plans

_____ physical plant/equipment

_____ staffing

_____ training

_____ unit program/activities review

_____ inmate programs

Unit managers have the latitude to alter post orders so that they more closely fit the mission of their unit. In cooperation with the major's staff, unit managers are responsible for maintaining inventory and accountability of all tools assigned to the unit, and should coordinate work-order requests for the repair of locks and security devices with the major's office.

Whenever possible, decisions regarding unit security matters should result from joint discussions between the major and the unit manager, such as relief coverage during unit correctional officers' lunch/supper period. When the unit manager and the major cannot agree, the deputy warden of programs will have final authority.

*Case Manager*—The unit case managers are under the direct supervision of the unit manager. They have an assigned caseload of inmates and are responsible for all case management matters that affect these individuals. Case managers also participate in other unit activities as assigned by the unit manager; however, they will not normally perform routine clerical duties.

Supervision, training, and technical assistance for unit case managers is the responsibility of the unit manager with assistance in specialist areas provided by the institution's case management coordinator (*see* page 161). While the unit manager has supervisory and monitoring responsibilities for his or her case managers, the unit manager will not always possess case management expertise. Therefore, it is imperative that the unit manager and the case management coordinator work together very closely so that each unit's case managers receives appropriate levels of training and technical assistance.

Case managers' responsibilities require developing and implementing social service-type programming for their caseload of inmates. This includes:

- completing classification/reclassification forms
- conducting individual/group counseling/therapy sessions
- visiting (at least weekly) inmates on their caseload who have been placed in the infirmary or in administrative or punitive segregation
- monitoring inmate progress through periodic formal and informal program reviews
- participating on various unit and institution committees when an inmate from their caseload is involved
- performing other duties as assigned by the unit manager, such as participating in the unit's admission and orientation program, handling the unit's volunteer program, and so forth

For the most part, case managers are concerned with external issues that affect inmates on their caseload, such as preparing documents for the parole board, dealing with outside agencies, preparing an inmate's visiting list, and so forth. A case manager will assist an inmate from his or her unit when that individual's own case manager is absent, and will serve as acting unit manager, when requested.

*Correctional Counselor*—A correctional counselor is a unit staff member who has been recruited from the ranks of the institution's correctional officers. He or she is a veteran member of the security staff (at the sergeant grade-level) who has been given additional training and no longer functions as a correctional officer. The primary focus of the correctional counselor's role is to help inmates deal more successfully with the daily problems of living in a prison.

Each correctional counselor is paired with a case manager and shares the same caseload of inmates. The counselor is under the direct supervision of the unit manager and will not be assigned correctional officer duties unless an emergency situation has been declared by the warden. Correctional counselors will serve as acting unit manager, when requested.

Correctional counselors have the following responsibilities:

- assist inmates on his or her caseload in resolving the day-to-day problems that may arise, using a variety of methods, such as:

  ______ formal/informal counseling sessions

  ______ individual and/or group counseling

  ______ crisis intervention

  ______ referral services, which require contacts with staff and inmates both on and off the unit. Consequently, correctional counselors should regularly (at least twice every week) tour the work and program sites of the inmates on their caseloads; and, when necessary, offer assistance to both inmates and the work/program supervisors

- develop general knowledge about prisoners in their unit and detailed information concerning inmates on their specific caseload
- serve as the hearing officer (or a member of the unit's disciplinary panel) which requires keeping abreast of policies and procedures
- serve as a voting member on the unit's classification committee
- as part of the unit's orientation program, interview newly admitted inmates, and participate in the program
- inspect the unit daily
- visit on a regular basis (such as once a week) inmates on their caseload who are in the infirmary or have been placed in administrative or punitive segregation
- log and distribute mail to unit inmates
- serve as a staff sponsor of an on-unit inmate group
- coordinate inmate telephone sign-up list (when such a procedure is used)
- attempt informal resolution of inmate grievances and distribute grievance forms
- conduct at least one unit-based program per week
- serve as the unit expert and coordinator on matters pertaining to:

  ——— inmate personal property, including incoming and outgoing package approvals

——— trust-fund activities, including inmate withdrawals and special purchase orders

- serve as policy and procedures expert on these topics when questions are raised by inmates, their families and friends, institution staff, other agencies, and the public

*Unit Secretary*—Each unit has its own secretary, who is permanently assigned to the unit. The unit secretary is directly supervised by, and works for, the unit manager; therefore, his or her office should be located in close proximity to the unit manager.

The unit secretary performs all clerical duties for the unit's staff. Specifically, this responsibility includes:

- typing reports, xeroxing, and performing other unit clerical functions
- entering information into the unit's/department's inmate database
- filing material in inmate files
- responding to written and telephonic communications from inmate families and the general public
- at the direction of the unit manager, serves as a recorder/participant on various unit committees
- at the direction of the unit manager, serves as a liaison between the unit and other institutions or departments

In regard to filing and handling inmate records, the unit secretary will receive training and quality control monitoring from the chief of the records office. A unit secretary's manual should be available for day-to-day reference and guidance.

Unit managers should encourage career development and a professional image for unit secretaries. Among the ways this can be accomplished are broadening the secretary's responsibilities and providing opportunities for him or her to participate in a variety of unit/institution activities.

*Unit Correctional Officers*—Correctional officers are assigned to a unit for not less than nine months. They may cycle from morning, to day, to evening shift before rotating out of the unit. The day and evening watch officers are under the supervision of the unit manager with input from the major.

In regard to the unit's correctional officers, unit managers:

- will be consulted and have meaningful input prior to the decision to place an officer in (or remove an officer from) his or her unit
- have written input into the annual performance rating of officers working the day and evening shifts. When a correctional officer rotates to a post outside of the unit, the unit manager writes an evaluation report that is placed in the

officer's personnel file; its contents are incorporated into the officer's annual performance rating

- may assign additional duties provided these do not interfere with the correctional officers' prime responsibilities for maintaining the unit's security and sanitation at levels that comply with department policy

Unit correctional officers supervise unit (inmate) orderlies and prepare any performance pay reports for these individuals. The officer is the primary staff member responsible for unit sanitation and inmate room/cell inspections.

At the end of every shift, the unit correctional officer makes a written, signed comment in a bound unit logbook (with numbered pages) concerning events occurring during his or her shift. All unit staff will read and initial these comments in the logbook when they come on duty.

The unit correctional officers are valuable members of the unit team. Correctional officers and unit staff are expected to communicate freely with one another. Unit managers shall ensure that maximum input is received from correctional officers assigned to the unit. This may be in writing or the officer may attend unit classification and program review meetings, if this can be arranged.

## Other Unit Staff

*Education Adviser*—The unit's education adviser is supervised directly by the supervisor of education. In collaboration with the unit manager, the supervisor of education assigns teachers to work on a part-time basis with unit staffs, for a minimum of four hours per week/per unit. The unit manager will have written input into the annual performance rating of this education department member.

The education adviser is the unit team's expert consultant regarding all education, vocational training, and recreation matters. This individual (who will not be assigned to more than two units) attends initial classification and program review (reclassification) meetings and also serves in a liaison capacity between the unit and the education department, such as ensuring that monthly progress reports on the unit's inmates are received in a timely fashion.

*Unit Psychologist*—In a general unit, the unit psychologist is a part-time team member. [In a special unit, this is a full-time position. In the latter instances, the unit manager is the psychologist's supervisor, while the chief psychologist has written input into this special unit staff member's annual performance rating.] He or she is under the direct supervision of the chief psychologist who, in collaboration with the unit manager, assigns a psychologist to work with each unit, for a minimum of eight hours per week/per unit. Unit managers have written input into their unit psychologist's annual performance evaluation concerning attendance at meetings, timeliness of reports, quality of interactions with other unit staff and inmates, and so forth.

A unit psychologist provides psychological services to inmates in not more than two general units. Such services include testing, diagnosis, therapy, and research and involves planning, organizing, and participating in group or individual counseling or therapy with inmates on the unit; training and monitoring of counseling conducted by other unit staff; and designing special needs programs.

## Nonunit Personnel

*Major*—The major is the institution department head who has primary responsibility for the facility's security. He or she serves as an adviser, consultant, and monitor for other department heads in matters pertaining to security issues. Due to an overlap in their areas of responsibility, unit managers and the major must maintain a cooperative relationship.

In the nonunit areas of the institution—such as outside inmate living quarters—the traditional centralized role of correctional services continues. Within units, the major's technical expertise and the first-hand knowledge of the unit manager need to be integrated; *see* Chart C (page 162).

Unit managers will have a persuasive voice in selecting correctional officers assigned to their unit. Correctional officers are assigned for nine months rotating through the morning, day, and evening shifts. Unit managers will be consulted before changes affecting their officers take place.

*Case Management Coordinator*—The case management coordinator is a resource person for both the institution's administrators and for unit management. This individual (under the supervision of the deputy warden for programs) is responsible for:

- ensuring quality case management activities
- providing technical assistance
- developing/delivering in-service training
- quarterly monitoring of the work of unit case managers, such as classification reports, out-of-facility transfers, parole board recommendations, court correspondence, etc.

The case management coordinator has no direct supervisory role over unit staff. He or she provides written input for each unit's case manager's annual performance ratings. There needs to be a close working relationship between this individual and the unit managers.

*Records Office*—In a computerized system, access to inmate records must be limited to those with a need-to-know that is determined in advance. There should be frequent changes of passwords so security will not be breached.

Other security measures should be developed by the MIS staff and any security breaches should be investigated and remedied promptly. In no case should inmates ever have access to their own or other inmates' records.

Centralized institutions have inmate records filed in a single office to which all other staff must go to obtain a prisoner's file and to which they return to replace the file. This is a time-consuming procedure, and often staff members may not have the inmate's file at hand, when it is needed.

# Chart C: Table of Organization

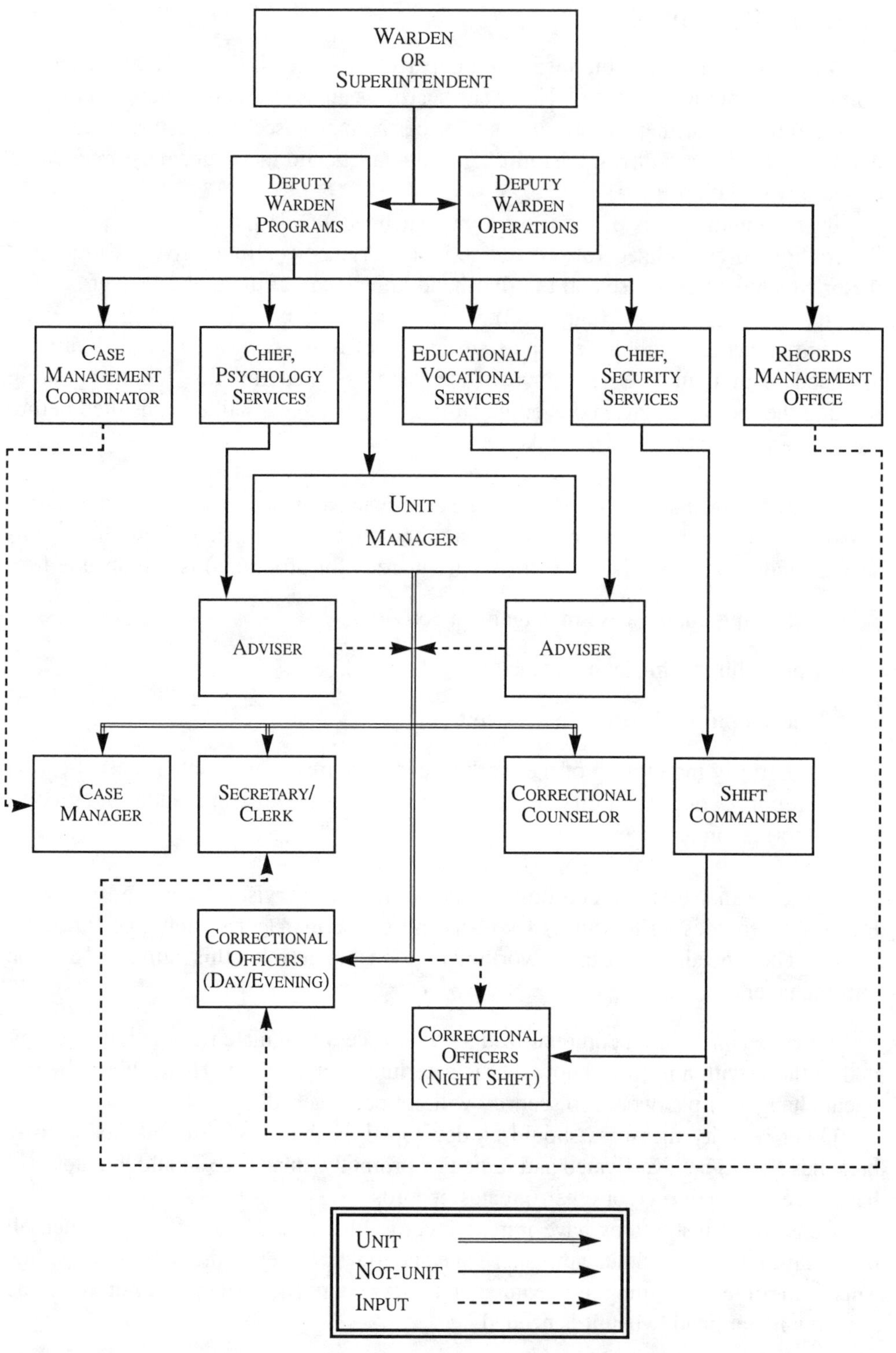

Under unit management, inmate files are decentralized. Special documents, such as original court papers, may be retained in a skeleton file at a centralized location, but copies of those papers also are placed in the inmate file located in a secure/fireproof area in the unit secretary's office. He or she receives training and periodic monitoring from the chief of the records office concerning records management (*see also* page 159).

*Other Facility Staff*—For the most part, the duties of all institution staff not mentioned remain the same under unit management. Modifications may be required due to changes in the chain of command (*see* page 153), but for the most part, current procedures continue in the:

——— Barber Shop

——— Business Office

——— Commissary

——— Education/Vocational Training/Recreation

——— Food Service

——— Laundry/Clothing Exchange

——— Library/Law Library

——— Maintenance

——— Medical/Dental/Infirmary Services

——— Prison Industries

——— Religious Services

——— Segregation

——— Warehouse, and so forth

# Managing A Unit

A functional unit has been likened to a "mini-institution" with the unit manager having responsibilities, which in many respects reflect those of a warden. This means that the unit manager must be knowledgeable about policy, safety and sanitation, personnel, supervision, training, security, case management, unit/institution programs, parole procedures, research, budget management, and so forth. Each unit manager will develop (in collaboration with the deputy warden for programs) a written, personalized annual training plan that specifically addresses areas in which he or she has little or no experience and for which management- and cross-training are needed.

## Management-By-Walking-Around

Management-by-walking-around is an effective managerial technique. To contribute to better prisoner supervision, facilitate informal staff/inmate interaction, and provide a mechanism for early problem identification, all unit managers, case managers, and correctional counselors are expected to tour their unit daily. These staff members also are expected to remain accessible to unit inmates during day and evening hours.

## Unit Staff Meetings

Unit staff meetings will be scheduled weekly; attendance is required by the unit manager, case managers, correctional counselors, and the unit secretary. The unit correctional officer(s), psychologist, and education adviser should be encouraged to attend.

The unit manager is responsible for ensuring that minutes of each meeting will be taken, and that copies are distributed to the deputy warden for programs and other staff, as appropriate. The unit secretary will maintain a file of past unit staff meeting minutes.

These weekly staff meetings provide an opportunity to:

- keep staff informed about current unit issues and concerns
- discuss new department policy and procedure statements
- modify current unit schedules and activities
- review unit monthly reports/statistics
- have unit staff and invited guests offer brief training sessions
- plan for the future
- promote a "team concept"

All unit personnel will be given an opportunity, and encouraged, to participate during the unit staff meetings, which will be chaired by the unit manager.

## Personnel Management

The following sections discuss several major areas for which the unit manager has managerial responsibility.

### Staff Orientation

The unit manager will be responsible for providing an orientation for all newly assigned unit staff, trainees, volunteers, and so forth. This requires creating a formal program (*see* Appendix, page 182) which, at a minimum, addresses the following:

- introduction to on-board staff and a unit tour
- discussion of staff roles and job expectations
- duty hours and the unit's activity schedule
- unit team's responsibilities for safety and sanitation, security, disciplinary proceedings, unit equipment, and so forth
- accountability for classification, inmate education/work assignments, program reviews, counseling/therapy, problem solving, parole planning, prerelease and release programs, and so forth
- a review of the unit plan

At the conclusion of the orientation agenda, the new staff member should sign and date a statement, which documents what has occurred; the original is placed in the employee's personnel file, and a copy is kept in a locked file on the unit.

## Duty Hours

Unit managers establish working hours for their unit's staff. In addition to correctional officer coverage, every unit is responsible for having personnel on duty twelve hours during the week and eight hours on weekends and holidays; *see* Chart D. This allows staff to become familiar with the total operation of the unit and to be available to inmates during leisure-time hours. The presence of staff at these times contributes to better control of prisoners. The work roster should be conspicuously posted on a glass-enclosed unit bulletin board for both staff and inmates to see.

## Chart D: Unit Staff Duty-hours Schedule (example)

| Employee | Sun | Mon | Tue | Wed | Thurs | Fri | Sat |
|---|---|---|---|---|---|---|---|
| Unit Manager | Off | 8:00-4 | 8:00-4 | 8:00-4 | 1:00-9 | 8:00-4 | Off |
| Case Manager #1 | 8:00-4 | 1:00-9 | 8:00-4 | 8:00-4 | 1:00-9 | Off | Off |
| Counselor #1 | Off | Off | 8:00-4 | 1:00-9 | 1:00-9 | 8:00-4 | 8:00-4 |
| Case Manager #2 | Off | Off | 1:00-9 | 8:00-4 | 1:00-9 | 8:00-4 | 8:00-4 |
| Counselor #2 | 8:00-4 | 1:00-9 | 8:00-4 | 8:00-4 | 1:00-9 | Off | Off |
| Secretary | Off | 8:00-4 | 8:00-4 | 8:00-4 | 1:00-9 | 8:00-4 | Off |
| Morning Officer | Off | 12AM-8 | 12AM-8 | 12AM-8 | 12AM-8 | 12AM-8 | Off |
| Day Officer | 8AM-4 | Off | Off | 8AM-4 | 8AM-4 | 8AM-4 | 8AM-4 |
| Evening Officer | 4PM-12 | 4PM-12 | 4PM-12 | 4PM-12 | Off | Off | 4PM-12 |

At least once every week, the unit manager, case manager(s), and correctional counselor(s) must work until 9:00 P.M. To stay abreast of activities in their unit and in the institution, unit managers must schedule themselves to work a weekend day and/or holiday at least once per quarter. Additionally, weekends and holidays will not be worked disproportionately by correctional counselors.

While it is important for unit managers to be sensitive to staff's work-hour needs, the ruling principle is the following:

**[ The duty hours of personnel are scheduled to meet the needs of the unit, not the wishes of the staff. ]**

## Annual Leave Schedule

Annual leave schedules will be developed so that uninterrupted services can be provided for inmates. For example, case manager #1 and correctional counselor #1 are not scheduled for annual leave at the same time. Unit managers should create leave schedules in advance for their unit staff. They should reflect an equitable distribution of "prime" vacation time.

A unit manager's own annual leave is scheduled/approved in advance by the deputy warden for programs. Whoever is the employee's official annual performance evaluation rater also approves annual leave.

When, for whatever reason, the unit manger is not on duty (between 8:00 A.M. and 9:00 P.M.), an acting unit manager, appointed by the unit manager, is in charge; appropriate written notification should be sent to other department heads and the deputy warden for programs.

## Employee Development

Unit managers should be aware of the strengths/weaknesses of their staff. From this information (in collaboration with each employee), they develop individualized training plans. Once staff needs have been identified, a plan of action should be initiated to secure the necessary training. Thus, training should be proactive rather than reactive. Such an approach fosters staff growth and enhances both unit and facility operations.

The unit manager should work closely with the institution's training officer in identifying potential inservice and outside resources to fulfill his or her staff's training needs. The following are areas in which unit personnel may need specialized training:

- unit managers:

  ——— unit management

  ——— correctional supervision

  ——— financial operations

  ——— personnel regulations

  ——— case management (if not a former case manager)

  ——— disciplinary board rules

- case managers:

  ——— thirty days' on-the-job training before assuming a caseload

——— case management

——— disciplinary board rules

- correctional counselors

  ——— forty-hour correctional counselor orientation course which includes: inmate discipline, intake screening, unit inmate orientation, classification and program review, central file rules, personal property operations, telephone procedures, mail and visiting operations, disciplinary board rules, grievance procedures, trust fund operations, and release procedures

  ——— forty-hour counseling training course delivered by the institution's psychology department within the counselor's first three months on duty

- unit secretaries:

  ——— within first month on duty, a minimum of sixteen-hours on-the-job training with an experienced unit secretary

  ——— unit secretary self-study course based on the unit secretary's manual

In addition, the unit manager should seek opportunities to provide informal staff training, such as during staff meetings and daily closeouts, establish unit task forces, put staff into "acting" roles, provide recognition for superior work, and so forth.

## Performance Ratings

It is important to make explicit who rates and who reviews the annual performance evaluations of unit management staff. This gives substance to written policy regarding supervisory responsibilities; Chart E (*see* page 168) displays this information.

## Inmate Management

Inmates come into corrections via three routes: (i) directly from the courts; (ii) as a consequence of a parole violation; or (iii) by transfer from another department or institution. All sentenced inmates—categories (i) and (ii)—will be processed by the Orientation and Indoctrination section of the Jamison facility.

Courts commit new offenders and recidivists. Those in the latter category who had a recent incarceration (within the past year) do not need the complete program for new admissions; nor do recent (within-one-year-of-release) parole violators. Such recently released persons should be processed rapidly through Orientation and Indoctrination and should be sent to an appropriately secure prison. If the person has been AIMS-classified, this process should be completed within seven days, since the AIMS classification is not redone. Individuals without an AIMS category stay in Orientation and Indoctrination for at least ten days in order to make an accurate AIMS categorization. (AIMS, which stands for Adult Internal Management System, is a method for classifying inmates based on their behavioral characteristics.)

## Chart E: Performance Ratings

| Employee Rated | Written Input | Official Rater | Reviewer |
|---|---|---|---|
| Case Management Coordinator | Unit Manager | Deputy Warden for Programs | Warden |
| Unit Manager | N/A | Deputy Warden for Programs | Warden |
| Case Manager | Case Management Coordinator | Unit Manager | Deputy Warden for Programs |
| Correctional Counselor | N/A | Unit Manager | Deputy Warden for Programs |
| Unit Secretary | N/A | Unit Manager | Deputy Warden for Programs |
| Unit Correctional Officer (Day/Evening) | Lieutenant | Unit Manager | Major |
| Unit Officer (Morning) | Unit Manager | Lieutenant | Major |
| Education Adviser | Unit Manager | Education Supervisor | Deputy Warden for Programs |
| Psychology Adviser (General Unit) | Unit Manager | Chief Psychologist | Deputy Warden for Programs |
| Psychology Adviser (Special) | Chief Psychologist | Unit Manager | Deputy Warden for programs |

New and returning released offenders, who have been in the community for more than one year, will require a complete Orientation and Indoctrination work-up; however, the AIMS portion of this process need not be repeated for any returnee who has been AIMS-classified on a prior occasion. This also holds for inmates received through transfer from another department or institution.

Thus, all designees from Orientation and Indoctrination should arrive with an AIMS classification category—"A", "B", "C", "D", or "E." Upon arrival, inmates will be assigned to a particular unit based on their AIMS category or (if the facility does not use a formal internal classification process) assigned randomly to living quarters based on the last digit of the inmate's register number. Once inmates have been assigned to a unit, they should not be moved permanently from it for as long as they remain at that facility. If the facility has a method by which it assigns new arrivals to particular units, then there should be an explicit procedure by which "mistakes" can be corrected. Such changes should not be easily achieved, should involve a committee which includes, at minimum, both the "receiving" and "losing" unit managers and the deputy warden for programs.

## Unit Security

As is true for all institution personnel, unit staff are correctional workers. They share a responsibility in helping to maintain the integrity of the facility's security systems. These shared duties include assisting with:

- unit shakedowns
- occasional lunch/supper relief
- accountability checks, and so forth

To foster an awareness of security issues, everyday as they come on duty, all unit staff will review and initial their unit officers' daily log. Unit managers also will review and initial everyday, the shift lieutenants' daily log.

## Inmate Orientation

Each unit is responsible for orienting its newly assigned inmates within five working days after arrival on the unit. Staff will deliver a formal program which, at a minimum, addresses:

- a review of institution/unit rules
- discussion of expectations
- introduction to on-board staff and a unit tour
- review of the unit's activity schedule
- distribution of facility's Inmate Handbook
- a bed assignment

Each staff member will sign/date the Inmate Orientation Checklist (*see* Appendix, page 183) after delivering his or her section. Following completion of the entire agenda, each inmate signs a statement documenting what has occurred. The form is dated and signed by the staff member coordinating the unit's orientation program, and it is then placed in the inmate's file.

## Classification/Reclassification/Program Review

Each unit will have its own unit classification committee. The committee meets on a regularly scheduled, weekly basis and consists of at least these unit staff members:

- the scheduled inmate's case manager and correctional counselor
- the unit secretary
- the unit manager, who will function as the chairperson

Whenever an inmate is being formally considered (in other words, is on the classification committee's agenda) he or she will be notified forty-eight hours in advance and will appear before the committee, in person.

If an inmate refuses to attend, he or she will be asked to sign a statement indicating this refusal. The inmate's case manger will witness, sign, and date the inmate's refusal statement, and inform the unit manager. If the inmate will not sign the refusal statement, this information will be noted on the refusal statement, dated and signed by the inmate's case manager, and countersigned by the unit manager.

Every inmate will appear before the unit classification committee at time intervals specified by department policy—but not less than once each year. Inmates may be seen by the unit classification committee more often, but only when this is requested in writing by a unit staff member.

The unit classification committee's authority will be spelled out clearly in department policy. In specified areas, the classification committee will have decision-making authority (such as changing an inmate's program) while in other areas the committee can only recommend changes that are decided upon by others (such as a transfer to another facility). Typically all within-unit and most within-institution decisions are made by the unit classification committee; recommendations are made regarding many outside-the-unit and all outside-the-institution activities, but these decisions are made by others.

# Inmate Disciplinary Process

Institutions will continue to have a facilitywide institution disciplinary board, which will handle all major rule violations. Each unit manager should serve as a voting member of this board, on a rotation basis. In addition, each unit will have its own unit disciplinary panel, which is the decision-making body on all minor disciplinary infractions (any rule violation for which the punishment is not disciplinary/punitive segregation) incurred by its unit's inmates. The unit manager chairs this three-person unit disciplinary panel, which also includes as voting members, the accused inmate's correctional counselor and another unit staff member selected by the unit manager.

When a major disciplinary report is written, a copy shall be sent to the accused inmate's unit manager. He or she will ensure that a written comment is forwarded to the institution disciplinary board within twenty-four hours so that this information is available during the decision-making process. The accused inmate's unit case manager will attend and may be one of the voting members on the institution disciplinary board if he or she is not involved in the disciplinary infraction, and will be notified about any action taken by the disciplinary board.

## Segregation/Protective Custody

As a result of being found "guilty" by the institution disciplinary board only, inmates may be confined in punitive segregation for a specified period. During this time, prisoners will be housed outside of their unit; following completion of the penalty, an inmate returns to the same unit. While in punitive segregation, the inmate remains on the caseload of his or her case manager and correctional counselor and will be visited by them.

Protective custody involves the long-term placement of a prisoner in a special environment where he or she is isolated from contact with other inmates. The decision to place an inmate into protective custody is made by the deputy warden for programs upon the recommendation of the inmate's unit classification committee.

Protective custody is a centralized program. It should have its own staff. The job descriptions of the institution's case management coordinator, chief psychologist, and records office chief should include responsibilities relating to the protective custody program. While in this program, inmates are no longer on their unit's caseload. Individuals in protective custody who are reinstated in the general population should be returned to their former unit, case manager, and counselor.

## Unit Prerelease/Release Programs

Every unit must offer its inmates an on-unit prerelease program. The program, which may be presented by either a case manager or joint case manager/correctional counselor, will be monitored by the unit manager.

The program will begin when an inmate is twelve months from a release date. It will include discussions about the release process; a sample checklist of the topics to be covered is located in the Appendix, page 184. Documentation of program participation will be maintained in a file by the unit secretary and a copy placed in the inmate's file folder.

While prerelease programs are common, release programs are not. A release program is concerned with the details of how a released inmate actually gets from the institution to his or her home, for example, how will the releasee get to the necessary public transportation?

When some prisoners are released at the completion of their sentence, they are picked up at the institution's sallyport by family and/or friends. On the last day that these inmates will be in the institution, their case manager should arrange a small in-unit "good-bye and good luck" ceremony; their correctional counselor can help make sure the releasee is all packed and ready to leave.

However, there are a number of to-be-released inmates for whom no one will come. In addition to the unit's "good-bye and good luck" ceremony, arrangements should be made for these individuals to be driven to the public transportation depot (bus, train, or plane) by their correctional counselor. The timing should be such that a small snack can be eaten together. The correctional counselor will gain considerable insight as to how releasees behave in a nonprison environment. Moreover, since the individual no longer will have to confront the pressure of living in a prison, very valuable information may be communicated as to what really goes on in the unit.

## Records Management

Inmate files contain all documents (or copies of documents) pertaining to the prisoner's background, court, and incarceration experiences. This confidential material should be maintained in a safe and secure setting (including computerized secure files); however, it also needs to be readily at hand for daily use by unit staff. Consequently, the unit manager (in collaboration with the chief of the records office and the unit secretary) needs to develop unit procedures for the following five areas:

(1) *Confidentiality.* An inmate's institutional file is confidential and should be handled in accordance with state and federal guidelines. Access to the file folder should be limited to properly authorized personnel having a demonstrated need to access it.

(2) *Security.* If files are computerized, there needs to be protection of access to them. If inmate files are not computerized, they should be stored in a fire-resistant cabinet located in a secure area in the unit secretary's office. Both the cabinet and the area will be kept locked when not in use. Under no circumstances should an inmate be permitted to be in this area.

(3) *Staff Access.* Access to an inmate's file, whether in hard copy or on computer, will be controlled by the unit manager and monitored by the unit secretary. A number of jurisdictions are changing (or have already completed converting) their records management process to include greater computerization. Thus, it involves not only data collection and storage, but also the day-to-day tasks of correspondence, storing individual inmate documents, and keeping all files current. As Federal Bureau of Prisons Regional Director Peter Carlson stated (December, 1998), "there still is a need for paper documentation." While some case managers input their own information directly into an inmate's file, others create paper documents which are given to unit secretaries to finish processing. Thus, while the increased use of computers has brought about some modifications in how inmate records are handled, the need for (and the basic functions of) unit secretaries has not changed in those units without complete computerization of inmate records. Availability, normally, is limited to the inmate's case manager, correctional counselor, and other staff members responsible for making custody, program, and work assignment decisions. A strict sign-out/sign-in should be established, which is monitored by the unit secretary.

(4) *File Maintenance.* The unit secretary is responsible for filing all material and keeping a unit inmate's record up to date. Training in, and periodic supervision of, this activity is the responsibility of the chief of the records office.

(5) *File Transfer.* When an inmate is transferred, the unit secretary is responsible for consolidating off-unit documents into the file. The complete file is then

signed over to the chief of the records office for transfer with the inmate. Files for released inmates will be archived in accord with department policy.

## Unit Management Reports

A systematic approach to evaluating unit management is necessary to determine whether its goals are being attained. Outcomes are analyzed with an eye towards refining current activities and programs so that overall effectiveness and efficiency are maximized.

One means of assessing unit programs and operations is by systematically collecting and evaluating demographic and statistical data. Valid conclusions can be drawn only if the information analyzed is both consistent and accurate. Data integrity is enhanced when those gathering it have a vested interest in learning about the results. Consequently, unit managers and their staff must become involved in the data collection process itself.

The gathering of consistent information is assured by having all units use the same monthly data reporting form. Combining the monthly reports from each unit provides the institution's administrators with a snapshot of the "state of the facility." It also offers unit managers a way to systematically monitor the operation of their unit. Monthly report results become an integral part of each unit's planning process. They are used to assess goal accomplishment, update the unit plan (*see* next section), and set future goals.

Each unit will collect, and report monthly on, information concerning its operation. This will consist of two types of material:

(1) numerical data regarding the unit's demographics, disciplinary reports, program enrollments/completions, and so forth

(2) text which describes accomplishments and problems that developed during the month and how they are being resolved, and progress made on previously reported problems

A standardized form will be used to report this information; *see* Appendix 1, pages 185-193. The completed form is due in the office of the deputy warden for programs within five working days from the end of the previous month. Submitting this report is the responsibility of the unit manager who may accomplish the task with assistance from other unit personnel.

# The Unit Plan

A unit plan contains specific information regarding the operation of a particular unit, especially, what makes the unit unique. Information which is standard for the department or the institution need not be addressed. Each unit develops its own unit plan, *see* Appendix 2 for an example. Writing this plan is the responsibility of the unit manager, with input from his or her staff. The completed unit plan is reviewed by the deputy warden for programs and approved by the warden. Subsequently, unit plans are updated, as needed, in order to remain current (at least once each year), and approved by the deputy warden for programs.

## Structure

Every unit has its own unit plan, which is a written document that describes how that unit will function. The plan reflects the goals and objectives of the unit and should be revised, as necessary.

The unit plan will be stored in the first division of a multipartitioned looseleaf binder. The binder is kept in an area easily accessible to the unit manager, who is responsible for its upkeep. Some parts in the binder will contain information which is not appropriate for release to inmates. However, sections I through IV of the unit plan should be written so that they can be disclosed to inmates and the interested public.

The binder is a six-part "working document" containing materials, which are necessary for the day-to-day operation of the unit. The information contained in the binder will help in strategic planning, monitoring unit operations, assessing levels of program success, and projecting the unit's future direction. Each six-part binder will contain the following:

(1) the unit plan (*see* next section, below)

(2) unit monthly/annual reports—previous unit monthly reports for the current year (the unit's annual report is attached to the prior twelve monthly reports and filed in the unit secretary's office)

(3) unit strategic plans (future architectural/program directions)

(4) memos from the unit manager (reverse chronological order)

(5) active correspondence not from the unit manager

(6) miscellaneous items

## Format

All unit plans will have seven sections, only I through IV of which are available to inmates: I - Unit Description, II - Unit Rules and Regulations, III - Programs and Services, IV - Unit Operations and Schedules, V - Unit Staffing, VI - Unit Emergency Plans, VII - Unit Records/Evaluation.

The following topical outline lists the essential components of a unit plan—all headings in boldface and *italics* must be included:

### Section I—Unit Description

A narrative describing what the unit looks like, its location and size, the type of inmates it houses, how it is staffed, and what it is attempting to accomplish.

A. *Unit Mission:* a paragraph which describes the purpose of the unit.

B. *Unit Objectives:* a list of statements of intent which, if accomplished, will indicate that the unit has fulfilled its mission, for example, if the unit houses a substance abuse program, one objective might be to "improve participants' self-esteem, as measured by an increase in the unit's inmate academic grade point average."

C. *Unit Description:*

1. Location (include a marked site plan)
2. Bed capacity and type (such as number of cells, dorms; single/double bunked)
3. Physical attributes (such as number of tiers, whether inside/outside cells/rooms; presence of corridor grilles/sallyports, recreation areas, and so forth)
4. Type of unit (such as general population, substance abuse, mental health, geriatric, AIMS category, and so forth)
5. Program approach (for example, in-unit programming philosophy/methods, such as a therapeutic community, and so forth)
6. Staffing pattern (titles, number of assigned staff; *see* Chart A, page 151)

## Section II—Unit Rules and Regulations

This section describes rules and regulations, with an emphasis on those unique to the unit. At a minimum, it will cover:

- room/cell assignment/changes (who makes them and documentation)
- inmate personal property (amount per inmate)
- wake-up/meals/counts/lights-out times (Sunday through Saturday schedule)
- laundry/barber shop/commissary (times, procedures)
- leisure-time/television/recreation (times, procedures)
- telephone calls/mail and packages (times, procedures)
- intra-unit visiting (times, procedures)
- quiet hours (times)

Facilities which have an Inmate Handbook that discusses important items, such as counts, clothing exchange, mail, commissary, family visiting, and so forth, need not repeat these in its unit plan; references should be listed (for example, *see* "Family Visiting in *Inmate Handbook*, page 99").

## Section III—Inmate Programs and Services

The unit plan should describe any of the following programs and services that differ from (or are not included among) the standard ones listed in the *Inmate Handbook*.

When a unit program is similar to the standard, the unit plan should just reference the *Inmate Handbook*. Additionally, for each program activity, the unit plan should describe who is responsible, when, and where the program is conducted, and so forth.

A. *Unit Admission and Orientation* (*see* page 169): The unit plan describes how this activity is accomplished; who is responsible for developing and delivering the program; when it occurs; how long it takes; the topics that are covered; the procedures in place to document each inmate's participation, and so forth.

B. *Health services* (includes medical, dental, mental health): When/where is sick-call/pill-line held? How are after-hours and/or emergency health services obtained?

C. *Classification* (includes reclassification/program reviews; *see* page 170): When and how often does this occur? Who initiates? Attends? Votes? How is documentation handled? What decisions/recommendations can the unit team make? To whom are recommendations sent and when are final results known? How is the inmate notified about results? How can an inmate appeal the results?

D. *Counseling* (individual and/or group): What in-unit counseling is conducted? How often are sessions held? Is the number of sessions limited or indefinite? How long are the sessions? Who leads these sessions? Is participation voluntary/involuntary?

E. *Self-help programs* (for example, aggression control, parenting): Describe what programs are conducted in the unit. How is the need for the program identified? Who conducts it? How often? What is the length of the sessions? What is the length of the program? What are the criteria for participation/completion?

F. *Grievance procedures*: How is the inmate informed about this program? How are forms obtained? What is/is not grievable? What are timeframes for a response? Are there further appeals?

G. *Visiting*: On what days? For how long? Any restrictions on the number of visits? How many visitors per inmate? Contact/noncontact visiting? Can family visit on unit? Are furloughs granted? If so, what are the criteria and procedures?

H. *Special events* (for example, unit picnic, awards ceremony): What special events does the unit conduct? How often? What is the criteria for participation?

I. *Prerelease/Release* (describe unit's prerelease and/or release program; *see* page 171): What is the criteria for admission? Who conducts the program?

J. *Other services*: Describe any unique contribution the unit makes to other programs/services, such as education/vocational training/prison industries, inmate organizations, library—legal/regular, religious services, and so forth.

## Section IV—Unit Operations and Schedules

All of the following items will be discussed in each unit's plan in terms of how the particular operation will function.

A. *Unit Safety and Sanitation*: Each unit manager will create and support a system which ensures that the highest levels of safety and sanitation are maintained in his or her unit. The activities of this operation will be described and will include:

- training provided to unit staff on how to recognize safety hazards, such as: electrical hazards, toxins, flammables, and unauthorized tools
- standards for unit sanitation—what they are and how (and by whom) compliance will be assessed
- unit sanitation supplies—requisition procedures and options available should problems develop
- a description of the duties of unit orderlies and how they will be selected, trained, paid, and supervised
- staff responsibilities for sanitation inspections, including who conducts them, when, how often, who receives inspection reports, and what follow-up occurs
- a description of the unit's recognition/reward program regarding sanitation

B. *Bed Assignment*: Each unit decides how its inmates will be assigned to a specific unit bed. The unit plan describes an allocation method that rewards positive behavior. Rather than seniority, assignment to favorable bed-space within the unit should be tied to tangible evidence of positive accomplishments (for example, no disciplinary reports, positive ratings on education and/or job assignment, and so forth.)

C. *Town Hall*: The key to a successful unit operation is communication. Staff need a mechanism for accurately informing inmates so that false rumors can be squelched; inmates need a way to bring to staff's attention unit-related problems and issues.

The unit manager should conduct a regularly scheduled (such as at least once a month, more frequent is better) town hall meeting attended by all unit staff and unit inmates. The unit plan should describe how this open forum to discuss unit issues and to share information will be accomplished, for example, when, where, and for how long the town hall will be scheduled, how its agenda will be developed, and how it will avoid becoming a gripe session.

D. *Inmate Council*: Many in corrections have problems with the idea of inmate councils, believing that they allow prisoners to develop a power base. Past difficulties of this nature were a consequence of poorly managed programs. Properly structured inmate councils avoid problems of this type and provide unit management with a very useful communications channel.

The unit plan should describe how an inmate council will operate, for example: criteria for election as a council member (such as no disciplinary report for past six months), length of council member's term (short, not to exceed three months), number of successive terms (two), role of the council ((i) meet weekly with unit staff, (ii) present issues, not plead own or another inmate's case, and (iii) help prepare agenda for town hall meeting).

E. *Unit Team Meeting* (*see* page 164): The unit manager will schedule a weekly team meeting at a time when ALL unit staff can attend; this should include unit correctional officer(s), if a relief arrangement can be set up. The purposes of this session are to (i) ensure that all unit personnel are informed about policy or procedure changes that may have been announced; (ii) provide staff with an opportunity to notify each other about unit operations and concerns pertaining to particular inmates; and, (iii) hear inmate concerns as expressed by the inmate council. The unit plan should describe how the team meeting will be conducted and how its objectives will be accomplished.

F. *Unit Disciplinary Panel*: Each unit will have a three-member unit disciplinary panel to handle minor disciplinary reports received by its inmates. In accord with the discussion on page 170, the unit plan describes the panel's operation, for example, where, when, and how often it will meet; who attends; how results are documented and communicated, and so forth.

G. *Staff Availability*: The unit plan will describe methods, which will ensure that personnel are accessible to inmates. For example, each staff member should post an "Open House" schedule.

H. *Unit Activities Schedule* (*see* Chart F): Each unit plan will contain a schedule of unit activities, which will be posted in a glass-enclosed bulletin board in the unit.

## Section V—Unit Staffing

A. *Lines of Authority*: The unit plan will contain schematics which show:

(i) the location of the unit manager in the institution's chain of command—*see* page 153

(ii) the unit's table of organization—*see* page 162

(iii) who does performance evaluations—*see* page 168

(iv) who approves annual leave—*see* page 166

B. *Positions and Roles*: Each unit will have its own full-time staff and designated part-time personnel. The unit plan will detail the number, type, and functions of each unit staff position; separate sections will be devoted to:

- unit manager—*see* page 153
- case managers—*see* page 157
- correctional counselors—*see* page 157

## Chart F: Unit Activities Schedule (example)

<table>
<tr><th>Time:</th><th>Sunday</th><th>Monday</th><th>Tuesday</th><th>Wednesday</th><th>Thursday</th><th>Friday</th><th>Saturday</th></tr>
<tr><td>6:30</td><td rowspan="3">Sleep In</td><td colspan="5">Early Morning Unit Activities</td><td rowspan="3">Sleep In</td></tr>
<tr><td>7:00</td><td colspan="5">Breakfast</td></tr>
<tr><td>7:30</td><td colspan="5">Free Time</td></tr>
<tr><td>8:00</td><td rowspan="2">Coffee Hour</td><td colspan="5" rowspan="8">Education & Vocational Training<br>Work Details<br>Industries</td><td rowspan="2">Breakfast</td></tr>
<tr><td>8:30</td></tr>
<tr><td>9:00</td><td rowspan="4">Protestant Church</td><td rowspan="6">House-keeping and Free Time</td></tr>
<tr><td>9:30</td></tr>
<tr><td>10:00</td></tr>
<tr><td>10:30</td></tr>
<tr><td>11:00</td><td rowspan="2">Brunch</td></tr>
<tr><td>11:30</td></tr>
<tr><td>12:00</td><td rowspan="2">Catholic Mass</td><td colspan="6" rowspan="2">Noon Meal</td></tr>
<tr><td>12:30</td></tr>
<tr><td>1:00</td><td rowspan="8">Religious Life School/ Gym or Outside Recreation</td><td colspan="5" rowspan="7">Education & Vocational Training<br>Work Details<br>Industries</td><td rowspan="5">Individual Counseling and Chores</td></tr>
<tr><td>1:30</td></tr>
<tr><td>2:00</td></tr>
<tr><td>2:30</td></tr>
<tr><td>3:00</td></tr>
<tr><td>3:30</td><td rowspan="3">Recreation and Gym</td></tr>
<tr><td>4:00</td></tr>
<tr><td>4:30</td><td colspan="5">Commissary</td></tr>
<tr><td>5:00</td><td colspan="7" rowspan="2">Evening Meal</td></tr>
<tr><td>5:30</td></tr>
<tr><td>6:00</td><td rowspan="7">Free Time</td><td rowspan="3">Group/ Individual Counseling</td><td rowspan="5">Individual Counseling</td><td rowspan="5">Group/ Individual Counseling</td><td rowspan="5">Team Meeting/ Unit Council</td><td rowspan="2">Hobby Shop</td><td rowspan="4">Free Time</td></tr>
<tr><td>6:30</td></tr>
<tr><td>7:00</td><td rowspan="5">Group/ Individual Counseling</td></tr>
<tr><td>7:30</td><td rowspan="4">Leisure Time Tournament</td></tr>
<tr><td>8:00</td><td rowspan="3">Movie</td></tr>
<tr><td>8:30</td><td rowspan="2">Group Prerelease</td><td rowspan="2">Leisure Activity</td><td rowspan="2">Town Hall</td></tr>
<tr><td>9:00</td></tr>
</table>

- unit secretary—*see* page 159
- correctional officer(s)—*see* page 159
- other assigned staff—*see* page 160

C. *Work Schedule*: The unit plan will display the work schedule for all full-time personnel; *see* page 165. It will also indicate the on-unit duty hours of all part-time personnel assigned to the unit.

## Section VI—Unit Emergency Plans

This section describes the unit's plans for dealing with rare, but often life-threatening situations, such as: fire, natural disasters, inmate escapes, homicide, suicide, disturbance control, and hostage situations.

A. *Unit Fire Escape Plan and Fire Drills*: This section includes a schematic of the unit's fire escape plan. It also requires the conspicuous posting in a glass-enclosed case of such escape-route schematics on each floor/section/tier of the unit.

The plan will discuss the frequency with which fire drills are to be held (at least one on each shift annually; in other words, a minimum of three) and the responsibilities of unit staff members on such occasions. All unit fire equipment will be visually checked during fire drills. A report of each fire drill will be maintained and a copy forwarded to the institution's safety manager.

B. *Escape/Disturbance Control*: This section describes the role of unit staff members when there is an emergency involving an inmate disturbance or escape.

C. *Homicide/Suicide*: This section contains a description of unit staff responsibilities when an emergency situation arises concerning an inmate homicide and/or suicide attempt. In regard to the latter, the plan should describe the role unit staff play in the facility's suicide prevention program.

## Section VII—Unit Evaluation/Research

A. *Evaluation*: This section of the unit plan describes the process by which data for each unit's monthly report will be:

- gathered (who collects what from where, how often, deadlines)
- entered onto the department's unit monthly report form—*see* Appendix pages 185-193—(who is responsible, and deadlines)
- where is each unit's monthly report sent? filed?
- by what deadline?

[*See also* discussion on page 173.]

B. *Research*: Staff members from the unit/facility may become involved in research projects that involve unit inmates. The unit plan should address this issue in terms of how such a project will be conducted. These plans should comply with the department's policy on research.

# Appendix

# Staff Orientation Agenda (example)

## Unit Staff Orientation Checklist

_____ Staff introductions
_____ Unit tour
_____ Position description/performance standards/rating process
_____ Hours/days of work; work schedule rotation, if any
_____ Unit annual leave schedule

_____ Unit sick-leave (who and when to contact if ill)
_____ Specific unit job expectations
_____ Roles of other unit/nonunit staff
_____ Unit plan (location, access, review)
_____ Unit rules and regulations

_____ Unit officers' log, bed/cell and unit inmate locator systems
_____ Inmate files (location, checkout system, security procedures)
_____ Copying equipment (location, information that can/cannot be copied)
_____ Unit team meetings (days, times, staff attending, purposes)
_____ Unit program activities/schedule

_____ Department policy/facility procedure statements (location, access)
_____ Unit inmate admission/orientation responsibilities
_____ Safety and sanitation role/expectations
_____ Unit staff security responsibilities
_____ Unit disciplinary panel

_____ Unit staff visibility in unit/institution
_____ Fire safety/evacuation procedures
_____ Role in orienting volunteers/interns/students, if applicable
_____ Inmate grievance procedures
_____ Data entry responsibilities/procedures

_____ Correspondence (drafts, reviews, approvals)
_____ Role on unit classification committee
_____ Role in intra- and interunit communications
_____ Release of information regulations
_____ Definitions of department "jargon" (for example, seg., shots, J & C)

| STAFF MEMBER'S SIGNATURE | DATE | UNIT MANAGER'S SIGNATURE |
|---|---|---|

# Inmate Orientation Agenda Checklist (example)

____________________ ______________

INMATE'S NAME REGISTER #

## Unit Manager

Security/Safety/Sanitation
Rights and Responsibilities
Unit Mission and Programs
Unit Organization and Staff Roles

DATE

STAFF SIGNATURE

---

## Case Manager

Sentence/Detainer Data/Custody/Security Levels
Programs—Education/Vocational Technical/Prison Industries/Recreation
Unit Disciplinary Panel/Institution Disciplinary Board
Classification and Program Reviews
In-unit Activities Schedule—Counseling/Therapy
Law Library/Grievance Procedures
Prerelease and Release Programs

DATE

STAFF SIGNATURE

---

## Correctional Counselor

Personal Appearance/Barbershop/Personal Property
Medical Services/Religious Services/Recreation
Work Assignments/Inmate Pay
Counseling/Problem Solving/Grievance Procedures
Commissary/Withdrawal of Funds
Mail/Visiting/Telephone Regulations
Town Hall/Inmate Council/Unit Bulletin Board

DATE

STAFF SIGNATURE

---

## Unit Officer

Counts/Searches/Accountability
Pass System/Controlled Movement
Fire Escape Procedures/Smoking Rules
Wake-up/Lights Out
Laundry/Clothing Exchange
Unit Orderlies/Sanitation Inspections
Within-/Between-unit Visiting

DATE

STAFF SIGNATURE

---

*I have been oriented in all the areas listed above and have had an opportunity to discuss them with unit staff.*

INMATE'S SIGNATURE / DATE

PROGRAM COORDINATOR'S SIGNATURE

# Inmate Prerelease Program Checklist (example)

______________________________ ________________

INMATE'S NAME REGISTER #

## Topics Discussed:

STAFF SIGNATURE / DATE

Release Destination ______________________________

Relocation (pros and cons) ______________________________

Release Plans: ______________________________

_____ Residence ______________________________

_____ Aftercare/Conditions of Supervision ______________________________

_____ Education/Vocational Technical Skills Documentation ______________________________

_____ Employment ______________________________

Personal Funds ______________________________

Disposition of Personal Property ______________________________

Disposition of Inmate Funds ______________________________

Release to Detainer ______________________________

Release Planning: ______________________________

_____ Gratuity ______________________________

_____ Clothing ______________________________

_____ Transportation ______________________________

_____ Personal Identification ______________________________

*I have been oriented in all the areas listed above and have had an opportunity to discuss them with unit staff.*

______________________________

INMATE'S SIGNATURE / DATE

______________________________

PROGRAM COORDINATOR'S SIGNATURE

# Unit Management—Monthly Report:

Facility________________________________

__________/______
Month / Year

Unit ________________

[ submit report within five working days from end of prior month. ]

## 1. In-unit population:

a. Number of inmates at 12:01 A.M. (first day of month) . . . . . . . . . . . . ______

b. Admissions to unit during month

(1) New commitments . . . . . . . . . . . . . . . . . . . . . . . ______

(2) Parole violator . . . . . . . . . . . . . . . . . . . . . . . . . . ______

(3) Others (specify__________________________) ______

(4) Total admissions to unit during month . . . . . . . . . . . . . . . . . . . ______

c. Transfers from unit during month

(1) Sent to less secure department facilities . . . . . . . ______

(2) Sent to more secure department facilities . . . . . . ______

(3) Total transfers within department for month . . . . . . . . . . . . . . . ______

d. Discharges from unit during month

(1) Number of inmates paroled . . . . . . . . . . . . . . . . ______

(2) Number of expired sentences . . . . . . . . . . . . . . . ______

(3) Number released to halfway house. . . . . . . . . . . ______

(4) Number released to other jurisdictions . . . . . . . . ______

(5) Total discharged from unit for month . . . . . . . . . . . . . . . . . . . . ______

e. Number of inmates at 11:59 P.M. (last day of month) . . . . . . . . . . . . . ______

## 2. Custody levels by race (number of inmates on last day of month):

| | Black | Hispanic | Native American | White | Other | Totals |
|---|---|---|---|---|---|---|
| Seven | | | | | | |
| Six | | | | | | |
| Five | | | | | | |
| Four | | | | | | |
| Three | | | | | | |
| Two | | | | | | |
| One | | | | | | |
| Totals | | | | | | |

## 3. Program activities:

a. Number of unit staff meetings (minutes required) during month . . . . ______

b. Number of town hall meetings during month. . . . . . . . . . . . . . . . . . . ______

c. Classification

(1) Number of initial classifications during month . . . . . . . . . . . . . ______

(2) Number of inmates seen for reclassification/program reviews during month . . . . . . . . . . . . . . . . . . . . . . . . . . . . . . . . . . . . . . . ______

(3) Number of parole hearings conducted during month . . . . . . . . . ______

d. Education

(1) Number of inmates currently enrolled first day of month. . . . . . ______

(2) Number of new enrollments during month. . . . . . . . . . . . . . . . . ______

(3) Number of GEDs completed during month . . . . . . . . . . . . . . . . ______

(4) Number of inmates dropped during month. . . . . . . . . . . . . . . . . ______

(5) Number of inmates currently enrolled last day of month . . . . . . ______

e. Inmate job assignments

(1) Number working in industry jobs on first day of month. . . . . . . ______

(2) Number working in industry jobs on  last day of month. . . . . . . ______

(3) Number in paid nonindustry jobs on first day of month . . . . . . . ______

(4) Number in paid nonindustry jobs on last day of month . . . . . . . ______

(5) Number on nonpaid work details first day of month . . . . . . . . . ______

(6) Number on nonpaid work details on last day of month . . . . . . . ______

(7) Number of unassigned inmates on first day of month . . . . . . . . ______

(8) Number of unassigned inmates on last day of month. . . . . . . . . ______

(9) Percent idleness (_____________/___________) . . . . . . . . . . . _____%
[the number from line 3.e.8 divided by line 1.e]

f. Counseling (scheduled, formal, in-unit sessions)

(1) Number of group sessions held during the month . . . . . . . . . . . ______

(2) Number of individual sessions held during the month . . . . . . . . ______

(3) Number of inmates enrolled on first day of the month. . . . . . . . ______

(4) Number of inmates enrolled on last day of the month . . . . . . . . ______

(5) Number of hours reported during the month . . . . . . . . . . . . . . . ______

g. Furloughs (at least one night away from facility)

(1) Number of total furlough requests submitted during the month. . ______

(2) Work training—number approved . . . . . . . . . . . . . . . . . . . . . . ______

(3) Resocialization—number approved . . . . . . . . . . . . . . . . . . . . . . ______

(4) Total number of furloughs approved during the month. . . . . . . . ______

## 4. Discipline (include only "guilty" findings):

a. Disciplinary reports

(1) Number of major reports during the month . . . . . . . . . . . . . . . . ______

(2) Number of minor reports during the month . . . . . . . . . . . . . . . . ______

(3) Number of inmates receiving major reports during the month . . ______

(4) Number of inmates receiving minor reports during the month . . ______

(5) Percent of major disciplinary reports (________/________) . . . _____%
[the number from line 4.a.3 divided by the number on line 1.e]

B. Segregation

(1) Number of inmates placed in punitive segregation during the month______

(2) Total number of days in punitive segregation during the month . . ______

C. Protective custody

(1) Number of inmates from unit in protective custody on first day of the month. . . . . . . . . . . . . . . . . . . . . . . . . . . . . . . . . . . . . . . ______

(2) Number of inmates placed in protective custody during the month ______

(3) Number of inmates returned to unit from protective custody during the month . . . . . . . . . . . . . . . . . . . . . . . . . . . . . . . . . ______

(4) Number of inmates from unit currently in protective custody on last day of the month. . . . . . . . . . . . . . . . . . . . . . . . . . . . . . ______

D. Grievances

(1) Total number submitted during the past month. . . . . . . . . . . . . . ______

(2) Number resolved informally (in unit). . . . . . . . . . . . . . . . . . . . . ______

(3) Number of inmates filing at least one during the month . . . . . . . ______

5. Positive accomplishments during the month:

6. New problems occurring during the month:

7. Progress made on previously mentioned problems:

8. Other:

# Instructions for Completing Monthly Report

(Form itself is on page 185)

Heading: Enter month and year for which report is being completed.
Enter facility name and unit name.

## 1. In-unit population:

a. Enter number of inmates on unit's count at 12:01 A.M. (first day of past month).

b.1. Enter number of new admissions to unit during past month.

b.2. Enter number of parole violators admitted to unit during past month.

b.3. Write in other type admissions during past month and enter their number.

b.4. Add (b.1) + (b.2) + (b.3) and enter total number of unit admissions.

c.1. Enter number of inmate transfers from unit to less secure facilities.

c.2. Enter number of unit inmates transferred to more secure department facilities.

c.3. Add (c.1) + (c.2) and enter total number of unit transfers.

d.1. Enter number of paroled inmates discharged from unit during month.

d.2. Enter number of inmates released at expiration of sentence.

d.3. Enter number of inmates released to halfway house during past month.

d.4. Enter number of inmates released to other jurisdictions (for example, to a detainer).

d.5. Add (d.1) + (d.2) + (d.3) + (d.4) and enter total number of unit discharges.

e. Enter number of inmates on unit's count at 11:59 P.M. (last day of past month).

## 2. Custody levels by race (chart):

First: Place one number in each cell of the chart, for example, first row, first column (in other words, custody level seven, race black). The number reflects how many black inmates with custody level seven were in the unit on the last day of the past month. In all, thirty-five (35) numbers should be entered into the chart's cells.

Second: For each of the seven (7) rows, add across and enter the total of the five numbers in the last column on the right.

Third: For each of the five (5) columns add down and enter the total of the seven numbers in the bottom row [total should equal second step total].

## 3. Program activities:

a. Enter number of unit staff meetings held during the past month.

b. Enter number of town hall meetings held during the past month.

c.1. Enter number of initial classification meetings held during the past month.

c.2. Enter number of inmates seen during the past month for reclassification/program reviews.

c.3. Enter number of parole hearings conducted during the past month.

d.1. Enter number of inmates enrolled in education on the first day of the past month.

d.2. Enter number of new enrollments in education during the past month.

d.3. Enter number of GEDs completed during the the past month.

d.4. Enter number of inmates dropped from education during the past month.

d.5. Enter number of inmates enrolled in education on the last day of the past month.

e.1. Enter number inmates on industry job assignments on the first day of the past month.

e.2. Enter number of inmates working in industry on the last day of the past month.

e.3. Enter number of inmates in paid nonindustry jobs on the first day of the past month.

e.4. Enter number of inmates in paid nonindustry jobs on the last day of the past month.

e.5. Enter number of inmates on nonpaid work details on the first day of the past month.

e.6. Enter number of inmates on nonpaid work details on the last day of the past month.

e.7. Enter number of unassigned inmates on the first day of the past month.

e.8. Enter number of unassigned inmates on the last day of the past month. [sum of lines 3.e.2 + 3.e.4. + 3.e.6 + 3.e.8 should equal line 1.e (last line page 1, above)]

e.9. For percent idleness:

- first, enter the number from line 3.e.8 (immediately above)
- second, enter the number from line 1.e (last line page 1, above)

- finally, divide the first number by the second number and enter the quotient (answer).

f.1. Enter number of group counseling sessions held during the past month.

f.2 Enter number of individual counseling sessions held during the past month.

f.3 Enter number of inmates enrolled in counseling on the first day of the month.

f.4. Enter number of inmates dropped from counseling during the past month.

f.5. Enter number of inmates enrolled in counseling on the last day of the month.

f.6. Enter total number of hours of counseling conducted during the past month.

g.1. Enter number of furloughs (at least one night away from facility) requested.

g.2. Enter number of work training furloughs approved during the past month.

g.3. Enter number of resocialization furloughs approved during the past month.

g.4. Add (g.2) + (g.3) and enter total number of furloughs approved during the month.

## 4. Discipline (include only "guilty" findings):

a.1. Enter number of major disciplinary reports inmates received during past month.

a.2. Enter number of minor disciplinary reports unit inmates received during month.

a.3. Enter number of inmates who received major disciplinary reports during month.

a.4. Enter number of inmates who received minor disciplinary reports during month.

a.5. For percent major disciplinary:

- first, enter the number from line 4.a.3 (above)
- second, enter the number from line 1.e (last line page 1, above)
- last, divide the first number by the second number and enter quotient (answer).

b.1. Enter number of unit inmates placed in punitive segregation during past month.

b.2. Enter total number of days unit's inmates spent in punitive segregation during month.

c.1. Enter number of inmates from unit who are in protective custody on first day of month.

c.2. Enter number of inmates placed in protective custody during past month.

c.3. Enter number of inmates returned to unit from protective custody during month.

c.4. Enter number of inmates from unit who are in protective custody on last day of month.

d.1. Enter total number of grievances submitted by unit inmates during past month.

d.2. Enter number of grievances resolved informally (in unit) during past month.

d.3. Enter number of inmates who filed at least one grievance during past month.

## Note:

- A comment is required every month in sections 5, 6, and 7. This will enable unit and administrative staff to track significant developing trends.

## 5. Narrative

- Write a brief narrative about the unit's positive accomplishments during the past month.

## 6. Problems

- Briefly discuss new problems that have arisen in the unit during the past month.

## 7. Progress

- Write a separate paragraph on each of the "problems" mentioned in section 6 of last month's report that indicates the amount of progress achieved.

## 8. Report

- Report on any other topics; for example, unit's upcoming special events or plans being made for same.

## Note:

- The unit count (item 1.e) should be the same as the custody levels by race overall total (item 2—right totals column and bottom totals row).
- Last month's unit count easily should convert into this month's unit count (item 1.e) after adding admissions (item 1.b.4) and subtracting transfers (item 1.c.3) and discharges (item 1.d.5).
- In other words, the unit's statistics must have integrity and show mathematical continuity from month to month.

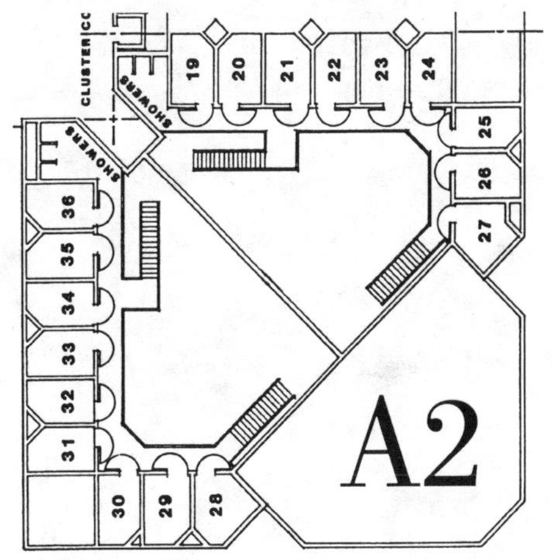


# Appendix 2

*South Dakota Department of Corrections*

## Sample Unit Plan

Ludeman Hall
Springfield State Prison

with additional commentary by
Robert B. Levinson, Ph.D.

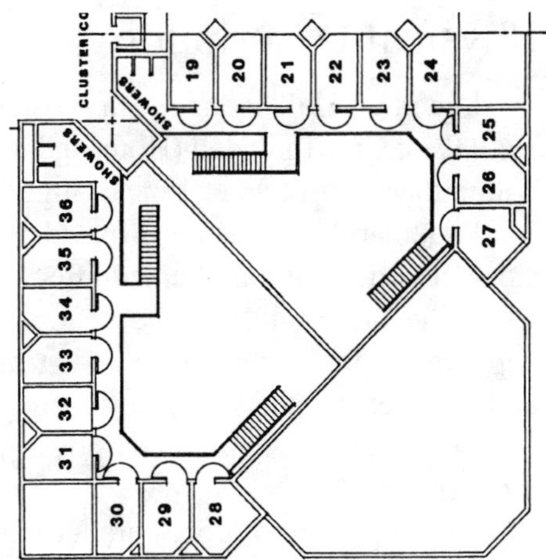


# Appendix 2

*This is an excellent unit plan and could serve as a model for other systems. Although an effort was made to note the positive aspects of Ludeman Hall's unit plan, in a critique of this nature the tendency is to focus on areas that need further work. This makes the overall comments sound much more negative than intended. The following comments should be read with this caveat in mind.—RBL*

## Section I: Ludeman Unit Description

### Mission/Purpose

The mission of Ludeman Hall at Springfield State Prison in South Dakota is the custody and care of its inmates. The goal of Ludeman Hall is to assist inmates and to provide incentives for prisoners to achieve the facility's goal of teaching inmates marketable job skills, along with job-seeking and job-keeping skills, in an effort to help each prisoner return to society with a realistic potential to become a responsible, self-reliant and tax-paying citizen.

### Unit Objectives

In addition to housing "typical" inmates, the Second Floor South of Ludeman Hall houses a therapeutic community. That program is designed to treat inmates with identified substance abuse problems, teach acceptance of the problem, and develop methods for dealing with these problems. Statistical data on this program is maintained by the Chemical Dependency Department.

***Comment***: Unit objectives need to mention how success in meeting these objectives will be measured.

## Physical Description—Location/Capacity/Attributes/Type

Ludeman Hall is among a cluster of buildings—Harmon Hall, East Crawford Hall, West Crawford Hall (Housing Units), and Montgomery Center (Food Service)—within the inner perimeter of Springfield State Prison.

Ludeman Hall was constructed as a university dormitory in 1962. It is a three-story masonry building named after Walter Ludeman, a former president of the college. The prison utilizes the south side of the first floor for its medical services department, which includes nursing offices, medical examination rooms, and dental and optometric clinics. The north side of the first floor has ten rooms for general population inmates—eight rooms house two inmates each and two rooms house four inmates each.

Unit supervisory offices are located between the two wings, as are a weight room and a laundry room used by building residents. The south side of the second floor serves as housing for male inmates in the Chemical Dependency Department's Therapeutic Community Program. It has nine rooms—eight housing two inmates each and one housing four inmates—plus a lounge/meeting room for Alcoholics Anonymous, Narcotics Anonymous, Gamblers Anonymous, and similar group activities. The north side of the second floor has nine two-person rooms and two four-person rooms for general population inmates.

The third floor has 20 rooms—16 house two inmates each and four house four inmates each. The total building capacity is 122 inmates. A day hall between the second floor wings has two pool tables for inmate recreation. A day hall between the third floor wings has card tables, a television viewing area and a concession stand. A desk area and a private office adjacent to the second floor day hall serve as a central activity site for correctional officers assigned to the unit team.

***Comment***: Physical description is very good; however, figures add up to 118 not 122 inmates.

## Physical Description—Program Approach

A forty-five- to sixty-minute general orientation session is held for each newly arriving group of inmates the day they enter Springfield Correctional Facility. The session includes an overview of Springfield State Prison and Ludeman Hall, discussion about classification and disciplinary procedures, introduction to supervisors with an outline of the primary responsibilities of each, and other topics that develop from questions. Each new arrival acknowledges participating in the session by signing a form. The case manager or the correctional counselor then conducts a brief, private interview with each new arrival to develop a program plan for the inmate.

In addition, two inmate residents also meet with new arrivals during their first evening in Ludeman Hall. Basically, the same prescribed topics are discussed, but from the inmate point of view. The pair of presenters are selected on the basis of longevity in Ludeman Hall, and their records of behavior and accomplishment.

Individual counseling is provided through the correctional counselor, with assistance from the case manager. The unit conducts its own Alcoholics Anonymous meeting each Wednesday evening and its own Gamblers Anonymous meeting every other

Tuesday evening, while the case manager holds a general topic, on-unit group session each Thursday afternoon.

Several inmates serve on the Ludeman Committee, an inmate organization which elects its own officers to stage recreational activities, such as card and pool tournaments, and operates a concession stand. Profits from Ludeman Committee activities are used for equipment and events to improve life for building residents. For example, much of the weight room equipment was purchased by the Ludeman Committee.

At present, Ludeman Hall houses inmates from all AIMS categories. About 25 percent of the residents are primarily involved in alcohol/drug treatment programs at any given time. About 60 percent are vocational students, while the remainder are assigned as members of the facility's work force.

The general philosophy which has been engendered in Ludeman Hall since unit management was introduced to Springfield Correctional Facility in February, 1991, and has centered around self-discipline, self-help, and self-responsibility. Residents, whose ages range from 16 to 73, are categorized by personal, educational, intellectual, and criminal history. A program plan is then developed in cooperation with the resident. The program plan first encourages residents to acknowledge their deficiencies and past failures and, secondly, to overcome them through participation in treatment and educational programs.

Toward that end, supervisory efforts tend toward guiding and teaching residents as opposed to babysitting them. All emphasis is placed upon demonstrating that success comes through goal setting, accepting responsibility for one's actions, hard work, a positive attitude, honesty, and community concern in the sense of unit involvement. Supervisory goals include teaching the strong that it is not right to exploit the weak, and teaching the weak how to successfully co-exist with the strong.

To this end, disciplinary action is consistent and firm. Residents quickly learn they cannot short-cut the system, nor the staff. They are treated as adults, with respect given as it is shown. They are made to look in the mirror, to see themselves as being responsible for their current situation, and assisted in finding a pathway which will lead them from prison existence to a productive life. Once on the pathway, they are encouraged, pushed, prodded, rewarded—whatever it takes; however, they are made to walk the pathway themselves.

***Comments:*** Program—Excellent! Who selects inmate orientors? How are inmates for Ludeman Committee selected? What role does unit staff play? Are there any plans for differential housing by AIMS category? Specify who develops program plan with inmate (should be case manager).This is very well done; among the best explanations I've read in a unit plan.

# Section II: Ludeman Unit Rules/Regulations

## Addressing Staff

A. Correctional officers must be addressed as Officer Jones, Mr. Jones, or Ms. Smith unless the inmate has prior permission from the officer to address him or her by his or her first name. Unit supervisors must be addressed as Mr. or

Ms. unless the inmate has prior permission to address him or her by his or her first name.

***Comment***: QUESTION: Shouldn't all inmates address all staff in the same way?

B. All staff members must be addressed in a courteous and respectful manner.

## Appeals/Classification/Grievances

A. Disciplinary decisions

1. Major and minor disciplinary decisions are board decisions that may be appealed to the CEO.
2. Inmates may appeal CEO decisions to the secretary of corrections.
3. Contact the correctional counselor for specific information.

***Comment***: Are any disciplinary decisions made by unit staff; for example, minor reports?

B. Classification decisions

1. Classification decisions may be appealed to the secretary of corrections.
2. Contact the correctional counselor for specific information.

C. Grievances

1. A grievance is a complaint against the substance or application of a written or unwritten Springfield State Prison policy or rule, or against an act or policy which an inmate believes violates higher personal and/or constitutional standards.
2. Any deviation in following the grievance procedure will result in grievance termination.
3. Submit a completed grievance form to the case manager.
   a. The case manager will attempt to informally resolve the grievance.
      (1) If the issue is resolved to the inmate's satisfaction, the grievance will be stopped at this stage.
      (2) If the issue is not resolved to the inmate's satisfaction, the grievance will be forwarded to the Springfield State Prison grievance board.
4. The inmate may appeal the grievance board's decision to the CEO.
5. The inmate may appeal the CEO's decision to the secretary of corrections.
6. Contact the case manager for specific information.

***Comment:*** There is no such thing as an unwritten policy or rule; if it is not written it does not exist. Specify where an inmate can get a grievance form (should be from the correctional counselor). Who sits on the Springfield State Prison grievance board? Is there representation from the inmate's unit?

## Cable Television

A. Each room is equipped with a cable television outlet to provide free cable services to the occupants.

B. Only one television may be connected to the cable outlet in each room.

***Comment:*** How it is determined which inmate's TV will be attached to the single cable TV outlet? How are program choices made? This has implications for AIMS-compatible room assignments.

C. Any resident who attempts to connect more than one television to a cable outlet, or otherwise tampers with a cable outlet, will be subject to disciplinary action.

D. Cable transmission/reception problems should be reported to a staff member for repair.

## Class Change Requests

A. Inmates requesting a change in schedule must complete a class change request.

1. Class change requests must be submitted to the case manager.

2. Class change requests are reviewed by the programs classification board.

***Comment:*** Specify who sits on programs classification board. This should be a function of the unit classification board.

3. The Programs classification board normally meets on Thursday.

***Comment:*** Does inmate appear in person before the program classification board? He should.

4. Inmates will be notified of the board's decision.

***Comment:*** How soon after the program classification board is the inmate notified? Is this documented?

5. If there are changes, inmates will be given a new schedule that takes effect on the following Monday.

6. Class changes within a department may be made by the department supervisor.

***Comment:*** The department supervisor should notify, in writing, that inmate has had a class change.

## Cleanliness and Grooming

A. Hair

1. Hair must be kept clean and neat. It must be restrained when an inmate is working in food service or the vocational shops.

2. A unit barbershop is located on Second Floor South.

    a. A professional barber generally is available on the unit on the first Monday of each month. A sign-up sheet is available at the barbershop door.

    b. An inmate barber generally is available on the unit. A schedule and sign-up sheet is available at the security desk.

***Comment:*** Specify who monitors unit barbershop sign-up list; should be a correctional officer.

## Clothing - Personal

A. Approved personal clothing is allowed.

B. Clothing must be sent in new and in the original container. The sales receipt must accompany the item. It may be sent via the U.S. Mail or a United Parcel Service-type carrier.

C. Refer to the Inmate Living Guide for a complete listing of allowed personal property items.

D. Altering personal or state clothing or property is not allowed. Persons who alter clothing are subject to disciplinary action.

## Clothing - State

A. Refer to the Inmate Living Guide for a complete listing of state-issued clothing.

B. All clothing, bedding, and linen issued to an inmate shall be the responsibility of the individual inmate, and that inmate shall be held accountable for its use and condition.

## Commissary

A. Procedures

1. Commissary day for Ludeman Hall residents is Thursday.

***Comment:*** Specify how inmate obtains commissary slip.

2. If there is a holiday on the scheduled commissary day, a notice will be posted to reflect any changes in the commissary schedule for that week.

3. Turn in both the white and pink copies of the commissary slips along with the laundry. Changes will be allowed on commissary orders, however, inmates must proceed to the end of the commissary line.

4. Remember to bring something in which to carry purchases.

5. Before leaving, check the bag to ensure all articles ordered are there. If there is a mistake, bring it to the attention of the commissary supervisor immediately.

6. Make-up day for commissary/laundry will be on Friday. No alternate day will be used. There will be no make-up day during weeks in which there is a state holiday. Commissary make-up day will be used only under the following guidelines:

   a. The inmate is off the facility grounds during regular commissary day and assigned time; for example, at a doctor's appointment.

   b. The inmate is making a unit-to-unit move and cannot make the regular commissary date of either unit.

***Comment:*** Why would an inmate make a "unit-to-unit move"? Should not occur except in very extraordinary circumstances which includes a detailed process which is documented.

   c. The inmate is confined in detention and has not attended commissary during that week.

   d. The inmate has had no funds in his spending account for at least two consecutive weeks and, during the third week, receives funds after the regular unit commissary day.

   e. The inmate is on the "frozen list" in excess of two consecutive weeks and, during the third week, receives funds after the regular unit commissary day.

***Comment:*** What is the "frozen list"? How does an inmate get placed on this list?

   f. The unit manager must approve make-up day in advance and deliver commissary slips to the commissary officer no later than 7 A.M. on Friday.

7. No inmate with spending overdrafts will be permitted to obtain commissary.

8. Inmates will be allowed to reduce their commissary list when the list cost exceeds the spending account limit. Inmates are required to go to the back of the commissary line after recalculating their commissary list.

9. Inmates are not allowed to attend commissary more than once per week.

## Committee Sales

A. Ludeman Committee Sales. The Ludeman Committee has been authorized to sell food items at posted times. Profits are placed in the Committee account and are used for housing improvements for Ludeman residents.

B. Various Committee Sales. Various organizations are permitted sales on a monthly basis. Representatives from the organizations will be available at designated times in the day hall for orders.

***Comment***: Need to explain how Ludeman Committee members are selected.

## Counts

A. Count times are posted on the bulletin board and are as follows:

***Comment*:** Specify who conducts counts; it should be a correctional officer.

1. Weekdays:

| | | | |
|---|---|---|---|
| 1st count | 7:15 AM | 3rd count | 5:00 PM |
| 2nd count | 11:40 AM | 4th count | 8:45 PM |

(Above counts are standing counts)

| | | | |
|---|---|---|---|
| 5th count | 10:30 PM | 7th count | 4:00 AM |
| 6th count | 12:30 AM | | |

(Above counts are nonstanding formal counts)

2. Weekends and Holidays:

| | | | |
|---|---|---|---|
| 1st count | 9:30 AM | 3rd count | 8:45 PM |
| 2nd count | 4:15 PM | | |

(Above counts are standing counts)

| | | | |
|---|---|---|---|
| 4th count | 10:30 PM | 6th count | 4:00 AM |
| 5th count | 12:30 AM | | |

(Above counts are nonstanding formal counts)

3. Informal counts are taken at random times throughout each day.

4. Gate counts are taken at all open recreation and program activity periods.

5. Disruption of any count is a rule violation.

B. Standing Count—Requirements

1. These are mandatory regulations. Disrupting a count in any way will not be tolerated. Those who disrupt a count will be subject to disciplinary action.

2. The inmate is required to stand outside his assigned room beneath his name tag.

3. The inmate's I.D. tag must be displayed where it is clearly visible.

4. The staff member conducting a count may ask for verbal identification.

5. All questions must be responded to; otherwise inmates are silent.

6. Radios, stereos, and televisions will be turned off during count.

7. Appropriate attire is required; inmates must be dressed from at least the waist down and be wearing shoes or slippers.

8. Inmates are required to remain in their assigned rooms with the doors closed until the count is cleared.

# Curfew

A. Curfew is at 10:30 P.M. seven days per week. The only reason a resident may leave his room between 10:30 P.M. and 6:00 A.M. is to use the restroom (no showering). Exceptions are made for kitchen workers, who may shower one-half hour before they are to report to work, and for unit work parties.

B. A resident who has a medical emergency between 10:30 P.M. and 6:00 A.M. should report to the security desk. If the fire alarm sounds, exit the building according to procedures.

## Daily Program Bulletin

A. A daily program bulletin is published every Friday showing the times for all activities during the following week. It is posted on the bulletin board. Activities may include: religious services, Alcoholics Anonymous/Narcotics Anonymous meetings, organization meetings, visits, and special events.

***Comment***: Daily program bulletin - an excellent idea!

## Day Hall Hours

A. The Ludeman Hall day hall hours are 6:00 A.M. to 10:30 P.M.

B. Walkman radios/tape players with headphones are allowed in the day hall.

C. No sleeping clothes are allowed in the day hall.

D. Shoes and appropriate attire must be worn.

## Dental Services

A. A request slip must be submitted addressed "Dentist." Reasons for the appointment must be stated on the request. Notification will be given concerning appointment times.

***Comment***: Specify how inmate gets dental request slip.

## Disciplinary Sanctions

A. Major Rule Violations

   1. *See* Inmate Living Guide

B. Minor Rule Violations

   1. *See* Inmate Living Guide

   2. Loss of recreation privileges

      a. Any inmate who has been assigned to loss of recreation may leave his room only to participate in the following activities:

         (1) Classes/graduation/work. Inmates may not work as referees, timers or in unit/recreation concession stands.

         (2) Group counseling/one-on-one sessions/AVP
         ***Comment***: Spell out what AVP stands for.

         (3) Laundry/commissary/packages, including downtown orders, consulting with property sergeant, placing property orders, etc.

         (4) Showers/restroom

         (5) Regular visits

         (6) Staff-initiated passes only. Including job service, copies, and unit passes.

         (7) Regularly scheduled church services/pipe ceremonies. Special sweat (if in honor of an immediate family member), memorial service (if an immediate family member of the person service is for)

         (8) Medications, including aspirin, Tylenol, Maalox

         (9) Sick call/emergencies (accidents, illness, etc.)

         (10) Advanced concessions. Inmates will receive items they have purchased from organizations prior to being on loss of recreation. These items will be delivered to their rooms.

      b. Inmates may not participate in the following activities while on loss of recreation:

(1) Recreation, including outside, armory, recreation center, bingo, unit weight rooms, etc. This does not include scheduled recreation classes.

(2) Program activities. Includes Alcoholics Anonymous/Narcotics Anonymous, inmate organizations, Bible study, parole communications, sweat lodge, movies, Christmas and other special programs, Ho Maza Singers/Dancers, pow wow, Christmas party, Winter Carnival, fun days, committee/organization projects, speaking engagements, such as COPE, guest at graduation, inmates's own wedding, guest at wedding, banquets, dinners, feeds, etc.

(3) Day hall privileges. Including concessions, organization sales, ice and pop. Inmates must be in their rooms, not the day hall, when waiting to go to rneals, sick call, classes, work, church/pipes, visits, etc.

(4) Telephone privileges

(5) Library passes. This does not include scheduled library classes.

(6) Barbershop privileges

## Downtown Orders

A. Slips listing items for downtown orders must be turned in to the property office by approximately 11:30 A.M. each Wednesday. Items will be purchased and can be picked up when notified.

***Comment***: Specify where inmates gets downtown order slip.

B. Only items on the allowable property list are permitted.

C. All purchases must be made at local vendors.

## Exits

A. Use the center staircase only.

B. Outer stairwells and exits are off limits except during emergencies, such as fires, etc. In case of fire, use the emergency exit nearest assigned room.

## Fire Alarms

A. Fire alarms are located on each floor of Ludeman Hall. They emit a loud, constant, piercing horn sound.

B. Evacuation maps are located on the wall at the entry way to each wing of the unit. Indicated routes should be followed in the event of a drill or an actual fire.

C. During a drill or an actual fire, a staff member is assigned to each floor of the unit to monitor and assist during evacuation.

D. Fire alarms are tested weekly during daytime hours. Inmates are not required to leave the unit for the fire alarm test.

E. If a fire alarm sounds when not being tested, inmates should exit the building according to designated routes and proceed to the street immediately in front of Ludeman Hall (east side). If evacuation to a more distant area is necessary, staff will direct the movement.

F. Tampering with fire alarms will result in disciplinary action.
***Comment***: Fire alarms section is excellent!

## Keys

A. A room key has been issued to each inmate. This key should be kept with the resident at all times. Unoccupied rooms should be locked at all times.

B. If a key is stolen or lost, it should be reported at the security desk immediately. A charge of $2.00 will be assessed for the replacement key.

## Kites/Request Slips

A. Kites are written requests that allow inmates to contact any staff member at the facility. Upon receipt, the staff member will contact the resident as soon as possible. The inmate must fill out the form completely, being specific regarding the request.

***Comment***: Specify how inmate obtains kite/request slips.

1. Outside Ludeman Hall. To contact any staff member off the housing unit, a kite must be filled out and dropped off at the security desk. Kites for off-unit distribution are taken to Gill Hall at the end of each shift.

2. Inside Ludeman Hall

   a. To contact any staff member on the housing unit, a kite may be filled out and dropped off at the security desk. This is to be done during day hall hours only.

   b. Ludeman Hall operates under an "open door" system. A resident may simply proceed to the office of the unit manager, the case manager, or the correctional counselor and knock. If the supervisor is available and unoccupied, he or she will respond.

B. If a room transfer is made, bring the laundry bag to the security desk for exchange.
***Comment***: How are inmate room transfers made? Is AIMS category taken into account? It should be.

## Laundry—Facility Services

A. Laundry day for Ludeman Hall residents is Thursday.

1. If the laundry drop-off day is missed, a resident must wait until the following week to turn in dirty laundry.

2. If there is a holiday on one of the laundry days, a notice will be posted to reflect any changes in the laundry schedule for that week.

3. Make sure the laundry slips are filled out properly, signed, and that they have the entire room number written on it. (Example: L103A) .

***Comment***: Specify how inmates obtain laundry slips.

4. Drop off laundry bags before 8:00 A.M.

5. Pick up laundry from 10:30 - 10:45 A.M.

   a. Before leaving, check the laundry bag to ensure all articles are there.
   b. If there is a mistake, bring it to the attention of the laundry supervisor immediately.

6. If a room transfer is made, bring the laundry bag to the security desk for exchange. Do not change the numbers on the laundry bags.

7. The following items are allowed to be turned into the laundry weekly (state issue only):

   a. 2 sheets and 1 pillowcase (must be turned in weekly)

   b. 4 bath towels and 4 washcloths

   c. 3 pair blue jeans and 3 blue shirts

   d. 4 white pants and 4 white shirts

      (1) Knots must be removed.

      (2) If you turn in more than allowed, the excess items will be returned unlaundered.

8. Blankets, jackets, and mattress pads will be laundered on a six-month basis. Notification will be posted. Any of these items turned in at unscheduled times will be returned unlaundered.

9. When state-issue clothing or linen needs replacement, a clothing and linen order form (a green slip) must be placed in the inmate's laundry bag along with the items which need replacing. These green slips do not need to be signed by a unit team member.

***Comment:*** Where does an inmate get the green slips?

10. Send a kite to "Laundry" concerning problems with state shoes. Notification will be given on exchange times.

11. Laundry time schedules are to be followed. Disciplinary action will be taken if not followed.

## Laundry—On Unit

A. Laundry—Personal

1. Put all personal laundry items, unbunched and turned right side out, in the mesh laundry bag. This bag is located in the room closet. Laundry bags are to be taken to the laundry room at the assigned times.

2. Personal laundry includes: personal jeans (not state issue), personal shirts, personal socks, personal sweats, personal shorts, socks, shirts, and underwear issued upon arrival, washcloths, personal bath and hand towels (not state issued), state shorts, state sweatshirt and state sweat pants.

3. State bedding, pillow cases, towels, washcloths, blankets, pillows, coats, and mattress pads are not allowed to be washed on the unit.

4. Laundry runners are responsible for washing and drying clothes in the personal mesh laundry bag, and notification when laundry is done. The laundry will be in the mesh bag, unfolded. The laundry bag will be picked up by the owner at the laundry room.

***Comment***: How are laundry runners selected?

5. If an allergy develops due to the laundry soap used, a medical order for different laundry soap must be obtained from the medical staff.

***Comment***: Excellent detail re: laundry!

## Library

A. A pass may be requested to go to the library between the hours of:

9:00 A.M.—11:00 A.M. Monday/Wednesday/Thursday/Friday

1:00 P.M.—4:00 P.M. Monday/Wednesday/Thursday/Friday

1:00 P.M.—4:00 P.M. Tuesday

B. Inmates may be paid for one scheduled library hour. Additional library hours will not be paid.

## Living Guide and Bulletin Boards

A. Read the Inmate Living Guide. Inmates are responsible for the information and knowing the rules and regulations of Springfield State Prison.

B. Read the bulletin board daily.

C. If in doubt or unsure about the rules and regulations, ask staff for assistance.

## Mail

A. A mailbox with a combination has been assigned. Keep the combination confidential. Ludeman Hall does not have enough mailboxes for every resident. Inmates not assigned a mail box will have their mail kept at the security desk.

B. If money is received via the mail, a receipt will be sent. The money will be placed in the inmate's account within two working days. Only money orders and cash are accepted through the mail. Personal checks are returned.

C. Personal property and packages will be opened, inspected for contraband, and inventoried in the presence of an inmate observer.

***Comment***: Why not open them in presence of inmate to whom mail is addressed, as is done with legal mail?

1. Allowable items received will be placed on the inmate's property card (when required). Any nonallowable items will be returned at the inmate's expense.

2. Legal mail will be opened in the presence of the receiving inmate, logged, inspected for contraband, and given directly to each inmate. The inmate's I.D. and signature will be required to obtain legal mail. Paper and legal envelopes are available at the desk.

D. All incoming mail will be opened, inspected for contraband, and all stamps, stickers, and/or foreign objects will be removed in the presence of an inmate observer.

E. Outgoing mail must be placed in the mail slot, during day hall hours, no later than 10:30 P.M. each day.

1. The resident's return address must be on all outgoing mail.

F. Incoming mail will be placed in the mailboxes by approximately 2:30 P.M. each day. Mail must be picked up during day hall hours only.

G. The correct address is:

Your Name
Springfield State Prison
Ludeman Hall
P.O. Box 389
Springfield, SD 57062

H. Confiscation notices will be received for any item confiscated from the mail. Inmates have the option of sending it out, giving it to Goodwill, or destroying it if the item is not cleared by the director of custody.

***Comment:*** Excellent detail regarding mail!

## Maintenance and Construction on Housing Units

A. Maintenance areas, tools, and equipment on the housing unit are off-limits for inmates, unless instructed otherwise.

B. Maintenance runners are available for minor maintenance repair.
***Comment***: How are maintenance runners selected?

C. If the assigned room or any issued state article is in need of major repair, a staff member must complete the maintenance request and give it to the unit manager.

## Meals

A. Normal meal times are as follows. Adjustments may be necessary under certain circumstances.

B. Weekdays:

| | |
|---|---|
| 5:55 - 6:25 | Breakfast |
| 11:50 - 12:20 | Lunch (rotate with Crawford) |
| 4:15 - 4:45 | Dinner |

C. Weekends:

| | |
|---|---|
| 9:45 - 10:15 | Brunch |
| 4:30 - 5:00 | Dinner |

D. Inmates are to be appropriately dressed when attending meals. No sweats, shorts, shower shoes, slippers, or sandals.

E. Inmates are permitted up to 30 minutes to eat their meal.

## Medical Lay-in

A. Any resident placed on medical lay-in by a nurse or physician will be excused from his work/school assignments. If a prisoner becomes so ill that the inmate must leave work or a class, the individual will be on lay-in status automatically. If the inmate must go back to the housing unit for Tylenol or aspirin, the inmate will be on lay-in status automatically. If an inmate becomes ill on Friday, Saturday, or Sunday to the extent a medical lay-in is necessary, the prisoner will be on lay-in status until 6:00 A.M. Monday. While an inmate is on a medical lay-in, he may leave his room only for meals and for activities specifically authorized in writing by a nurse or doctor. To leave under other circumstances is a violation of Springfield State Prison rules. Any inmate placed on medical lay-in status automatically stays on that status until 6:00 A.M. the following day. Medical staff are the only personnel authorized to take an inmate off medical lay-in prior to 6:00 A.M. If the medical staff does this, a termination of the medical lay-in must be obtained from the medical staff and turned in at the security desk of the housing unit. Medical staff will determine attendance at sick call.

B. Activities that are allowed on medical lay-in: (Unless specially prohibited by a nurse or physician):

- Meals
- Unit passes
- Restroom
- Shower
- Tylenol/aspirin/Maalox/medication
- Must stand for count

C. Activities that are not allowed on medical lay-in: (Unless specially ordered by nurse or physician):

- Work
- Classes
- Group counseling
- Laundry/commissary
- Visits
- Packages
- Regularly scheduled church services/pipe ceremonies
- Concessions
- Recreation
- Program activities
- Day hall privileges including pop/ice
- Telephone privileges
- Library passes
- Haircuts and beauty shop privileges
- Room cleaning supplies
- Off unit one-on-one sessions

## Medical Services

A. Sick Call

1. A sick call request must be filled out upon arrival at sick call. A nurse must be seen before a doctor's appointment will be scheduled.

2. Sick call is at 7:30 A.M. on weekdays. It is held in Ludeman Hall, First Floor South.

B. Medications

1. Medications are distributed at Health Services at posted times. Read the bulletin board for correct times. Evening medications and weekend medications are given on the unit at approximately 9:30 P.M.

2. Report to the security desk with a glass of water and inmate I.D. card to request medication.

   a. Wearing of sleeping apparel is not allowed when picking up medication.

3. If an inmate is allowed to keep medication in an assigned room, specific rules are explained by the medical staff and must be followed at all times.

4. Insulin is self-administered at Health Services.

C. Medication Schedule

1. Self-dispensed medications are given for self-administration.

2. Controlled medications/PRNs are dispensed on the housing units by medical staff at posted times.
***Comment***: Spell out PRN.

3. Over-the-counter medications may be picked up at Health Services at post medication distribution times. A self-charting system is utilized.

## Mental Health Services

Mental health services are available. Correctional counselor and/or medical staff will assist in obtaining these services.

## Movements

A. An "unauthorized area" is any area an inmate does not have staff authorization to be in.

B. Inmates are required to take the most direct route to their destination. It is a violation of Springfield State Prison rules to cut across the grass; traffic is confined to sidewalks.

## Optometric Care

A request slip must be submitted and addressed: "Optometrist." The reasons for the appointment must be stated on the request.

## Pictures

A. Pictures/photographs may not be in frames. Pictures/photographs may be attached to the bulletin board or in a photo album only. No explicit sexual pictures may be displayed.

***Comment***: Pictures—"explicit sexual pictures" may have many different interpretations; suggest specify no nudity.

B. Facility photographs must observe Springfield Correctional Facility's one foot rule between inmates.

***Comment***: Explain "Springfield Correctional Facility's one foot rule."

## Recreation

A. Off-unit recreation facilities

1. Armory recreation

    a. No articles are allowed to be taken; such as letters, cups, drinking glasses, food items, pop, candy, gum, tokens, craft items, books, magazines, personal board games, cards, state towels, or tobacco products.

    b. Portable radios/tape players (with headphones), keys, I.D., and personal towels are allowed.

    c. Smoking or chewing of tobacco is not permitted in the armory.

    d. Slam dunking of basketballs is not allowed.

    e. No street shoes are allowed on the armory floor.

2. Library recreation

    a. No articles are allowed to be taken, for example, letters, cups, drinking glasses, food items, pop, candy, gum, tokens, craft items, books, magazines, personal board games, cards, or tobacco products.

    b. Smoking or chewing tobacco is not permitted in the library.

3. Outside recreation yard

    a. Limited articles are allowed to be taken.

        (1) Letters, food items, or craft items are not allowed.

        (2) Portable radios/tape players and stereos, keys, I.D., drinking glass, tokens, cigarettes, and lighter are allowed.

b. Inmates playing volleyball are required to wear shoes.

c. Lying down or leaning on elbows is prohibited.

d. When sitting at a picnic table, male and female inmates must sit on opposite sides of the table.

4. Special programs and events

a. No articles are allowed to be taken, such as letters, cups, drinking glasses, food items, tokens, craft items, or tobacco products.

b. Keys and I.D. are allowed.

5. General rules

a. Inmates taking coats, jackets, and sweat shirts to recreation will either wear the garment or lay it on the floor, bench, chair, etc.

b. Clothing will not be draped across the inmates' legs, hung on the back of a chair, or draped over the end of a table.

B. Unit recreation

1. Day hall

a. The television must be played at a low volume, with channel selection by popular vote.

b. A variety of board games may be checked-out from a designated inmate runner. Games must be returned to the designated runner when completed; no hoarding. Ask at the security desk for the name of the designated runner currently in charge of checking out the games.

***Comment:*** Unit recreation—How is inmate runner selected? Who monitors this function?

c. All pool table equipment is available near the pool table.

2. Weight room

a. Hours are:

8:00 A.M.—9:30 P.M. Monday - Friday

7:00 A.M.—9:30 P.M. Weekends/Holidays

b. Personal stereos and fans are permissible.

c. No more than six inmates, plus the weight room runner, may be in the weight room at any given time.

d. A resident should not use the weight room more than one hour daily to ensure that a maximum number of residents have the opportunity to utilize it.

e. Any resident who abuses weight room privileges will be subject to a rule infraction report.

## Religious Services

A. Scheduled services include:

| | |
|---|---|
| Catholic services | Saturday 8:00 - 9:15A.M. |
| Protestant services | Sunday 8:00 - 9:15A.M. |
| Pipe ceremony | Sunday 7:30 - 9:00A.M. |

## Rooms

A. Rooms will be assigned by the unit manager or the correctional counselor. Requests for roommates will be considered.

***Comment***: Is AIMS or another internal classification system used in making room assignments? It should be.

B. Room changes ordinarily will be made on Monday.

1. Change requests must be received by 3:30 P.M. Thursday to take place the following Monday.

***Comment***: Who approves room changes? Why are such changes made?

C. Room changes generally will occur following 7:15 A.M. count.

D. Inmates must turn in their old room key, their laundry bag, and their net bag at the security desk after the 7:15 A.M. count on the morning of the change.

E. Assigned rooms may be locked when not occupied to protect property.

F. Between the 7:15 A.M. count and 10:30 P.M. count an occupied room must be left unlocked unless the occupant has permission from a staff member to lock it.

G. Between the 10:30 P.M. and 7:15 A.M. count, rooms may be locked.

H. At the discretion of the unit staff, doors may be left part way open during hot weather.

I. Inmates and the room of the inmates are subject to search at any time.

1. The inmate need not be present when the room is searched. If the inmate is not present, two officers will conduct the search. In an emergency, one officer may conduct the search.

***Comment:*** Who decides when it is an emergency?

2. An inmate is responsible for all articles found in his room. Joint occupancy denotes both individuals are responsible.

J. In two-man rooms, inmates are to sleep with feet towards the door. In four-man rooms, inmates are to sleep with their head towards the door.

K. Inmates are not allowed in rooms other than their assigned room. Visiting must be done in the day hall, not in any doorway, hallway, or bathroom.

L. Residents are responsible for the cleanliness of the room.

1. Bunks will be made when not occupied.

2. Nothing may be taped or fastened in any manner or hung from room walls, fixtures, or furnishings. Blankets, towels, clothing, and so forth will not be hung on the end of bunks.

3. Notify the floor runner to check out cleaning materials. The inmate runner will provide necessary cleaning supplies and will lock the items in the runner's closet upon their return. Defacing or damaging living quarters is in violation of Springfield State Prison rules.

M. Personal radios, stereos, and televisions will be played at low volume at all times. All electrical items must be turned off when a room is unoccupied.

N. Two cardboard boxes are allowed for storage of books and/or personal papers and letters. They may be used as stereo stands; however, any empty boxes found in a room will be considered unauthorized items.

O. Possession of unauthorized items is not allowed. Inmate should not accumulate items, such as pop cans, tobacco cans, and so forth.

## Sexual Contact

A. Sexual contact is forbidden. This includes holding hands, hugging, kissing, caressing—any form of touching. This pertains to contact between females, between males, and between males and females.

B. All inmates must maintain a minimum distance of one foot between each other at all times.

## Smoking

A. On-unit smoking is permitted in assigned rooms only.

B. Off-unit smoking is permitted in designated areas only.

## Telephones

A. Telephones are located on each floor. Inmates are permitted to use only the telephone located on the floor on which they live, between the hours of 6:00 A.M. and 10:30 P.M., daily.

B. Upon arrival in Ludeman Hall, each resident receives a form to establish a personal identification number (PIN) for placing collect calls on the unit telephones. Additional information is available at the security desk.

***Comment***: Specify who monitors/coordinates inmate-call telephone log; correctional officer? correctional counselor?

## Town Hall Meetings

A. An hour-long town hall meeting may be conducted in the third floor day room beginning at approximately 5:15 P.M. on the third Thursday of each month.

1. The purpose of the session is to provide answers to questions regarding rules or aspects of facility life which affect the inmate population in general, and is modeled after the federal prison system's town hall meeting.
2. Residents requesting a special topic and/or a "guest respondent," for example, the health services director or the food services supervisor, must make such requests by noon of the first Thursday of each month.
3. All questions must be presubmitted in written form. The deadline for submitting questions is noon of the second Thursday of each month. Questions will not be taken from the floor. Questions may address any topic regarding Ludeman Hall and Springfield State Prison; however, questions which are too broad in scope to answer will not be addressed.
4. Town hall meeting topic requests and questions should be submitted to the correctional counselor.
5. If no questions are submitted by noon of the second Thursday of the month, there will be no town hall meeting that month.

***Comment:*** Weekly or biweekly would be better. Written questions are an excellent idea! Do not cancel town hall meeting if no questions are submitted. It's a two-way street for communication. Unit staff should use town hall meetings to convey information, changes, and so forth to inmates.

***Comment:*** Attendance at town hall meeting is mandatory for inmates; there should be no "coming and going." Schedule town hall meeting and unit staff meeting so that they do not conflict; one should not cause the other to be canceled. Town hall meetings should be held whether or not inmates have submitted questions; otherwise, inmates (not staff) are in control.

## Track Assignments

A. Each resident will participate in a full-time track whenever possible.

1. Assignment shall be based on an individual's needs assessment and on a commitment from the resident.

   a. The track may include a combination of work assignments and academic, vocational, and other classes, with the goal of filling at least twenty-four (24) hours weekly.

   b. Current core tracks are:

      (1) General Equivalency Diploma (GED) program

      (2) Vocational education program

      (3) Work program

      (4) Prison industry

      (5) Chemical dependency treatment

2. All inmate schedules must be followed.

***Comment***: The track idea is excellent! Who establishes content of track? It should be unit classification board with input from unit's education person.

## Visits

A. Visiting hours are as follows:

| | |
|---|---|
| Weekends and holidays | 11:00 A.M.—3:45 P.M. |
| Friday evenings | 6:30 P.M.—8:15 P.M. |
| Tuesdays and Thursdays | 2:15 P.M.—4:15 P.M. |

B. All regular visits will take place in the visit room. The visit room is located on the first floor of the library. All visits must begin at least thirty minutes prior to the end of visiting hours.

C. Handshaking, kissing, and embracing may take place at the beginning and the end of each visit only. Above the table hand holding is allowed during the visit (*see* appropriate contact regulations posted at the desk in the visiting room).

D. Inmates are subject to a strip search upon leaving the visiting area.

E. Inmates will be pat searched.

F. Inmates will not be allowed to use the restroom.

G. Smoking is not permitted.

H. No personal property or packages will be allowed.

I. Inmates must conduct themselves in a quiet and orderly manner.

J. Inmates must maintain any visiting children under strict supervision at all times.

K. Inmates will not greet or say goodbye to visitors near the visitor's entrance; this must be done at the table.

L. Attorney/clergy visits may take place in Gill Hall.

M. Coats, jackets, caps, hats, scarf, and gloves are not allowed to be worn in the visiting room.

    1. Coats are hung in the inmate entrance. I.D. card, comb, and room key may be taken to a visit.

    2. Consult the Inmate Living Guide [not included in this book] for additional information.

## Unit Management

Position responsibilities: unit management is an approach to managing correctional institutions which decentralizes control over inmates. Primary decision-making for issues which concern inmates is given to the unit team which works with them daily in their housing units. It allows the unit team to specialize; they can closely supervise inmates by concentrating resources.

A. Unit Manager

    1. The unit manager ultimately is responsible for all decisions made, actions taken, and for the overall functioning of the unit. It is essential all information is forwarded to the unit manager for review. It is also equally important that the unit manager share all information with all members of the unit team. With proper communication, the unit team will be cohesive, informed, and effective.

    2. Duties of the unit manager include:

        - Developing/coordinating unit safety and security measures
        - Supervising multidisciplinary unit team members
        - Administering unit budget
        - Coordinating unit operations with other Springfield State Prison departments
        - Acting as liaison with private and public agencies

- Preparing required reports to DOC, Springfield State Prison administration and other agencies
- Instituting and managing personnel schedules and time sheets
- Developing appropriate training schedules and programs
- Conducting semiannual performance evaluations
- Developing, implementing, and updating unit policy and procedures
- Attending senior staff and facility policy review meetings
- Reviewing and approving informal counts and safety checks
- Conducting unit team meetings

***Comment*:** Specify frequency of unit team meetings; should be weekly (biweekly OK)

- Developing and implementing unit programs
  - Chairing security classification board hearings
  - Reviewing and approving program classification hearings
- Chairing minor disciplinary board hearings
  - Chairing furlough board hearings
- Interviewing as part of unit staff hirings

B. Case manager

1. The case manager develops, in cooperation with the unit team, an individual program plan for all incoming inmates and monitors each resident until his release.
2. Duties of the case manager include:

   Interviewing new inmates to obtain personal history, educational social-economic background

   ***Comment:*** Security classification, program classification and furloughs should be combined and become the function of the unit classification: board, for example, 1 not 3 meetings. Specify that the unit classification board meets weekly.

   - Preparing parole reports and progress reports
   - Conducting a weekly inmate group session
   - Assisting with program classification activities

- Assisting with minor disciplinary board
- Coordinating and reviewing furlough applications
- Preparing and coordinating release plans and forms
- Making referrals to medical and mental health specialists
- Acting as liaison to federal agencies
- Acting as liaison to state agencies, tracking holds and detainers
- Conducting orientation for new residents
- Maintaining inmate files

***Comment*:** Maintaining inmate files should be unit secretary's duty.

- Maintaining and updating visitor lists
- Coordinating inmate grievance system

***Comment:*** Inmate grievances typically are handled by the correctional counselor.

- Coordinating inmate classes/work scheduling
- Supervising unit runners

***Comment***: Supervising unit runners and janitors is correctional officer's duty.

- Coordinating unit maintenance, safety, and sanitation activities

***Comment*:** Unit-sanitation inspection is correctional counselor duty.

- Conducting quarterly safety inspections.
- Supervising Ludeman Committee
- Monitoring unit programming activities
- Acting as unit manager in unit manager's absence

C. Correctional counselor

1. The correctional counselor ensures security procedures are maintained by all unit staff. This position provides counseling to assigned inmates on institutional adjustment, program planning, personal problems, and assists in the development of individual program plans.

2. Duties of the correctional counselor include:

- Administering counseling services for unit residents
- Compiling/preparing security classification data
- Directing unit program classification activities

***Comment:*** Correctional counselor—Program classification activities are case manager duties.

- Coordinating work release, house arrest, and community alternatives programs

***Comment:*** Work release, house arrest, and community alternatives are case manager functions.

- Preparing progress reports

***Comment:*** Parole progress reports are the case manager's responsibility; the correctional counselor can assist.

- Representing inmates (if requested) at major disciplinary hearings
- Assisting with minor disciplinary board
- Conducting orientation for new residents
- Assisting with unit room assignments
- Maintaining inmate unit files

***Comment:*** Maintaining inmate files is the unit secretary's duty.

- Maintaining and updating visitor lists

***Comment:*** This is the case manager's duty.

- Preparing and coordinating release plans and forms

***Comment:*** Preparing release plans/forms is the case manager's responsibility; the correctional counselor can assist. The correctional counselor's duties include visiting inmates at program or work sites on a regular basis.

- Making referrals to medical and mental health specialists
- Acting as liaison to federal agencies
- Acting as liaison to state agencies
- Coordinating unit town meeting activities
- Monitoring unit programming activities
- Acting as unit manager in unit manager's absence

D. Hours

1. Unit manager—The unit manager normally will be available from 9:00 A.M. to 6:00 P.M. to assist in matters that cannot be accomplished by the case manager, correctional counselor, or other unit team members.
   ***Comment:*** The unit manager should work until 9:00 P.M. at least once every week and on some weekends.

2. Case manager and correctional counselor—The case manager and the correctional counselor generally maintain an open door policy. They work a rotating shift. Each week, one is on the unit from 12:30 P.M. to 9:00 P.M.

Monday through Friday. The other is on the unit from 9:30 A.M. to 6:00 P.M. Saturday and Sunday, and from 8:00 A.M. to 4:30 P.M. three weekdays.

E. Springfield State Prison Administration

Superintendent

Deputy Superintendent

Assistant Superintendent for Operations

Assistant Superintendent for Programs

Director of Custody

Ludeman Unit Manager

Harmon Unit Manager

East Crawford Unit Manager

West Crawford Unit Manager

Training, Industry, Education Coordinator

Director of Vocational Education

Academic Principal

Director of Physical Plant

Director of Food Service

Director of Health Services

Ludeman Hall Unit Team

Unit Manager

Case Manager

Correctional Counselor

Five Correctional Officers

***Comment***: 1) Administration—To whom does the unit manager report? Is it same person to which the director of custody reports? Including a table of organization would help; 2) Ludeman Hall should have a unit secretary; and 3) Excellent detail in the unit management section!

# Section III—Ludeman Programs and Services

## Unit Admission/Orientation

Refer to: (1) Attachments 1 and 2 [not included in this book]
***Comment*:** Admission/orientation checklists are excellent! Is there anything similar for new staff?

## Health Services

Refer to: (1) Section II

## Classification

Refer to: *South Dakota Department of Corrections Inmate Classification Manual*—1993 Edition

## Counseling

The case manager conducts weekly, hour-long, general topic group session 3:00 P.M. Wednesday. (Participation last quarter: 12) This person maintains open door policy for one-on-one sessions.

The correctional counselor maintains an open door policy for one-on-one sessions, averages 215 inmate contacts per month, and sees each unit resident at least once monthly.

## Self-help Programs

Ludeman Hall Alcoholics Anonymous, 7:00 P.M. Wednesday: participation last quarter: 7-11

Ludeman Hall Gamblers Anonymous 7:00 P.M. every other Tuesday: 3 attended initial meeting

## Grievance Procedures

Refer to: Inmate Living Guide, Section II, and Policy and Procedure

## Visiting

Refer to: Inmate Living Guide, Section II, and Policy and Procedure

# Section IV—Ludeman Operations and Schedules

## Unit Safety and Sanitation

Thirteen inmate runners, supervised by the case manager and an assigned unit correctional officer, perform daily maintenance, janitorial, and laundry duties. For specific tasks, refer to Attachment 3 [not included in this book].

Safety/sanitation inspections are conducted weekly by the case manager, monthly by a facility custodial supervisor who coordinates supply and equipment inventories, and annually by the facility safety committee. The weekly and annual inspections are documented, with the weekly reports being submitted to the unit manager.
***Comment***: Unit safety/sanitation—Excellent! Handling these inspections is typically duty of correctional counselor.

## Bed Assignment

Refer to: (1) Section II

## Unit Team Meeting

Ludeman Hall team meeting, 2:00 P.M., Thursday; weekly participation: 3 unit supervisors 4 (of 5) unit correctional officers

***Comment:*** Unit team meeting-weekly participation. Who are "3 Unit Supervisors?" Is this AW's unit manager's meeting? Unit team meeting is with Ludeman unit staff, for example, LTM, CM, CC and any COs that can attend.

If the unit manager is absent, the acting unit manager conducts the unit team meeting; it is not cancelled. Attendance at unit team meetings is mandatory for the unit manager, the correctional manager, and the correctional counselor; correctional officers attend if available.

## Unit Disciplinary Board

Refer to: Inmate Living Guide, Section II, and Policy and Procedure

## Staff Availability

Refer to (1) Section II

# Ludeman Statistics/Memos/Miscellaneous

Please review pages 228-233 for sample documents.

# MEMORANDUM

TO: Ludeman Unit Team
SUBJECT: Cable TV Repairs
FROM: Dean Vik, Unit Manager
DATE: 04 August

Effective immediately, a maintenance order should be filled out and forwarded to the business office for any and all repair/equipment replacement work required on the cable TV system in Ludeman Hall. Please make certain these maintenance orders carry the signature of a unit supervisor as well as your own. Some have been going up to Gill Hall without a unit supervisor's signature and have been returned to us.

# Minutes of Ludeman Unit Supervisory Meeting

## August 12—2:00 Memo

(1) No agenda...

— Officers Fisher, Novotny, Rouse and Huisman present for general discussion.

— One camera/monitor plus an extra camera have arrived. The camera/monitor will be passed around to the other three housing units and to custody for feasibility testing in different areas, for example, in the hard cells and in the visit room. The extra camera, running off the Ludeman monitor, will be operational in the Health Services hallway by next Monday.

— Training in the use of a portable Breathalyzer will be held at 9:30 A.M. Thursday, Aug. 19. Most lieutenants and sergeants, as well as interested unit supervisors, will be trained. The Breathalyzer will be used for "quick response" situations, and will not replace UA tests. Inmates who are given a breathalyzer test will also receive UAed in a timely manner, as backup.

— Sex offenders no longer will be sent to the Cottage, only to the West Farm. This means the average waiting period to get to the West Farm probably will be around five months after the classification date.

# LUDEMAN HALL FIRST FLOOR LIVING CRITERIA ELIGIBILITY

Disciplinary: No more than 1 minor rule violation the past 6 months.

Any first-floor resident convicted of 2 minor rule violations during any 6-month period will be relocated to an upstairs room or to another housing unit.

No major rule violations during the past 1 year.

Any first-floor resident convicted of a major rule violation will be relocated to an upstairs room or to another housing unit

Programs: Must be engaged in or have graduated from a vocational course.

Any first floor resident not already a vocational graduate who withdraws from or is permanently suspended from a vocational course will be relocated to an upstairs room or to another housing unit.

Financial: Must demonstrate financial responsibility.

Any first-floor resident whose name appears on the "frozen list" will be relocated to an upstairs room or to another housing unit.

First-floor living criteria—Rule violations or other reasons should never result in transfer to another housing unit. If inmate cannot make in Ludeman Hall, then transfer to another facility is in order; do not "pass around" problem cases.

# Exit Survey Form

You are about to leave Springfield State Prison. We would appreciate learning your opinion about some aspects of Springfield State Prison. Your honest opinion is preferred. Through it, we might be able to improve services for other inmates still at the facility and those who will be here in the future.

Did you complete a vocational course? Yes _____ No_____

On a scale of 1 (poor) to 10 (excellent), rate the quality of the course. _____

Do you think the course will be of benefit in your future? Yes _____ No_____

Did you complete an alcohol/drug program? Yes _____ No_____

On a scale of 1 (poor) to 10 (excellent), rate the quality of the program. _____

At which facility did you prefer being? Penitentiary _____ Prison _____

Which facility served your needs/problems best? Penitentiary _____ Prison _____

On a scale of 1 (poor) to 10 (excellent) rate:

Ludeman Hall officers (guards) overall helpfulness to you _______

Ludeman Hall overall helpfulness to you _______

The quality of the food service department at Springfield State Prison _______

The quality of the medical service department at Springfield State Prison _______

The quality of the commissary at Springfield State Prison _______

The quality of the business office (inmate accounts) at Springfield State Prison _______

***Comment*:** The exit survey form is an excellent idea! Might want to include items for the staff to fill-in (on second sheet), regarding the inmate's disciplinary behavior, program achievements, and so forth.

# LUDEMAN ROOM CLEAN-UP ORDER

Your room has been identified as one which is in need of cleaning. This notice is to inform you the room will be reinspected for general cleanliness in approximately 24 hours. If your room fails that inspection, the inspecting staff member may:

1) Grant a time extension up to 24 hours for you to remedy specific problems.
2) File a Rule Infraction Report. The charge would involve Rule #72 (Failure to comply with a "cell clean-up notice" within a 24 hour period), and possibly other charges.

If a Rule Infraction Report is filed and you are found guilty by the disciplinary board, in addition to traditional penalties, such as loss of recreation or fines, you may be assigned to a different room.

In addition to general cleaning, it has been determined:

1) Entire room or portion needs to be painted (specify) ___________. You have been granted _____________ time to complete.
2) Floor needs to be waxed _________. You have been granted ___________ time to complete.
3) Floor needs to be stripped and waxed __________. You have been granted _____________ time to complete.
4) Walls need to be washed ___________. You have been granted ___________ time to complete.
5) Windows need to be washed ___________. You have been granted _________ time to complete.
6) Curtains need to be washed ___________. You have been granted _________ time to complete.
7) Repairs needed:

   Item:____________________________ Time to complete:_______________

   Item:____________________________ Time to complete:_______________

Date:_______________ Time: _______________

Name: _____________________________________ #_________________

_____________________________________________

Signed

> Accumulation of three of these notices within a 60 day period will result in an automatic Rule Infraction Report.

# LUDEMAN HALL
# WEEKLY SECURITY CHECKLIST

Date: ________________

| | OFFICER | CHECK | ITEM |
|---|---|---|---|
| 1. | ______________ | ______ | Security telephones all floors |
| 2. | ______________ | ______ | Roof Hatches/Padlocks |
| 3. | ______________ | ______ | Security screens/outside |
| 4. | ______________ | ______ | Crawl tunnels |
| 5. | ______________ | ______ | Security doors to mechanical rooms |
| 6. | ______________ | ______ | Emergency exit alarms/north center exit alarm |
| 7. | ______________ | ______ | All fuse boxes locked including janitor closet boxes |
| 8. | ______________ | ______ | Janitor/closets for fire hazards (debris, paper, combustible items) |
| 9. | ______________ | ______ | Janitor/Utility supply-storage closets for fire hazards |
| 10. | ______________ | ______ | Utility closets locked/clean/no hazards |
| 11. | ______________ | ______ | Fire extinguishers full and in proper locations |
| 12. | ______________ | ______ | Fire alarm indicator lights in entrances working |
| 13. | ______________ | ______ | SCBAs full and in proper locations, Masks/straps serviceable<br>Unit 1______ lbs. Unit 2______ lbs. |
| 14. | ______________ | ______ | Boxes in weight rooms locked |
| 15. | ______________ | ______ | Check/restock orange first aid bag |
| 16. | ______________ | ______ | Security lights working all floors |

Comments: ________________________________________________

__________________________________________________________

Supervisor's Signature: ______________________________

Officer('s) Signature(s): ______________________________

______________________________

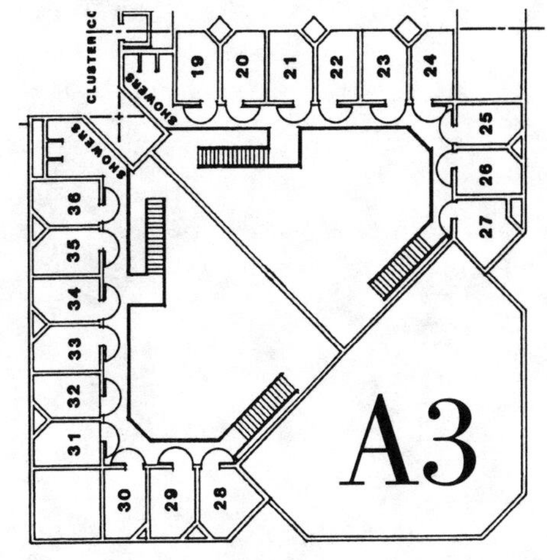


# Appendix 3

## Unit Management Audit Form

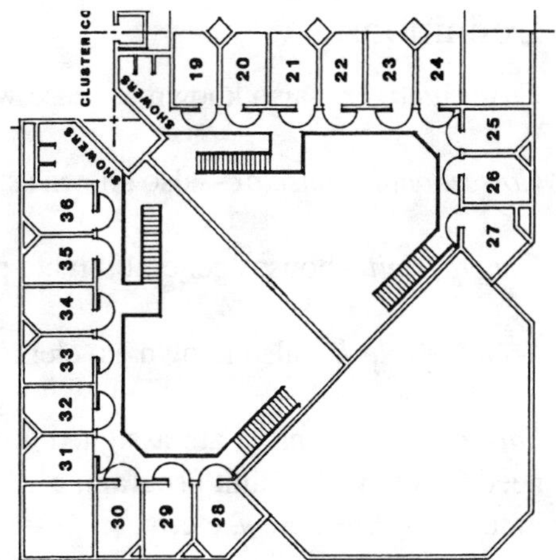


# Appendix 3

## Unit Management Audit Form

### Instructions

The following pages contain audit items relating to unit management. One rating score—**0, 1, 2,** or **3**—should be circled for each item. When there are two items with the same number (e.g., 1a and 1b), circle 'NA' for one of them and then rate the other item by circling 0, 1, 2, or 3.

Cues for using the rating scores: 0, 1, 2, or 3

**Circle "0"** if the practice is nonexistent [items left BLANK will be scored "zero"].

**Circle "1"** if the practice is followed 50 percent of the time or less.

**Circle "2"** if the practice is followed more than 50 percent but less than 100 percent of the time OR if it does not meet the "ideal" or "preferable" criteria specified in the item.

**Circle "3"** if practice fully complies with the item and meets any "ideal" or "preferable" level, if one is specified.

**Write-in "NA"** if item does not apply and, briefly, explain why; such items are not included when points are totaled.

## Definitions

*Case manager*—also known as: case worker, counselor, etc.

*Correctional counselor*—also known as: liaison officer, inmate relations coordinator, etc.

*General unit*—houses general inmate population.

*Secretary/clerk*—also known as: clerk/correctional officer

*Special unit*—Inmates are assigned to these living quarters when they have a special need for the within-unit program; e.g., substance abuse, mental health, etc.; but NOT industry, kitchen crew, etc.

***Please ENTER (print):***

______________________________ ___________________________________
Auditor's Name Institution's Name

Audit Date____/____/____ Unit Name__________________________________

# Unit Management Audit Form

0 = Noncompliance
1 = Minimal compliance
2 = Substantial compliance
3 = Full compliance

## *Section I*: Unit Size and Staffing (#1-17)

Circle ONE

|  | | |
|---|---|---|
| 1a | General unit—consists of two caseloads; i.e., total number of inmates not more than 250—ideal 150-160. | 0 1 2 3 N/A |
| | OR | |
| 1b | Special program unit—consists of one caseload; i.e., total number of inmates not more than 125—ideal 50-75. | 0 1 2 3 N/A |
| 2 | Each unit has one full-time unit manager. | 0 1 2 3 |
| 3a | General unit—has two full-time case managers. | 0 1 2 3 N/A |
| | OR | |
| 3b | Special program unit—has at least one full-time case manager. | 0 1 2 3 N/A |
| 4a | General unit—has two full-time correctional counselors (liaison officers). | 0 1 2 3 N/A |
| | OR | |
| 4b | Special program unit—has at least one full-time correctional counselor (liaison officer). | 0 1 2 3 N/A |

# Unit Management Audit Form

0 = Noncompliance
1 = Minimal compliance
2 = Substantial compliance
3 = Full compliance

| | Circle One |
|---|---|
| **5a** General unit has at least a half-time mental health staff person assigned to it. | 0 1 2 3<br>N/A |
| OR | |
| **5b** Special program unit has a full-time mental health staff person assigned to it. | 0 1 2 3<br>N/A |
| **6** Each unit is assigned one full-time secretary/clerk. | 0 1 2 3 |
| **7** Unit has (on duty and in the unit) at least one correctional officer per shift, twenty-four hours a day, seven days per week. | 0 1 2 3 |
| **8** Shift commander assigns correctional officers to all unit posts (including relief assignments); unit manager has input into assignments to posts within his/her unit. | 0 1 2 3 |
| **9** Except for relief officer(s), no correctional officer is assigned to one unit for less than nine months—correctional officers may rotate through different shifts (morning, day, evening) within the same unit. | 0 1 2 3 |
| **10** In addition to its full-time staff, each unit has an identified staff member in other institution departments who provides services to the unit on a regularly scheduled basis; e.g., education, chaplaincy, psychology, recreation, etc. | 0 1 2 3 |

# Unit Management Audit Form

0 = Noncompliance
1 = Minimal compliance
2 = Substantial compliance
3 = Full compliance

Circle ONE

|  | Circle ONE |
| --- | --- |
| 11 All full-time unit staff share the responsibility for evening and weekend coverage of the unit. | 0 1 2 3 |
| 12 Office space in (preferable), or proximate to, the unit is available for the following full-time unit staff members: unit manager, case managers, mental health person, and secretary. | 0 1 2 3 |
| 13 All offices are appropriately equipped to facilitate the occupant's ability to conduct his/her responsibilities; e.g, desk, chairs, telephone, file cabinet, typewriter/computer, copier, etc. | 0 1 2 3 |
| 14 Unit manger's office is large enough to hold unit team and unit classification meetings (preferable), or this size private space is available elsewhere in the unit. | 0 1 2 3 |
| 15 Unit secretary's office is located close to the unit manager's office. | 0 1 2 3 |
| 16 Unit secretary's office includes an area designed to hold unit inmate files safely and securely; e.g., contains a vault. | 0 1 2 3 |
| 17 Unit case managers' offices and office used by mental health staff person are designed to provide the necessary privacy for one-on-one counseling/therapy sessions. | 0 1 2 3 |

# Unit Management Audit Form

0 = Noncompliance
1 = Minimal compliance
2 = Substantial compliance
3 = Full compliance

## *Section II*: Unit Staff Responsibilities— Unit Manager (#18-40)

| | Circle One |
|---|---|
| **18** Unit manager position is at the department head level. | 0 1 2 3 |
| **19** Unit manager participates on institution committees, promotion boards, serves as the institution duty officer (on rotation), and performs other duties, as assigned. | 0 1 2 3 |
| **20** Unit manager and chief of security report directly to the same supervisor. | 0 1 2 3 |
| **21** Institution administrator responsible for unit management holds a weekly meeting with all the unit managers. | 0 1 2 3 |
| **22** Unit manager is responsible for all within-unit security, safety, sanitation, supervision, and programming of inmates. | 0 1 2 3 |
| **23** Each unit manager has a budget (cost center) which can be used to fund in-unit activities when authorized in writing by the unit manager; assumes prior approval for the activity by the unit manager's supervisor. | 0 1 2 3 |
| **24** The unit manager has developed a written unit orientation program which is presented to staff assigned to his/her unit—including part-time personnel—within the first week after being appointed to the unit. | 0 1 2 3 |

# Unit Management Audit Form

0 = Noncompliance
1 = Minimal compliance
2 = Substantial compliance
3 = Full compliance

| Item | Circle One |
|---|---|
| 25 Unit manager conducts (preferably) and/or participates in, an orientation program for all new unit staff members. | 0 1 2 3 |
| 26 Unit manager develops a unit admission/orientation program (conducted by unit staff) and delivered, within 5 days of admission, to the unit's newly admitted inmates. | 0 1 2 3 |
| 27 Unit manager schedules coverage of unit, using all full-time unit staff, for twelve hours Monday through Friday; preferably until ten P.M. | 0 1 2 3 |
| 28 Unit manager schedules coverage of unit for at least eight hours on Saturdays, Sundays, and holidays—any full-time unit staff may be assigned. | 0 1 2 3 |
| 29 Unit manager has prepared a written schedule (and distributed copies to appropriate facility staff) indicating who is "acting" when the unit manager is off duty; e.g., day/evening hours, sick leave, vacation, etc. | 0 1 2 3 |
| 30 Unit manager is responsible for directing, scheduling, and monitoring the training given all full-time unit staff. | 0 1 2 3 |
| 31 With input from other unit staff, unit manager develops unit schedule, which specifies times when all regular, within-unit activities will occur. | 0 1 2 3 |

# Unit Management Audit Form

0 = Noncompliance
1 = Minimal compliance
2 = Substantial compliance
3 = Full compliance

Circle ONE

| | |
|---|---|
| 32 Unit manager (or acting unit manager) reviews and initials unit correctional officer's log book daily. | 0 1 2 3 |
| 33 Unit manager conducts weekly unit team meetings—scheduled so that all full-time members of the unit staff can attend. | 0 1 2 3 |
| 34 At least monthly (preferably, weekly) unit manager conducts unit "town hall" meeting with all unit inmates and as many unit staff as possible in attendance. | 0 1 2 3 |
| 35 Unit manager meets at least monthly (preferably, weekly) with the unit's inmate council (dorm/tier reps.). | 0 1 2 3 |
| 36 Unit manager attends (and, preferably, chairs) weekly unit classification team meeting. | 0 1 2 3 |
| 37 Unit manager writes (or has written input into) the annual performance evaluation for all unit staff and part-time personnel. | 0 1 2 3 |
| 38 The unit manager writes the annual performance ratings for the case managers, counselors, and secretary (with input from others, where appropriate; e.g., from the case-manager coordinator). | 0 1 2 3 |

# Unit Management Audit Form

0 = Noncompliance
1 = Minimal compliance
2 = Substantial compliance
3 = Full compliance

## *Section III*: Unit Staff Responsibilities—Case Manager (#41-61)

| Item | Circle One |
|---|---|
| 39 Unit manager has input into the annual performance rating of the unit's correctional officers. | 0 1 2 3 |
| 40 Unit manager receives monthly performance reports from the work and/or academic supervisor for all inmates in his/her unit. | 0 1 2 3 |
| 41 Each unit case manager has his/her own caseload of unit inmates, which is identical to the one managed by a correctional counselor. | 0 1 2 3 |
| 42 Every case manager participates (possibly on a rotation basis) in the unit's admission/orientation program for all inmates newly admitted to the unit. | 0 1 2 3 |
| 43 Each case manager conducts an individual interview with every inmate assigned to his/her caseload—within 24 hours after such an assignment has been made (in the absence of the case manager, it is done by the correctional counselor). | 0 1 2 3 |
| 44 Case manager develops initial visiting list for each new admission and handles any subsequent add-ons, deletions, and/or special visits (subject to unit manager's approval). | 0 1 2 3 |
| 45 Based on interview information and a review of each inmate's file, each case manager prepares an individualized treatment program (in collaboration with every newly admitted prisoner). | 0 1 2 3 |

# Unit Management Audit Form

0 = Noncompliance
1 = Minimal compliance
2 = Substantial compliance
3 = Full compliance

| Item | Circle One |
|---|---|
| **46** Each case manager completes necessary classification instrument(s) in a timely fashion for presentation at an upcoming unit-classification team meeting, within 30 days after an inmate's admission. | 0 1 2 3 |
| **47** Each case manager reviews monthly reports received from the education/work/training supervisors concerning in-program progress for all inmates on his/her caseload. | 0 1 2 3 |
| **48** Each case manager holds individual "debriefing" session with inmates on his/her caseload after every meeting inmate has with a formal unit or institution committee. | 0 1 2 3 |
| **49** Each case manager completes necessary reclassification instrument(s) in a timely fashion, for presentation at an upcoming unit-classification team meeting—not to exceed one year since prior classification review. | 0 1 2 3 |
| **50a** In a general unit, every inmate is seen by his/her case manager for an individual interview at least once every three months—which is documented. | 0 1 2 3 N/A |
| OR | |
| **50b** In a special unit, every inmate is seen by his/her case manager for an individual interview at least once every two months (preferably monthly)—which is documented. | 0 1 2 3 N/A |
| **51** Each case manager conducts formal (30-90 minute), regularly scheduled, (at least weekly) individual/group counseling/therapy with some of the unit inmates on his/her caseload—which is documented. | 0 1 2 3 |

# UNIT MANAGEMENT AUDIT FORM

0 = NONCOMPLIANCE
1 = MINIMAL COMPLIANCE
2 = SUBSTANTIAL COMPLIANCE
3 = FULL COMPLIANCE

CIRCLE ONE

| Item | Circle One |
| --- | --- |
| 52 Each case manager attends and (preferably) is a voting member, at any formal unit or institution committee meetings which involves an inmate on his/her caseload. | 0 1 2 3 |
| 53 During any stay exceeding five days in punitive segregation for a violation of institution rules, every inmate is visited at least once by his/her case manager. | 0 1 2 3 |
| 54 Each case manager is involved (and participates) in the development and delivery of all on-unit programs. | 0 1 2 3 |
| 55 Each case manager is involved in enlisting the aid of, and coordinating program activities for, community volunteers. | 0 1 2 3 |
| 56 Each case manager participates in the gathering of information to update and/or evaluate within-unit programs. | 0 1 2 3 |
| 57 Each case manager prepares and/or assists in the preparation of any weekly/monthly/annual statistical and narrative reports concerning unit activities. | 0 1 2 3 |
| 58 Each case manager assists other unit staff members in the performance of their duties—including correctional officers, secretary, correctional counselors, and the unit manager. | 0 1 2 3 |

# Unit Management Audit Form

0 = Noncompliance
1 = Minimal compliance
2 = Substantial compliance
3 = Full compliance

## *Section IV*: Unit Staff Responsibilities—Correctional Counselor (#62-75) Circle One

| Item | Circle One |
|---|---|
| 59 Each case manager "backs up"—assists inmates on the caseload of—the other (within unit) case manager when that case manager is absent. | 0 1 2 3 |
| 60 Each case manager serves as acting unit manager when so requested by the unit manager, during the latter's absence. | 0 1 2 3 |
| 61 The case manager coordinator serves in a quality-control role, periodically reviewing the work of every case manager at least annually (preferably quarterly). | 0 1 2 3 |
| 62 Each correctional counselor is responsible for managing a caseload of inmates, which he/she shares with a case manager. | 0 1 2 3 |
| 63 The primary role for each correctional counselor at which he/she spends the most time) is attempting to resolve the day-to-day concerns of every inmate on his/her caseload. | 0 1 2 3 |
| 64 Each correctional counselor regularly (at least twice every week) tours work and program assignment areas of inmates on his/her caseload and, when necessary, offers guidance to both staff and prisoners. | 0 1 2 3 |
| 65 Each correctional counselor sees every inmate on his/her caseload at least once every month for (at minimum) a 15 minute interview; small-group interviews are okay when the caseload is big. | 0 1 2 3 |

# Unit Management Audit Form

0 = Noncompliance
1 = Minimal compliance
2 = Substantial compliance
3 = Full compliance

Circle ONE

| Item | Circle ONE |
|---|---|
| 66 Each correctional counselor attends and is a voting member, at any formal unit (and, preferably, institution) meetings which involve an inmate on his/her caseload. | 0 1 2 3 |
| 67 Unless personally involved in the incident, each correctional counselor serves as a hearing officer at all in-unit disciplinary hearings concerning inmates on his/her caseload. | 0 1 2 3 |
| 68 Each correctional counselor serves as the initial contact (i.e., source of form) for any inmate on his/her caseload wishing to file a formal grievance. | 0 1 2 3 |
| 69 During any stay exceeding three days in punitive segregation for a violation of institution rules, every inmate is visited at least once by his/her correctional counselor. | 0 1 2 3 |
| 70 Each correctional counselor conducts formal/informal (i.e., planned/unplanned) group/individual counseling sessions with some of the inmates on his/her caseload—which is documented. | 0 1 2 3 |
| 71 Each correctional counselor works with the unit's recreation specialist helping to run intra- and interunit leisure-time and other sport tournaments, held at least quarterly. | 0 1 2 3 |
| 72 Each unit is inspected regularly (at least weekly, preferably daily) by a correctional counselor, who recommends to the unit manager methods for maintaining a secure, safe, and clean living environment. | 0 1 2 3 |

# Unit Management Audit Form

0 = Noncompliance
1 = Minimal compliance
2 = Substantial compliance
3 = Full compliance

## *Section V*: Unit Staff Responsibilities—Secretary/Clerk (#76-86)

| Item | Circle ONE |
|---|---|
| 73 Each correctional counselor assists other unit staff in performing their duties—including correctional officers, case managers, secretary—at the direction of the unit manager. | 0 1 2 3 |
| 74 Each correctional counselor prepares and/or assists in the preparation of any weekly/monthly/annual statistical and narrative reports concerning unit activities. | 0 1 2 3 |
| 75 Each correctional counselor serves as acting unit manager when so requested by the unit manager during the latter's absence. | 0 1 2 3 |
| 76 The unit secretary is responsible for the unit's inmate files and for monitoring access to them. | 0 1 2 3 |
| 77 Files are maintained in a secure area on the unit to which no inmate has access. | 0 1 2 3 |
| 78 File material is filed by the unit secretary in accord with department policies. | 0 1 2 3 |
| 79 The unit secretary conducts a unit file count—at the start of the day and the end of the day—to ensure that no files are missing and makes appropriate entries into a bound, page-numbered logbook. | 0 1 2 3 |

# Unit Management Audit Form

0 = Noncompliance
1 = Minimal compliance
2 = Substantial compliance
3 = Full compliance

Circle ONE

| Item | Circle ONE |
|---|---|
| 80 The records office manager serves in a quality control role, periodically reviewing every unit secretary's inmate files—at least quarterly, preferably monthly. | 0 1 2 3 |
| 81 The unit secretary schedules in-unit interviews and committee meetings, at the direction of the unit manager. | 0 1 2 3 |
| 82 The unit secretary serves on various unit committees, as directed by the unit manager. | 0 1 2 3 |
| 83 The unit secretary types unit correspondence and unit reports, as directed by the the unit manager. | 0 1 2 3 |
| 84 The unit secretary responds with routine written and verbal communications to the public and to unit inmate families, subject to approval by unit manager. | 0 1 2 3 |
| 85 At direction of unit manager, the unit secretary is responsible for keeping current the unit plan and the unit's institution manual of policies and procedures. | 0 1 2 3 |
| 86 The unit secretary functions as a liaison between the unit and other units and institutional departments. | 0 1 2 3 |

# UNIT MANAGEMENT AUDIT FORM

0 = NONCOMPLIANCE
1 = MINIMAL COMPLIANCE
2 = SUBSTANTIAL COMPLIANCE
3 = FULL COMPLIANCE

## *SECTION VI*: UNIT STAFF RESPONSIBILITIES—CORRECTIONAL OFFICER (#87-94)

| Item | CIRCLE ONE |
|---|---|
| 87 The unit correctional officer has primary responsibility for monitoring inmate adherence to institution/unit procedures concerning unit security and sanitation, prisoner accountability, and custody regulations. | 0 1 2 3 |
| 88 The unit correctional officer signs bound, page-numbered logbook when coming on-duty, and initials messages left by staff during the previous 24 hours. | 0 1 2 3 |
| 89 The unit correctional officer supervises the unit orderlies and helps prepare their monthly performance and inmate pay reports. | 0 1 2 3 |
| 90 The unit correctional officer regularly tours the unit and recommends to the unit manager ways to improve operations, particularly in the correctional officers' areas of primary responsibility. | 0 1 2 3 |
| 91 The unit correctional officer provides both positive and negative information concerning unit inmates to other unit staff members, preferably in written form. | 0 1 2 3 |
| 92 When possible, the unit correctional officer attends unit classification team meetings and/or other unit team activities. | 0 1 2 3 |
| 93 The unit correctional officer assists in the preparation of any weekly/monthly/annual statistical and narrative reports concerning unit activities. | 0 1 2 3 |

# Unit Management Audit Form

0 = Noncompliance
1 = Minimal compliance
2 = Substantial compliance
3 = Full compliance

## *Section VII*: Unit Plan (#95-117)

| | Circle ONE |
|---|---|
| 94 The unit correctional officer signs the logbook when going off-duty, and must write a comment concerning activities occurring during his/her shift. | 0 1 2 3 |
| 95 For every unit, there is a unit plan written by the unit manager and his/her staff, which has been approved (in writing) by the warden; a copy of its plan is kept in the unit. | 0 1 2 3 |
| 96 There is documentation that the unit plan is reviewed annually, and if necessary, updated, as appropriate. | 0 1 2 3 |
| 97 All updates and/or modifications of the unit plan have been approved, in writing, by the warden. | 0 1 2 3 |
| 98 The unit plan follows the format dictated by central office policies concerning unit management and unit plans. | 0 1 2 3 |
| 99 The unit plan contains a description of the unit which includes information about its location and size. | 0 1 2 3 |
| 100 The unit plan describes the type of inmates housed in the unit and/or the selection criteria used to place prisoners on the unit. | 0 1 2 3 |

# Unit Management Audit Form

0 = Noncompliance
1 = Minimal compliance
2 = Substantial compliance
3 = Full compliance

| | Circle ONE |
|---|---|
| 101 The unit plan specifies the staffing pattern for the unit. | 0 1 2 3 |
| 102 The unit plan specifies the bed capacity of the unit. | 0 1 2 3 |
| 103 The unit plan explains the mission of the unit. | 0 1 2 3 |
| 104 The unit plan contains a list of specific objectives the unit intends to accomplish during the current year. | 0 1 2 3 |
| 105 The objectives contained in the unit plan relate to the unit's mission, and are written so that they are measurable. | 0 1 2 3 |
| 106 The unit plan contains a current staff roster. | 0 1 2 3 |
| 107 The unit plan contains a timetable, that displays the work schedule for all unit staff members. | 0 1 2 3 |

# UNIT MANAGEMENT AUDIT FORM

0 = NONCOMPLIANCE
1 = MINIMAL COMPLIANCE
2 = SUBSTANTIAL COMPLIANCE
3 = FULL COMPLIANCE

| Item | CIRCLE ONE |
|---|---|
| 108 The unit plan contains a listing of rules and regulations which are unique to the unit. | 0 1 2 3 |
| 109 Written plans govern inmate council procedures; e.g., criteria for nomination, time in office (short), replacement if "guilty" of disciplinary report, can succeed self only once, role in town hall meetings, etc. | 0 1 2 3 |
| 110 The unit plan contains a current schedule of within-unit programs and activities; e.g., unit admission/orientation, classification, team reviews, counseling, town hall, prerelease, inmate organizations, special events, etc. | 0 1 2 3 |
| 111 For each activity, the unit plan lists the name of the staff member responsible for it, and provides an indication of when and where the activity is conducted. | 0 1 2 3 |
| 112 The unit plan contains information about "routine" procedures such as: meal rotation, commissary schedule, sick call, mail, telephone, barbershop, law library, recreation, visiting, leisure-time activities, counts, wake-up, etc. | 0 1 2 3 |
| 113 The unit plan describes the unit's fire safety and periodic fire drill procedures, and specifies who is responsible for conducting and reporting these activities. | 0 1 2 3 |
| 114 The unit plan includes emergency plans which list staff duties during escapes, natural disasters, inmate disturbances, hostage situation, homicide/suicide, etc. | 0 1 2 3 |

# UNIT MANAGEMENT AUDIT FORM

0 = NONCOMPLIANCE
1 = MINIMAL COMPLIANCE
2 = SUBSTANTIAL COMPLIANCE
3 = FULL COMPLIANCE

## *SECTION VIII*: UNIT ADMISSION/ORIENTATION (#118-126)

| | CIRCLE ONE |
|---|---|
| 115 There is a description in the unit plan of how unit sanitation will be maintained which specifies responsibilities of both staff supervisors and inmate orderly crews. | 0 1 2 3 |
| 116 The unit plan specifies the number and frequency of documented in-unit inspections (in addition to those required by department of corrections' policy) to be conducted by unit staff—at least once each week. | 0 1 2 3 |
| 117 There is a section in the unit plan which contains samples of all required statistical and narrative reports, and lists when each is due and who is responsible for meeting the deadline. | 0 1 2 3 |
| 118 Upon staff's initial assignment to the unit, a formal admission/orientation program is conducted under the direction of the unit manager. | 0 1 2 3 |
| 119 The unit's admission/orientation program is also presented to consultants, volunteers, student interns, and others who provide services for the unit on a regular basis. | 0 1 2 3 |
| 120 There is a written method by which inmates are assigned to units after being admitted to the institution. | 0 1 2 3 |
| 121 Inmates newly admitted to the unit will be seen for an intake interview within 24 hours of arrival; preferably, the intake session is conducted by the inmate's case manager or correctional counselor. | 0 1 2 3 |

# UNIT MANAGEMENT AUDIT FORM

0 = NONCOMPLIANCE
1 = MINIMAL COMPLIANCE
2 = SUBSTANTIAL COMPLIANCE
3 = FULL COMPLIANCE

## *SECTION IX*: UNIT CLASSIFICATION TEAM (#127-136)

CIRCLE ONE

| Item | Circle One |
|---|---|
| 122 In addition to the institution's admission/orientation program, inmates newly admitted to the unit participate in a formal orientation program conducted by unit staff. | 0 1 2 3 |
| 123 There are written outlines which list the topics to be covered during the unit's admission/orientation programs for staff and for inmates. | 0 1 2 3 |
| 124 Following completion of the unit's admission/orientation programs, every participant signs a form which lists the topics that were covered during the orientation session(s). | 0 1 2 3 |
| 125 After being admitted to a unit, an inmate continues to receive services from that unit's staff as long as he/she remains at the facility. | 0 1 2 3 |
| 126 Inmates are not to be reassigned to another unit unless the decision is made by an institutionwide committee (appointed by the warden) the majority of whose members are not staff from the 'gaining' and 'losing' units. | 0 1 2 3 |
| 127 Unit classification team meetings are scheduled so that (except for unit correctional officers) all other full-time unit staff can, and do, attend. | 0 1 2 3 |
| 128 The number and titles of unit staff participating during the unit's classification team meetings are in conformity with written department of corrections' policy statements. | 0 1 2 3 |

# Unit Management Audit Form

0 = Noncompliance
1 = Minimal compliance
2 = Substantial compliance
3 = Full compliance

| Item | Circle One |
|---|---|
| 129 The type of decisions the unit classification team can make is specified in written department of corrections' policy statements [there is no further review or approval of a decision]. | 0 1 2 3 |
| 130 The type of recommendations the unit classification team can make is specified in written department of corrections' policy statements [recommendations are reviewed and approved before they become final]. | 0 1 2 3 |
| 131 All within-unit assignment decisions are made by the unit classification team. | 0 1 2 3 |
| 132 Decisions concerning outside-the-unit programs are made by the unit classification team in collaboration with a representative from the other department/program area. | 0 1 2 3 |
| 133 Newly admitted inmates appear before the unit classification team—for initial classification (or a progress review)—within one month after placement in the unit. | 0 1 2 3 |
| 134a At a minimum, every inmate in a general unit meets formally with the unit's classification team at least annually, more often is preferable. | 0 1 2 3 N/A |
| OR | |
| 134b At a minimum, every inmate in a special unit meets formally with the unit's classification team every six months, more often is preferable. | 0 1 2 3 N/A |

# UNIT MANAGEMENT AUDIT FORM

0 = NONCOMPLIANCE
1 = MINIMAL COMPLIANCE
2 = SUBSTANTIAL COMPLIANCE
3 = FULL COMPLIANCE

## *SECTION X*: UNIT DISCIPLINARY PROCESS (#137-143)

CIRCLE ONE

| Item | Circle One |
|---|---|
| 135 Within three working days following an appearance at the unit classification team session, every inmate receives a written form containing the decisions/recommendations reached and the date scheduled for his/her next meeting. | 0 1 2 3 |
| 136 Inmates are permitted to meet with the unit classification team prior to their next next scheduled date, but only when such action has been recommended, in writing, by a unit staff member. | 0 1 2 3 |
| 137 The unit's disciplinary hearing officer(s) has been formally trained in the procedures required by the department of corrections' policy for handling the inmate disciplinary process. | 0 1 2 3 |
| 138 All disciplinary reports received by any of the unit's inmates are reviewed by unit staff (preferably, before the disciplinary hearing is held). | 0 1 2 3 |
| 139 In accord with department of corrections' written policy, the unit makes the final disposition on a specified class of disciplinary offenses—except if it involves inmates from two different units. | 0 1 2 3 |
| 140 When the disciplinary incident involves inmates from two or more units, the case is decided by the institutionwide disciplinary board with, at least, written (preferably in-person) input by staff from the involved units. | 0 1 2 3 |
| 141 For all disciplinary offenses which are not decided at the unit level, unit staff append a written comment and, within 24 hours, forward the disciplinary report to an institutionwide disciplinary board for final disposition. | 0 1 2 3 |

# Unit Management Audit Form

0 = Noncompliance
1 = Minimal compliance
2 = Substantial compliance
3 = Full compliance

## *Section XI*: Unit Monitoring and Evaluation (#144-148)

| | Circle ONE |
|---|---|
| 142 Unit staff routinely participate in the institutionwide disciplinary board hearings when they involve an inmate from their unit. | 0 1 2 3 |
| 143 The unit receives a monthly report (within three days after the end of the month) concerning the unit's performance in regard to disciplinary activity during the previous month. | 0 1 2 3 |
| 144 There is a monthly unit report which is completed by every unit manager and sent to the supervisor of the unit management program within five days after the end of the month. | 0 1 2 3 |
| 145 The monthly unit report consists of two major sections: statistical and narrative. | 0 1 2 3 |
| 146 The statistical section of the monthly unit report contains subsections which report data on (at least) population, program participation, disciplinary, and segregation activity. | 0 1 2 3 |
| 147 The narrative section of the monthly unit report contains subsections dealing with, at least: positive accomplishments, new problems, and progress made on previous problems. | 0 1 2 3 |
| 148 Every unit manager prepares an annual unit report which: (1) summarizes the past year; (2) includes a section dealing with unit plan objectives that were and were not accomplished, and, (3) lists next year's unit objectives. | 0 1 2 3 |

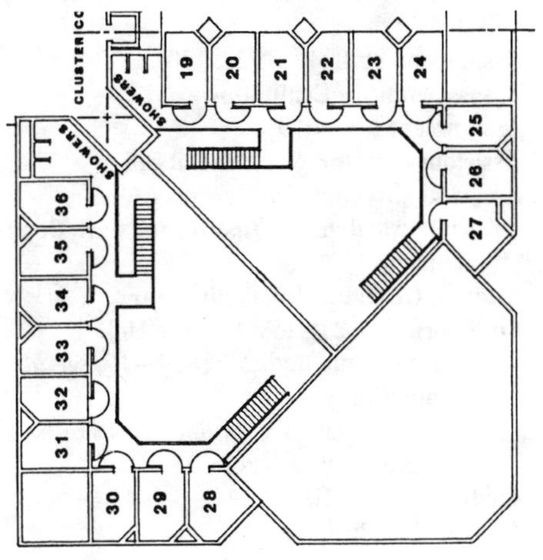
CLUSTER C
SHOWERS
SHOWERS
19
20
21
22
23
24
25
26
27
28
29
30
31
32
33
34
35
36

# Index

## A

# D

# I



# J



# K

# T

# V



# W



# Y



# Z

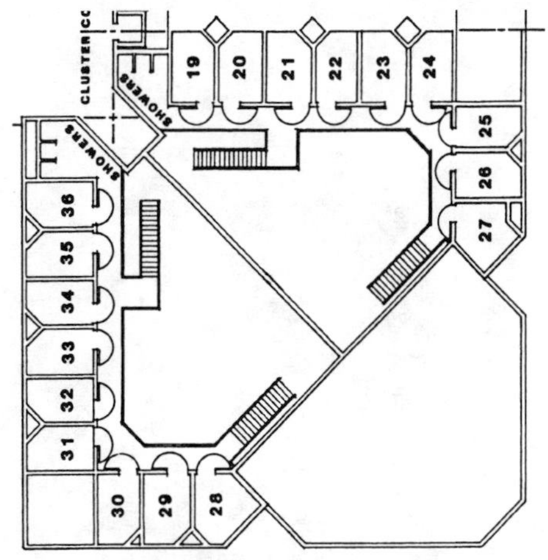


# About the Author

As a psychology intern (at a $100/month less room and board), Bob Levinson began employment in corrections more than forty years ago. Since then, he has acquired a wife, a Ph.D., three children, and two grandchildren. In addition to changes in roles, responsibilities, and recompense, Dr. Levinson has worked—as a full-time employee or a consultant—for municipal, county, state, and federal agencies, and for both private for-profit and nonprofit companies. His longest period of employment was with the Federal Bureau of Prisons, from which he retired as Deputy Assistant Director for Inmate Programs after twenty-two years of service. In this capacity, he is one of the individuals most responsible for the development and implementation of unit management.

For the past fifteen years, he has been an independent consultant working with the American Correctional Association as its special projects manager. In addition to psychology/mental health issues, Dr. Levinson has focused on other areas in corrections, such as objective classification (both external and internal) and unit management. Recent government-funded projects that he has led or been involved in as a researcher, concerned the following areas: the use of technology in corrections, prison gangs, community-based programs for juveniles, and under eighteen-year-olds in adult prisons.